COMPUTER
SYSTEM DESIGN

COMPUTER SYSTEM DESIGN

System-on-Chip

Michael J. Flynn

Wayne Luk

A JOHN WILEY & SONS, INC., PUBLICATION

Library of Congress Cataloging-in-Publication Data:

Flynn, M. J. (Michael J.), 1934–
    Computer system design : system-on-chip / Michael J. Flynn, Wayne Luk.
        p. cm.
    Includes bibliographical references and index.
    ISBN 978-0-470-64336-5 (hardback)
 1. Systems on a chip. I. Luk, Wayne. II. Title.
    TK7895.E42F65 2011
    004.1–dc22

                                                        2010040981

oBook ISBN: 9781118009925
ePDF ISBN: 9781118009901
ePub ISBN: 9781118009918

CONTENTS

PREFACE

The next generation of computer system designers will be concerned more about the elements of a system tailored to particular applications than with the details of processors and memories.

Such designers would have rudimentary knowledge of processors and other elements in the system, but the success of their design would depend on their skills in making system-level trade-offs that optimize the cost, performance, and other attributes to meet application requirements.

This text is organized to introduce issues in computer system design, particularly for system-on-chip (SOC). Managing such design requires knowledge of a number of issues, as shown in Figure 1.

After Chapter 1, the introduction chapter, Chapter 2 looks at issues that define the design space: area, speed, power consumption, and configurability. Chapters 3–5 provide background knowledge of the basic elements in a system: processor, memory, and interconnect.

The succeeding chapters focus on computer systems tailored to specific applications and technologies. Chapter 6 covers issues in customizing and configuring designs. Chapter 7 addresses system-level trade-offs for various applications, bringing together earlier material in this study. Finally, Chapter 8 presents future challenges for system design and SOC possibilities.

The tools that illustrate the material in the text are still being developed. The Appendix provides an overview of one such tool. Since our tools are evolving, please check from time to time to see what is available at the companion web site: www.soctextbook.com.

Moreover, material useful for teaching, such as slides and answers to exercises, is also being prepared.

This book covers a particular approach to computer system design, with emphasis on fundamental ideas and analytical techniques that are applicable to a range of applications and architectures, rather than on specific applications, architectures, languages, and tools. We are aware of complementary treatments on these and also on other topics, such as electronic system-level design, embedded software development, and system-level integration and test. We have included brief descriptions and references to these topics where appropriate; a more detailed treatment can be covered in future editions or in different volumes.

SOC is a quickly developing field. Although we focused on fundamental material, we were forced to draw a line on the inclusion of the latest

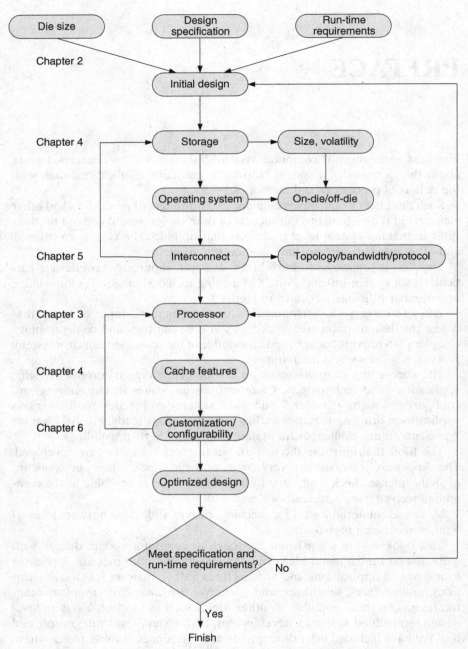

Figure 1   An approach to SOC system design described in this book.

technological advances for the sake of completing the book. Such advances, instead, are captured as links to relevant sources of information at the companion web site described above.

Many colleagues and students, primarily at Imperial College London and Stanford University, have contributed to this book. We are sorry that we are not able to mention them all by name here. However, a number of individuals deserve special acknowledgment. Peter Cheung worked closely with us from the beginning; his contributions shaped the treatment of many topics, particularly those in Chapter 5. Tobias Becker, Ray Cheung, Rob Dimond, Scott Guo, Shay Ping Seng, David Thomas, Steve Wilton, Alice Yu, and Chi Wai Yu contributed significant material to various chapters. Philip Leong and Roger Woods read the manuscript many times carefully and provided many excellent suggestions for improvement. We also greatly benefited from comments by Jeffrey Arnold, Peter Boehm, Don Bouldin, Geoffrey Brown, Patrick Hung, Sebastian Lopez, Oskar Mencer, Kevin Rudd, and several anonymous reviewers. We thank Kubilay Atasu, Peter Collingbourne, James Huggett, Qiwei Jin, Adrien Le Masle, Pete Sedcole, and Tim Todman, as well as those who prefer to remain anonymous, for their invaluable assistance.

Last, but not least, we thank Cassie Strickland, of Wiley, and Janet Hronek, of Toppan Best-set, for their help in the timely completion of this text.

LIST OF ABBREVIATIONS AND ACRONYMS

AC	Autonomous chip
A/D	Analog to digital
AES	Advanced Encryption Standard
AG	Address generation
ALU	Arithmetic and logic unit
AMBA	Advanced Microcontroller Bus Architecture
ASIC	Application-specific integrated circuit
ASIP	Application-specific instruction processor
ASOC	Autonomous system-on-chip
AXI	Advanced eXtensible Interface
BC	Branch conditional
BIST	Built-in-self-test
BRAM	Block random access memory
BTB	Branch target buffer
CAD	Computer aided design
CBWA	Copy-back write allocate cache
CC	Condition codes
CFA	Color filter array
CGRA	Coarse-grained reconfigurable architecture
CIF	Common Intermediate Format
CISC	Complex instruction set computer
CLB	Configurable Logic Block
CMOS	Complementary metal oxide semiconductor
CORDIC	COordinate Rotation Digital Computer
CPI	Cycles per instruction
CPU	Central processing unit
DCT	Discrete Cosine Transform
DDR	Double data rate
DES	Data Encryption Standard
3DES	Triple Data Encryption Standard

DF	Data fetch
DMA	Direct memory access
DRAM	Dynamic random access memory
DSP	Digital signal processing (or processor)
DTMR	Design Target Miss Rates
ECC	Error correcting code
eDRAM	Embedded dynamic random access memory
EX	Execute
FIFO	First in first out
FIR	Finite impulse response
FO4	Fan-out of four
FP	Floating-point
FPGA	Field programmable gate array
FPR	Floating-point register
FPU	Floating-point unit
GB	Giga bytes, a billion (10^9) bytes
GIF	Graphics interface
GPP	General-purpose processor
GPR	General-purpose register
GPS	Global Positioning System
GSM	Global System for Mobile Communications
HDTV	High definition television
HPC	High performance computing
IC	Integrated circuit
ICU	Interconnect interface unit
ID	Instruction decode
IF	Instruction fetch
ILP	Instruction-level parallelism
I/O	Input/output
IP	Intellectual property
IR	Instruction register
ISA	Instruction set architecture
JPEG	Joint Photographic Experts Group (image compression standard)
Kb	Kilo bits, one thousand (10^3) bits
KB	Kilo bytes, one thousand bytes
L1	Level 1 (for cache)
L2	Level 2 (for cache)
LE	Logic Element

LRU	Least recently used
L/S	Load-store
LSI	Large scale integration
LUT	Lookup table
Mb	Mega bits, one million (10^6) bits
MB	Mega bytes, one million bytes
MEMS	Micro electro mechanical systems
MIMD	Multiple instruction streams, multiple data streams
MIPS	Million instructions per second
MOPS	Million operations per second
MOS	Metal oxide semiconductor
MPEG	Motion Picture Experts Group (video compression standard)
MTBF	Mean time between faults
MUX	Multiplexor
NOC	Network on chip
OCP	Open Core Protocol
OFDM	Orthogonal Frequency-Division Multiplexing
PAN	Personal area network
PCB	Printed circuit board
PLCC	Plastic leaded chip carrier
PROM	Programmable read only memory
QCIF	Quarter Common Intermediate Format
RAM	Random access memory
RAND	Random
RAW	Read-after-write
rbe	Register bit equivalent
RF	Radio frequency
RFID	Radio frequency identification
RISC	Reduced instruction set computer
R/M	Register-memory
ROM	Read only memory
RTL	Register transfer language
SAD	Sum of the absolute differences
SDRAM	Synchronous dynamic random access memory
SECDED	Single error correction, double error detection
SER	Soft error rate
SIA	Semiconductor Industry Association
SIMD	Single instruction stream, multiple data streams
SMT	Simultaneous multithreading

SOC	System on chip
SRAM	Static random access memory
TLB	Translation look-aside buffer
TMR	Triple modular redundancy
UART	Universal asynchronous receiver/transmitter
UMTS	Universal mobile telecommunications system
UV	Ultraviolet
VCI	Virtual Component Interface
VLIW	Very long instruction word
VLSI	Very large scale integration
VPU	Vector processing unit
VR	Vector register
VSIA	Virtual Socket Interface Alliance
WAR	Write after read
WAW	Write after write
WB	Write back
WTNWA	Write-through cache, no write allocate

1 Introduction to the Systems Approach

1.1 SYSTEM ARCHITECTURE: AN OVERVIEW

The past 40 years have seen amazing advances in silicon technology and resulting increases in transistor density and performance. In 1966, Fairchild Semiconductor [84] introduced a quad two input NAND gate with about 10 transistors on a die. In 2008, the Intel quad-core Itanium processor has 2 billion transistors [226]. Figures 1.1 and 1.2 show the unrelenting advance in improving transistor density and the corresponding decrease in device cost.

The aim of this book is to present an approach for computer system design that exploits this enormous transistor density. In part, this is a direct extension of studies in computer architecture and design. However, it is also a study of system architecture and design.

About 50 years ago, a seminal text, *Systems Engineering—An Introduction to the Design of Large-Scale Systems* [111], appeared. As the authors, H.H. Goode and R.E. Machol, pointed out, the system's view of engineering was created by a need to deal with complexity. As then, our ability to deal with complex design problems is greatly enhanced by computer-based tools.

A system-on-chip (SOC) architecture is an ensemble of processors, memories, and interconnects tailored to an application domain. A simple example of such an architecture is the Emotion Engine [147, 187, 237] for the Sony PlayStation 2 (Figure 1.3), which has two main functions: behavior simulation and geometry translation. This system contains three essential components: a main processor of the reduced instruction set computer (RISC) style [118] and two vector processing units, VPU0 and VPU1, each of which contains four parallel processors of the single instruction, multiple data (SIMD) stream style [97]. We provide a brief overview of these components and our overall approach in the next few sections.

While the focus of the book is on the system, in order to understand the system, one must first understand the components. So, before returning to the issue of system architecture later in this chapter, we review the components that make up the system.

Computer System Design: System-on-Chip, First Edition. Michael J. Flynn and Wayne Luk.
© 2011 John Wiley & Sons, Inc. Published 2011 by John Wiley & Sons, Inc.

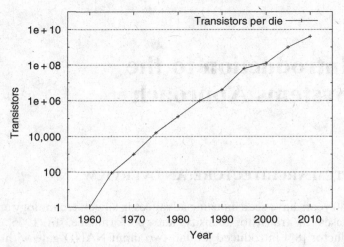

Figure 1.1   The increasing transistor density on a silicon die.

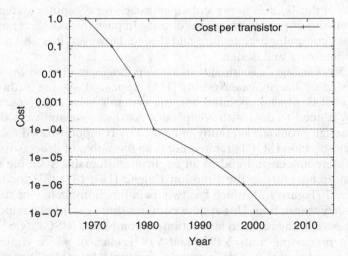

Figure 1.2   The decrease of transistor cost over the years.

1.2   COMPONENTS OF THE SYSTEM: PROCESSORS, MEMORIES, AND INTERCONNECTS

The term *architecture* denotes the operational structure and the user's view of the system. Over time, it has evolved to include both the functional specification and the hardware implementation. The system architecture defines the system-level building blocks, such as processors and memories, and the

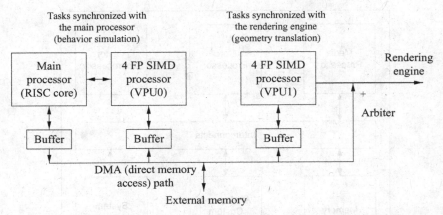

Figure 1.3 High-level functional view of a system-on-chip: the Emotion Engine of the Sony PlayStation 2 [147, 187].

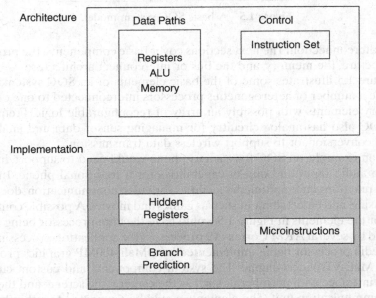

Figure 1.4 The processor architecture and its implementation.

interconnection between them. The processor architecture determines the processor's instruction set, the associated programming model, its detailed implementation, which may include hidden registers, branch prediction circuits and specific details concerning the ALU (arithmetic logic unit). The implementation of a processor is also known as *microarchitecture* (Figure 1.4).

The system designer has a programmer's or user's view of the system components, the system view of memory, the variety of specialized processors, and

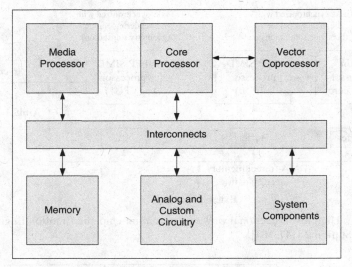

Figure 1.5 A basic SOC system model.

their interconnection. The next sections cover basic components: the processor architecture, the memory, and the bus or interconnect architecture.

Figure 1.5 illustrates some of the basic elements of an SOC system. These include a number of heterogeneous processors interconnected to one or more memory elements with possibly an array of reconfigurable logic. Frequently, the SOC also has analog circuitry for managing sensor data and analog-to-digital conversion, or to support wireless data transmission.

As an example, an SOC for a smart phone would need to support, in addition to audio input and output capabilities for a traditional phone, Internet access functions and multimedia facilities for video communication, document processing, and entertainment such as games and movies. A possible configuration for the elements in Figure 1.5 would have the core processor being implemented by several ARM Cortex-A9 processors for application processing, and the media processor being implemented by a Mali-400MP graphics processor and a Mali-VE video engine. The system components and custom circuitry would interface with peripherals such as the camera, the screen, and the wireless communication unit. The elements would be connected together by AXI (Advanced eXtensible Interface) interconnects.

If all the elements cannot be contained on a single chip, the implementation is probably best referred to as a system on a board, but often is still called a SOC. What distinguishes a system on a board (or chip) from the conventional general-purpose computer plus memory on a board is the specific nature of the design target. The application is assumed to be known and specified so that the elements of the system can be selected, sized, and evaluated during the design process. The emphasis on selecting, parameterizing, and configuring system components tailored to a target application distinguishes a system architect from a computer architect.

In this chapter, we primarily look at the higher-level definition of the processor—the programmer's view or the instruction set architecture (ISA), the basics of the processor microarchitecture, memory hierarchies, and the interconnection structure. In later chapters, we shall study in more detail the implementation issues for these elements.

1.3 HARDWARE AND SOFTWARE: PROGRAMMABILITY VERSUS PERFORMANCE

A fundamental decision in SOC design is to choose which components in the system are to be implemented in hardware and in software. The major benefits and drawbacks of hardware and software implementations are summarized in Table 1.1.

A software implementation is usually executed on a general-purpose processor (GPP), which interprets instructions at run time. This architecture offers flexibility and adaptability, and provides a way of sharing resources among different applications; however, the hardware implementation of the ISA is generally slower and more power hungry than implementing the corresponding function directly in hardware without the overhead of fetching and decoding instructions.

Most software developers use high-level languages and tools that enhance productivity, such as program development environments, optimizing compilers, and performance profilers. In contrast, the direct implementation of applications in hardware results in custom application-specific integrated circuits (ASICs), which often provides high performance at the expense of programmability—and hence flexibility, productivity, and cost.

Given that hardware and software have complementary features, many SOC designs aim to combine the individual benefits of the two. The obvious method is to implement the performance-critical parts of the application in hardware, and the rest in software. For instance, if 90% of the software execution time of an application is spent on 10% of the source code, up to a 10-fold speedup is achievable if that 10% of the code is efficiently implemented in hardware. We shall make use of this observation to customize designs in Chapter 6.

Custom ASIC hardware and software on GPPs can be seen as two extremes in the technology spectrum with different trade-offs in programmability and

TABLE 1.1 Benefits and Drawbacks of Software and Hardware Implementations

	Benefits	Drawbacks
Hardware	Fast, low power consumption	Inflexible, unadaptable, complex to build and test
Software	Flexible, adaptable, simple to build and test	Slow, high power consumption

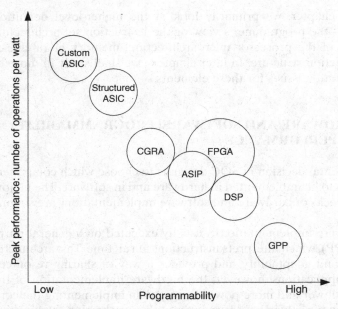

Figure 1.6   A simplified technology comparison: programmability versus performance. GPP, general-purpose processor; CGRA, coarse-grained reconfigurable architecture.

performance; there are various technologies that lie between these two extremes (Figure 1.6). The two more well-known ones are application-specific instruction processors (ASIPs) and field-programmable gate arrays (FPGAs).

An ASIP is a processor with an instruction set customized for a specific application or domain. Custom instructions efficiently implemented in hardware are often integrated into a base processor with a basic instruction set. This capability often improves upon the conventional approach of using standard instruction sets to fulfill the same task while preserving its flexibility. Chapters 6 and 7 explore further some of the issues involving custom instructions.

An FPGA typically contains an array of computation units, memories, and their interconnections, and all three are usually programmable in the field by application builders. FPGA technology often offers a good compromise: It is faster than software while being more flexible and having shorter development times than custom ASIC hardware implementations; like GPPs, they are offered as off-the-shelf devices that can be programmed without going through chip fabrication. Because of the growing demand for reducing the time to market and the increasing cost of chip fabrication, FPGAs are becoming more popular for implementing digital designs.

Most commercial FPGAs contain an array of fine-grained logic blocks, each only a few bits wide. It is also possible to have the following:

- *Coarse-Grained Reconfigurable Architecture (CGRA).* It contains logic blocks that process byte-wide or multiple byte-wide data, which can form building blocks of datapaths.
- *Structured ASIC.* It allows application builders to customize the resources before fabrication. While it offers performance close to that of ASIC, the need for chip fabrication can be an issue.
- *Digital Signal Processors (DSPs).* The organization and instruction set for these devices are optimized for digital signal processing applications. Like microprocessors, they have a fixed hardware architecture that cannot be reconfigured.

Figure 1.6 compares these technologies in terms of programmability and performance. Chapters 6–8 provide further information about some of these technologies.

1.4 PROCESSOR ARCHITECTURES

Typically, processors are characterized either by their application or by their architecture (or structure), as shown in Tables 1.2 and 1.3. The requirements space of an application is often large, and there is a range of implementation options. Thus, it is usually difficult to associate a particular architecture with a particular application. In addition, some architectures combine different implementation approaches as seen in the PlayStation example of Section 1.1. There, the graphics processor consists of a four-element SIMD array of vector processing functional units (FUs). Other SOC implementations consist of multiprocessors using very long instruction word (VLIW) and/or superscalar processors.

TABLE 1.2 Processor Examples as Identified by Function

Processor Type	Application
Graphics processing unit (GPU)	3-D graphics; rendering, shading, texture
Digital signal processor (DSP)	Generic, sometimes used with wireless
Media processor	Video and audio signal processing
Network processor	Routing, buffering

TABLE 1.3 Processor Examples as Identified by Architecture

Processor Type	Architecture/Implementation Approach
SIMD	Single instruction applied to multiple functional units (processors)
Vector (VP)	Single instruction applied to multiple pipelined registers
VLIW	Multiple instructions issued each cycle under compiler control
Superscalar	Multiple instructions issued each cycle under hardware control

From the programmer's point of view, sequential processors execute one instruction at a time. However, many processors have the capability to execute several instructions concurrently in a manner that is transparent to the programmer, through techniques such as pipelining, multiple execution units, and multiple cores. Pipelining is a powerful technique that is used in almost all current processor implementations. Techniques to extract and exploit the inherent parallelism in the code at compile time or run time are also widely used.

Exploiting program parallelism is one of the most important goals in computer architecture.

Instruction-level parallelism (ILP) means that multiple operations can be executed in parallel within a program. ILP may be achieved with hardware, compiler, or operating system techniques. At the loop level, consecutive loop iterations are ideal candidates for parallel execution, provided that there is no data dependency between subsequent loop iterations. Next, there is parallelism available at the procedure level, which depends largely on the algorithms used in the program. Finally, multiple independent programs can execute in parallel.

Different computer architectures have been built to exploit this inherent parallelism. In general, a computer architecture consists of one or more interconnected processor elements (PEs) that operate concurrently, solving a single overall problem.

1.4.1 Processor: A Functional View

Table 1.4 shows different SOC designs and the processor used in each design. For these examples, we can characterize them as general purpose, or special purpose with support for gaming or signal processing applications. This functional view tells little about the underlying hardware implementation. Indeed, several quite different architectural approaches could implement the same generic function. The graphics function, for example, requires shading, rendering, and texturing functions as well as perhaps a video function. Depending

TABLE 1.4 Processor Models for Different SOC Examples

SOC	Application	Base ISA	Processor Description
Freescale e600 [101]	DSP	PowerPC	Superscalar with vector extension
ClearSpeed CSX600 [59]	General	Proprietary ISA	Array processor of 96 processing elements
PlayStation 2 [147, 187, 237]	Gaming	MIPS	Pipelined with two vector coprocessors
ARM VFP11 [23]	General	ARM	Configurable vector coprocessor

Instruction

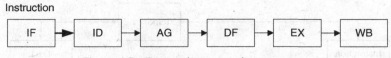

Figure 1.7 Instruction execution sequence.

on the relative importance of these functions and the resolution of the created images, we could have radically different architectural implementations.

1.4.2 Processor: An Architectural View

The architectural view of the system describes the actual implementation at least in a broad-brush way. For sophisticated architectural approaches, more detail is required to understand the complete implementation.

Simple Sequential Processor   Sequential processors directly implement the sequential execution model. These processors process instructions sequentially from the instruction stream. The next instruction is not processed until all execution for the current instruction is complete and its results have been committed.

The semantics of the instruction determines that a sequence of actions must be performed to produce the specified result (Figure 1.7). These actions can be overlapped, but the result must appear in the specified serial order. These actions include

1. fetching the instruction into the instruction register (IF),
2. decoding the opcode of the instruction (ID),
3. generating the address in memory of any data item residing there (AG),
4. fetching data operands into executable registers (DF),
5. executing the specified operation (EX), and
6. writing back the result to the register file (WB).

A simple sequential processor model is shown in Figure 1.8. During execution, a sequential processor executes one or more operations per clock cycle from the instruction stream. An instruction is a container that represents the smallest execution packet managed explicitly by the processor. One or more operations are contained within an instruction. The distinction between instructions and operations is crucial to distinguish between processor behaviors. Scalar and superscalar processors consume one or more instructions per cycle, where each instruction contains a single operation.

Although conceptually simple, executing each instruction sequentially has significant performance drawbacks: A considerable amount of time is spent on overhead and not on actual execution. Thus, the simplicity of directly implementing the sequential execution model has significant performance costs.

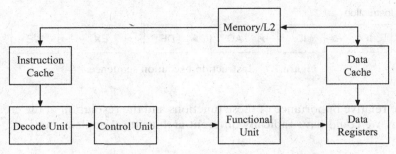

Figure 1.8 Sequential processor model.

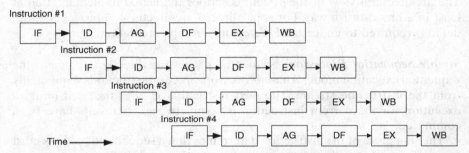

Figure 1.9 Instruction timing in a pipelined processor.

Pipelined Processor Pipelining is a straightforward approach to exploiting parallelism that is based on concurrently performing different phases (instruction fetch, decode, execution, etc.) of processing an instruction. Pipelining assumes that these phases are independent between different operations and can be overlapped—when this condition does not hold, the processor stalls the downstream phases to enforce the dependency. Thus, multiple operations can be processed simultaneously with each operation at a different phase of its processing. Figure 1.9 illustrates the instruction timing in a pipelined processor, assuming that the instructions are independent.

For a simple pipelined machine, there is only one operation in each phase at any given time; thus, one operation is being fetched (IF); one operation is being decoded (ID); one operation is generating an address (AG); one operation is accessing operands (DF); one operation is in execution (EX); and one operation is storing results (WB). Figure 1.10 illustrates the general form of a pipelined processor. The most rigid form of a pipeline, sometimes called the static pipeline, requires the processor to go through all stages or phases of the pipeline whether required by a particular instruction or not. A dynamic pipeline allows the bypassing of one or more pipeline stages, depending on the requirements of the instruction. The more complex dynamic pipelines allow instructions to complete out of (sequential) order, or even to initiate out of order. The out-of-order processors must ensure that the sequential consistency of the program is preserved. Table 1.5 shows some SOC pipelined "soft" processors.

TABLE 1.5   SOC Examples Using Pipelined Soft Processors [177, 178]. A Soft Processor Is Implemented with FPGAs or Similar Reconfigurable Technology

Processor	Word Length (bit)	Pipeline Stages	I/D-Cache* Total (KB)	Floating-Point Unit (FPU)	Usual Target
Xilinx MicroBlaze	32	3	0–64	Optional	FPGA
Altera Nios II fast	32	6	0–64	—	FPGA
ARC 600 [19]	16/32	5	0–32	Optional	ASIC
Tensilica Xtensa LX	16/24	5–7	0–32	Optional	ASIC
Cambridge XAP3a	16/32	2	—	—	ASIC

*Means configurable I-cache and/or D-cache.

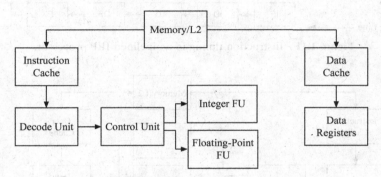

Figure 1.10   Pipelined processor model.

ILP   While pipelining does not necessarily lead to executing multiple instructions at exactly the same time, there are other techniques that do. These techniques may use some combination of static scheduling and dynamic analysis to perform concurrently the actual evaluation phase of several different operations, potentially yielding an execution rate of greater than one operation every cycle. Since historically most instructions consist of only a single operation, this kind of parallelism has been named ILP (instruction level parallelism).

Two architectures that exploit ILP are *superscalar* and *VLIW* processors. They use different techniques to achieve execution rates greater than one operation per cycle. A superscalar processor dynamically examines the instruction stream to determine which operations are independent and can be executed. A VLIW processor relies on the compiler to analyze the available operations (OP) and to schedule independent operations into wide instruction words, which then execute these operations in parallel with no further analysis.

Figure 1.11 shows the instruction timing of a pipelined superscalar or VLIW processor executing two instructions per cycle. In this case, all the instructions are independent so that they can be executed in parallel. The next two sections describe these two architectures in more detail.

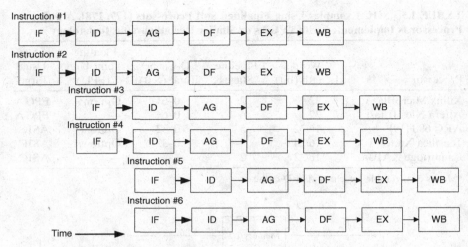

Figure 1.11 Instruction timing in a pipelined ILP processor.

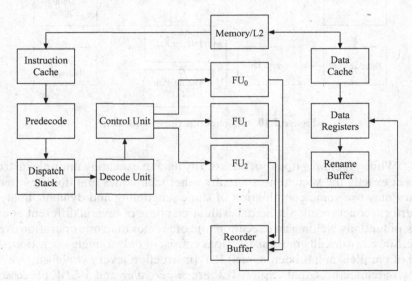

Figure 1.12 Superscalar processor model.

Superscalar Processors Dynamic pipelined processors remain limited to executing a single operation per cycle by virtue of their scalar nature. This limitation can be avoided with the addition of multiple functional units and a dynamic scheduler to process more than one instruction per cycle (Figure 1.12). These superscalar processors [135] can achieve execution rates of several instructions per cycle (usually limited to two, but more is possible depending on the application). The most significant advantage of a superscalar processor is that processing multiple instructions per cycle is done transparently to the user, and that it can provide binary code compatibility while achieving better performance.

Compared to a dynamic pipelined processor, a superscalar processor adds a scheduling instruction window that analyzes multiple instructions from the instruction stream in each cycle. Although processed in parallel, these instructions are treated in the same manner as in a pipelined processor. Before an instruction is issued for execution, dependencies between the instruction and its prior instructions must be checked by hardware.

Because of the complexity of the dynamic scheduling logic, high-performance superscalar processors are limited to processing four to six instructions per cycle. Although superscalar processors can exploit ILP from the dynamic instruction stream, exploiting higher degrees of parallelism requires other approaches.

VLIW Processors   In contrast to dynamic analyses in hardware to determine which operations can be executed in parallel, VLIW processors (Figure 1.13) rely on static analyses in the compiler.

VLIW processors are thus less complex than superscalar processors and have the potential for higher performance. A VLIW processor executes operations from statically scheduled instructions that contain multiple independent operations. Because the control complexity of a VLIW processor is not significantly greater than that of a scalar processor, the improved performance comes without the complexity penalties.

VLIW processors rely on the static analyses performed by the compiler and are unable to take advantage of any dynamic execution characteristics. For applications that can be scheduled statically to use the processor resources effectively, a simple VLIW implementation results in high performance. Unfortunately, not all applications can be effectively scheduled statically. In many applications, execution does not proceed exactly along the path defined

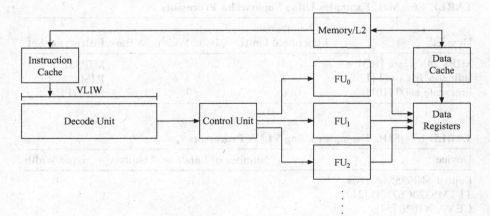

Figure 1.13   VLIW processor model.

by the code scheduler in the compiler. Two classes of execution variations can arise and affect the scheduled execution behavior:

1. delayed results from operations whose latency differs from the assumed latency scheduled by the compiler and
2. interruptions from exceptions or interrupts, which change the execution path to a completely different and unanticipated code schedule.

Although stalling the processor can control a delayed result, this solution can result in significant performance penalties. The most common execution delay is a data cache miss. Many VLIW processors avoid all situations that can result in a delay by avoiding data caches and by assuming worst-case latencies for operations. However, when there is insufficient parallelism to hide the exposed worst-case operation latency, the instruction schedule has many incompletely filled or empty instructions, resulting in poor performance.

Tables 1.6 and 1.7 describe some representative *superscalar* and *VLIW processors*.

SIMD Architectures: Array and Vector Processors   The SIMD class of processor architecture includes both array and vector processors. The SIMD processor is a natural response to the use of certain regular data structures, such as vectors and matrices. From the view of an assembly-level programmer, programming SIMD architecture appears to be very similar to programming a simple processor except that some operations perform computations on aggregate data. Since these regular structures are widely used in scientific programming, the SIMD processor has been very successful in these environments.

The two popular types of SIMD processor are the array processor and the vector processor. They differ both in their implementations and in their data

TABLE 1.6   SOC Examples Using Superscalar Processors

Device	Number of Functional Units	Issue Width	Base Instruction Set
MIPS 74K Core [183]	4	2	MIPS32
Infineon TriCore2 [129]	4	3	RISC
Freescale e600 [101]	6	3	PowerPC

TABLE 1.7   SOC Examples Using VLIW Processors

Device	Number of Functional Units	Issue Width
Fujitsu MB93555A [103]	8	8
TI TMS320C6713B [243]	8	8
CEVA-X1620 [54]	30	8
Philips Nexperia PNX1700 [199]	30	5

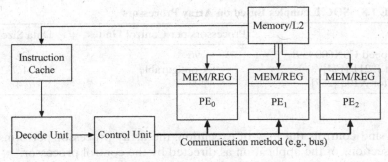

Figure 1.14 Array processor model.

organizations. An array processor consists of many interconnected processor elements, each having their own local memory space. A vector processor consists of a single processor that references a global memory space and has special function units that operate on vectors.

An array processor or a vector processor can be obtained by extending the instruction set to an otherwise conventional machine. The extended instructions enable control over special resources in the processor, or in some sort of coprocessor. The purpose of such extensions is to enable increased performance on special applications.

Array Processors The array processor (Figure 1.14) is a set of parallel processor elements connected via one or more networks, possibly including local and global interelement communications and control communications. Processor elements operate in lockstep in response to a single broadcast instruction from a control processor (SIMD). Each processor element (PE) has its own private memory, and data are distributed across the elements in a regular fashion that is dependent on both the actual structure of the data and also the computations to be performed on the data. Direct access to global memory or another processor element's local memory is expensive, so intermediate values are propagated through the array through local interprocessor connections. This requires that the data be distributed carefully so that the routing required to propagate these values is simple and regular. It is sometimes easier to duplicate data values and computations than it is to support a complex or irregular routing of data between processor elements.

Since instructions are broadcast, there is no means local to a processor element of altering the flow of the instruction stream; however, individual processor elements can conditionally disable instructions based on local status information—these processor elements are idle when this condition occurs. The actual instruction stream consists of more than a fixed stream of operations. An array processor is typically coupled to a general-purpose control processor that provides both scalar operations as well as array operations that are broadcast to all processor elements in the array. The control processor performs the scalar sections of the application, interfaces with the outside

TABLE 1.8   SOC Examples Based on Array Processors

Device	Processors per Control Unit	Data Size (bit)
ClearSpeed CSX600 [59]	96	32
Atsana J2211 [174]	Configurable	16/32
Xelerator X10q [257]	200	4

world, and controls the flow of execution; the array processor performs the array sections of the application as directed by the control processor.

A suitable application for use on an array processor has several key characteristics: a significant amount of data that have a regular structure, computations on the data that are uniformly applied to many or all elements of the data set, and simple and regular patterns relating the computations and the data. An example of an application that has these characteristics is the solution of the Navier–Stokes equations, although any application that has significant matrix computations is likely to benefit from the concurrent capabilities of an array processor.

Table 1.8 contains several array processor examples. The ClearSpeed processor is an example of an array processor chip that is directed at signal processing applications.

Vector Processors   A vector processor is a single processor that resembles a traditional single stream processor, except that some of the function units (and registers) operate on vectors—sequences of data values that are seemingly operated on as a single entity. These function units are deeply pipelined and have high clock rates. While the vector pipelines often have higher latencies compared with scalar function units, the rapid delivery of the input vector data elements, together with the high clock rates, results in a significant throughput.

Modern vector processors require that vectors be explicitly loaded into special vector registers and stored back into memory—the same course that modern scalar processors use for similar reasons. Vector processors have several features that enable them to achieve high performance. One feature is the ability to concurrently load and store values between the vector register file and the main memory while performing computations on values in the vector register file. This is an important feature since the limited length of vector registers requires that vectors longer than the register length would be processed in segments—a technique called strip mining. Not being able to overlap memory accesses and computations would pose a significant performance bottleneck.

Most vector processors support a form of result bypassing—in this case called chaining—that allows a follow-on computation to commence as soon as the first value is available from the preceding computation. Thus, instead of waiting for the entire vector to be processed, the follow-on computation can be significantly overlapped with the preceding computation that it is dependent on. Sequential computations can be efficiently compounded to behave as if they were a single operation, with a total latency equal to the latency of the first operation with the pipeline and chaining latencies of the remaining operations, but none of the start-up overhead that would be incurred without chaining. For example, division could be synthesized by chaining a reciprocal with a multiply operation. Chaining typically works for the results of load operations as well as normal computations.

A typical vector processor configuration (Figure 1.15) consists of a vector register file, one vector addition unit, one vector multiplication unit, and one vector reciprocal unit (used in conjunction with the vector multiplication unit to perform division); the vector register file contains multiple vector registers (elements).

Table 1.9 shows examples of vector processors. The IBM mainframes have vector instructions (and support hardware) as an option for scientific users.

Multiprocessors Multiple processors can cooperatively execute to solve a single problem by using some form of interconnection for sharing results. In

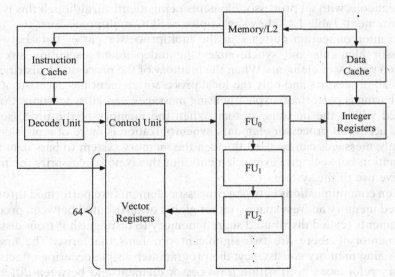

Figure 1.15 Vector processor model.

TABLE 1.9 SOC Examples Using Vector Processor

Device	Vector Function Units	Vector Registers
Freescale e600 [101]	4	32 Configurable
Motorola RSVP [58]	4 (64 bit partitionable at 16 bits)	2 streams (each 2 from, 1 to) memory
ARM VFP11 [23]	3 (64 bit partitionable to 32 bits)	4 × 8, 32 bit

Configurable implies a pool of N registers that can be configured as p register sets of N/p elements.

TABLE 1.10 SOC Multiprocessors and Multithreaded Processors

SOC	Machanick [162]	IBM Cell [141]	Philips PNX8500 [79]	Lehtoranta [155]
Number of CPUs	4	1	2	4
Threads	1	Many	1	1
Vector units	0	8	0	0
Application	Various	Various	HDTV	MPEG decode
Comment	Proposal only		Also called Viper 2	Soft processors

this configuration, each processor executes completely independently, although most applications require some form of synchronization during execution to pass information and data between processors. Since the multiple processors share memory and execute separate program tasks (MIMD [multiple instruction stream, multiple data stream]), their proper implementation is significantly more complex then the array processor. Most configurations are homogeneous with all processor elements being identical, although this is not a requirement. Table 1.10 shows examples of SOC multiprocessors.

The interconnection network in the multiprocessor passes data between processor elements and synchronizes the independent execution streams between processor elements. When the memory of the processor is distributed across all processors and only the local processor element has access to it, all data sharing is performed explicitly using messages, and all synchronization is handled within the message system. When the memory of the processor is shared across all processor elements, synchronization is more of a problem—certainly, messages can be used through the memory system to pass data and information between processor elements, but this is not necessarily the most effective use of the system.

When communications between processor elements are performed through a shared memory address space—either global or distributed between processor elements (called distributed shared memory to distinguish it from distributed memory)—there are two significant problems that arise. The first is maintaining memory consistency: the programmer-visible ordering effects on memory references, both within a processor element and between different processor elements. This problem is usually solved through a combination of hardware and software techniques. The second is cache coherency—the programmer-invisible mechanism to ensure that all processor elements see the same value for a given memory location. This problem is usually solved exclusively through hardware techniques.

The primary characteristic of a multiprocessor system is the nature of the memory address space. If each processor element has its own address space (distributed memory), the only means of communication between processor elements is through message passing. If the address space is shared (shared memory), communication is through the memory system.

The implementation of a distributed memory machine is far easier than the implementation of a shared memory machine when memory consistency and cache coherency are taken into account. However, programming a distributed memory processor can be much more difficult since the applications must be written to exploit and not to be limited by the use of message passing as the only form of communication between processor elements. On the other hand, despite the problems associated with maintaining consistency and coherency, programming a shared memory processor can take advantage of whatever communications paradigm is appropriate for a given communications requirement, and can be much easier to program.

1.5 MEMORY AND ADDRESSING

SOC applications vary significantly in memory requirements. In one case, the memory structure can be as simple as the program residing entirely in an on-chip read-only memory (ROM), with the data in on-chip RAM. In another case, the memory system might support an elaborate operating system requiring a large off-chip memory (system on a board), with a memory management unit and cache hierarchy.

Why not simply include memory with the processor on the die? This has many attractions:

1. It improves the accessibility of memory, improving both memory access time and bandwidth.
2. It reduces the need for large cache.
3. It improves performance for memory-intensive applications.

But there are problems. The first problem is that DRAM memory process technology differs from standard microprocessor process technology, and would cause some sacrifice in achievable bit density. The second problem is more serious: If memory were restricted to the processor die, its size would be correspondingly limited. Applications that require very large real memory space would be crippled. Thus, the conventional processor die model has evolved (Figure 1.16) to implement multiple robust homogeneous processors sharing the higher levels of a two- or three-level cache structure with the main memory off-die, on its own multidie module.

From a design complexity point of view, this has the advantage of being a "universal" solution: One implementation fits all applications, although not necessarily equally well. So, while a great deal of design effort is required for such an implementation, the production quantities can be large enough to justify the costs.

An alternative to this approach is clear. For specific applications, whose memory size can be bounded, we can implement an integrated memory SOC. This concept is illustrated in Figure 1.17 (also recall Figure 1.3).

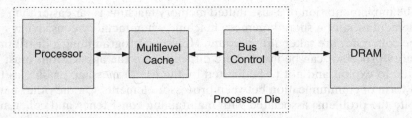

Figure 1.16   Processors with memory off-die.

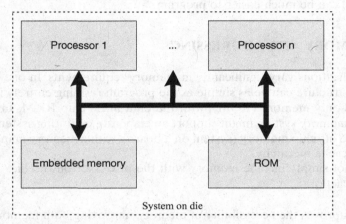

Figure 1.17   System on a chip: processors and memory.

A related but separate question is: Does the application require virtual memory (mapping disk space onto memory) or is all real memory suitable? We look at the requirement for virtual memory addressing in the next section.

Finally, the memory can be centralized or distributed. Even here, the memory can appear to the programmer as a single (centralized) shared memory, even though it is implemented in several distributed modules. Several memory considerations are listed in Table 1.11.

The *memory system* comprises the physical storage elements in the memory hierarchy. These elements include those specified by the instruction set (registers, main memory, and disk sectors) as well as those elements that are largely transparent to the user's program (buffer registers, cache, and page mapped virtual memory).

1.5.1 SOC Memory Examples

Table 1.12 shows a number of different SOC designs and their cache and memory configuration. It is important for SOC designers to consider whether to put RAM and ROM on-die or off-die. Table 1.13 shows various examples of SOC embedded memory macro cell.

TABLE 1.11   SOC Memory Considerations

Issue	Implementation	Comment
Memory placement	On-die	Limited and fixed size
	Off-die	System on a board, slow access, limited bandwidth
Addressing	Real addressing	Limited size, simple OS
	Virtual addressing	Much more complex, require TLB, in-order instruction execution support
Arrangement (as programmed for multiple processors)	Shared memory	Requires hardware support
	Message passing	Additional programming
Arrangement (as implemented)	Centralized	Limited by chip considerations
	Distributed	Can be clustered with a processor or other memory modules

TABLE 1.12   Memory Hierarchy for Different SOC Examples

SOC	Application	Cache Size	On-Die/ Off-Die	Real/ Virtual
NetSilicon NET + 40 [184]	Networking	4-KB I-cache, 4-KB D-cache	Off	Real
NetSilicon NS9775 [185]	Printing	8-KB I-cache, 4-KB D-cache	Off	Virtual
NXP LH7A404 [186]	Networking	16-KB I-cache, 8 KB D-Cache	On	Virtual
Motorola RSVP [58]	Multimedia	Tile buffer memory	Off	Real

1.5.2   Addressing: The Architecture of Memory

The user's view of memory primarily consists of the addressing facilities available to the programmer. Some of these facilities are available to the application programmer and some to the operating system programmer. Virtual memory enables programs requiring larger storage than the physical memory to run and allows separation of address spaces to protect unauthorized access to memory regions when executing multiple application programs. When virtual addressing facilities are properly implemented and programmed, memory can be efficiently and securely accessed.

Virtual memory is often supported by a memory management unit. Conceptually, the physical memory address is determined by a sequence of (at least) three steps:

TABLE 1.13 Example SOC Embedded Memory Macro Cell (See Chapter 4 for the Discussion on Cell Types)

Vendor	Cell Type (Typical)	SOC User (Typical)
Virage Logic	6T (SRAM)	SigmaTel/ARM
ATMOS	1T (eDRAM)	Philips
IBM	1T (eDRAM)	IBM

Note: T refers to the number of transistors in a 1-bit cell.

1. The application produces a *process address*. This, together with the *process or user ID*, defines the *virtual address*: *virtual address = offset + (program) base + index*, where the *offset* is specified in the instruction while the *base* and *index* values are in specified registers.

2. Since multiple processes must cooperate in the same memory space, the process addresses must be coordinated and relocated. This is typically done by a segment table. Upper bits of the *virtual address* are used to address a segment table, which has a (predetermined) *base* and *bound* values for the process, resulting in a *system address*: *system address = virtual address + (process) base*, where the *system address* must be less than the *bound*.

3. *Virtual versus real.* For many SOC applications (and all generic systems), the memory space exceeds the available (real) implemented memory. Here the memory space is implemented on disk and only the recently used regions (pages) are brought into memory. The available pages are located by a page table. The upper bits of the system address access a page table. If the data for this page have been loaded from the disk, the location in memory will be provided as the upper address bits of the "real" or physical memory address. The lower bits of the real address are the same as the corresponding lower bits of the virtual address.

Usually, the tables (segment and page) performing address translation are in memory, and a mechanism for the translation called the translation lookaside buffer (TLB) must be used to speed up this translation. A TLB is a simple register system, usually consisting of between 64 and 256 entries, that saves recent address translations for reuse. A small number of (hashed) virtual address bits address the TLB. The TLB entry has both the real address and the complete virtual address (and ID). If the virtual address matches, the real address from the TLB can be used. Otherwise, a *not-in-TLB* event occurs and a complete translation must occur (Figure 1.18).

1.5.3 Memory for SOC Operating System

One of the most critical decisions (or requirements) concerning an SOC design is the selection of the operating system and its memory management function-

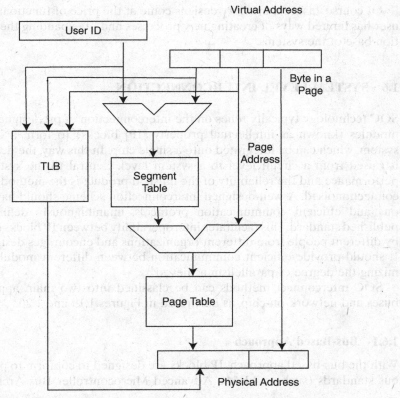

Figure 1.18 Virtual-to-real address mapping with a TLB bypass.

TABLE 1.14 Operating Systems for SOC Designs

OS	Vendor	Memory Model
uClinux	Open source	Real
VxWorks (RTOS) [254]	Wind River	Real
Windows CE	Microsoft	Virtual
Nucleus (RTOS) [175]	Mentor Graphics	Real
MQX (RTOS) [83]	ARC	Real

ality. Of primary interest to the designer is the requirement for virtual memory. If the system can be restricted to a real memory (physically, not virtually addressed) and the size of the memory can be contained to the order of 10s of megabytes, the system can be implemented as a true system on a chip (all memory on-die). The alternative, virtual memory, is often slower and significantly more expensive, requiring a complex memory management unit. Table 1.14 illustrates some current SOC designs and their operating systems.

Of course, fast real memory designs come at the price of functionality. The user has limited ways of creating new processes and of expanding the application base of the systems.

1.6 SYSTEM-LEVEL INTERCONNECTION

SOC technology typically relies on the interconnection of predesigned circuit modules (known as intellectual property [IP] blocks) to form a complete system, which can be integrated onto a single chip. In this way, the design task is raised from a circuit level to a system level. Central to the system-level performance and the reliability of the finished product is the method of interconnection used. A well-designed interconnection scheme should have vigorous and efficient communication protocols, unambiguously defined as a published standard. This facilitates interoperability between IP blocks designed by different people from different organizations and encourages design reuse. It should provide efficient communication between different modules maximizing the degree of parallelism achieved.

SOC interconnect methods can be classified into two main approaches: buses and network-on-chip, as illustrated in Figures 1.19 and 1.20.

1.6.1 Bus-Based Approach

With the bus-based approach, IP blocks are designed to conform to published bus standards (such as ARM's Advanced Microcontroller Bus Architecture

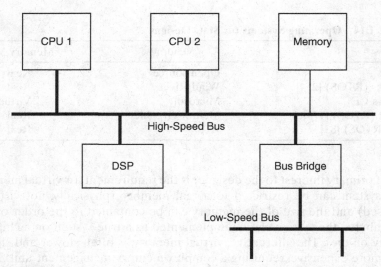

Figure 1.19 SOC system-level interconnection: bus-based approach.

[AMBA] [21] or IBM's CoreConnect [124]). Communication between modules is achieved through the sharing of the physical connections of address, data, and control bus signals. This is a common method used for SOC system-level interconnect. Usually, two or more buses are employed in a system, organized in a hierarchical fashion. To optimize system-level performance and cost, the bus closest to the CPU has the highest bandwidth, and the bus farthest from the CPU has the lowest bandwidth.

1.6.2 Network-on-Chip Approach

A network-on-chip system consists of an array of switches, either dynamically switched as in a crossbar or statically switched as in a mesh.

The crossbar approach uses asynchronous channels to connect synchronous modules that can operate at different clock frequencies. This approach has the advantage of higher throughput than a bus-based system while making integration of a system with multiple clock domains easier.

In a simple statically switched network (Figure 1.20), each node contains processing logic forming the core, and its own routing logic. The interconnect scheme is based on a two-dimensional mesh topology. All communications between switches are conducted through data packets, routed through the router interface circuit within each node. Since the interconnections between switches have a fixed distance, interconnect-related problems such as wire delay and cross talk noise are much reduced. Table 1.15 lists some interconnect examples used in SOC designs.

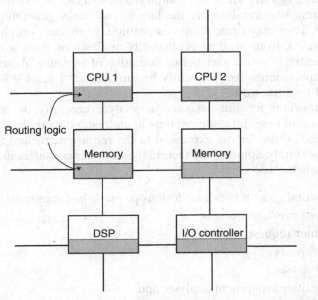

Figure 1.20   SOC system-level interconnection: network-on-chip approach.

TABLE 1.15 Interconnect Models for Different SOC Examples

SOC	Application	Interconnect Type
ClearSpeed CSX600 [59]	High Performance Computing	ClearConnect bus
NetSilicon NET +40 [184]	Networking	Custom bus
NXP LH7A404 [186]	Networking	AMBA bus
Intel PXA27x [132]	Mobile/wireless	PXBus
Matsushita i-Platform [176]	Media	Internal connect bus
Emulex InSpeed SOC320 [130]	Switching	Crossbar switch
MultiNOC [172]	Multiprocessing system	Network-on-chip

1.7 AN APPROACH FOR SOC DESIGN

Two important ideas in a design process are figuring out the requirements and specifications, and iterating through different stages of design toward an efficient and effective completion.

1.7.1 Requirements and Specifications

Requirements and specifications are fundamental concepts in any system design situation. There must be a thorough understanding of both before a design can begin. They are useful at the beginning and at the end of the design process: at the beginning, to clarify what needs to be achieved; and at the end, as a reference against which the completed design can be evaluated.

The system requirements are the largely externally generated criteria for the system. They may come from competition, from sales insights, from customer requests, from product profitability analysis, or from a combination. Requirements are rarely succinct or definitive of anything about the system. Indeed, requirements can frequently be unrealistic: "I want it fast, I want it cheap, and I want it now!"

It is important for the designer to analyze carefully the requirements expressions, and to spend sufficient time in understanding the market situation to determine all the factors expressed in the requirements and the priorities those factors imply. Some of the factors the designer considers in determining requirements include

- compatibility with previous designs or published standards,
- reuse of previous designs,
- customer requests/complaints,
- sales reports,
- cost analysis,
- competitive equipment analysis, and
- trouble reports (reliability) of previous products and competitive products.

The designer can also introduce new requirements based on new technology, new ideas, or new materials that have not been used in a similar systems environment.

The system specifications are the quantified and prioritized criteria for the target system design. The designer takes the requirements and must produce a succinct and definitive set of statements about the eventual system. The designer may have no idea of what the eventual system will look like, but usually, there is some "straw man" design in mind that seems to provide a feasibility framework to the specification. In any effective design process, it would be surprising if the final design significantly resembles the straw man design.

The specification does not complete any part of the design process; it initializes the process. Now the design can begin with the selection of components and approaches, the study of alternatives, and the optimization of the parts of the system.

1.7.2 Design Iteration

Design is always an iterative process. So, the obvious question is how to get the very first, initial design. This is the design that we can then iterate through and optimize according to the design criteria. For our purposes, we define several types of designs based on the stage of design effort.

Initial Design   This is the first design that shows promise in meeting the key requirements, while other performance and cost criteria are not considered. For instance, processor or memory or input/output (I/O) should be sized to meet high-priority real-time constraints. Promising components and their parameters are selected and analyzed to provide an understanding of their expected idealized performance and cost. Idealized does not mean ideal; it means a simplified model of the expected area occupied and computational or data bandwidth capability. It is usually a simple linear model of performance, such as the expected million instructions per second (MIPS) rate of a processor.

Optimized Design   Once the base performance (or area) requirements are met and the base functionality is ensured, then the goal is to minimize the cost (area) and/or the power consumption or the design effort required to complete the design. This is the iterative step of the process. The first steps of this process use higher-fidelity tools (simulations, trial layouts, etc.) to ensure that the initial design actually does satisfy the design specifications and requirements. The later steps refine, complete, and improve the design according to the design criteria.

Figure 1.21 shows the steps in creating an initial design. This design is detailed enough to create a component view of the design and a corresponding projection of the component's expected performance. This projection is, at this

```
1. Understand functional, cost, and real-time requirements.
2. Identify key requirements that the design must meet.
3. Prioritize the selection of processor, memory, and interconnect
   components based on their impact on key requirements.
4. Evaluate whether key requirements are met.
5. If yes, then initial design is completed.
6. If no, then try a different component selection; go to step 3.
```

Figure 1.21   The SOC initial design process.

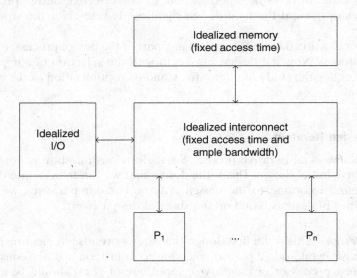

n idealized processors (P) selected by function

Figure 1.22   Idealized SOC components.

step, necessarily simplified and referenced to here as the idealized view of the component (Figure 1.22).

System performance is limited by the component with the least capability. The other components can usually be modeled as simply presenting a delay to the critical component. In a good design, the most expensive component is the one that limits the performance of the system. The system's ability to process transactions should closely follow that of the limiting component. Typically, this is the processor or memory complex.

Usually, designs are driven by either (1) a specific real-time requirement, after which functionality and cost become important, or (2) functionality and/or throughput under cost–performance constraints. In case (1), the real-time constraint is provided by I/O consideration, which the processor–memory–interconnect system must meet. The I/O system then determines the performance, and any excess capability of the remainder of the system is usually used to add functionality to the system. In case (2), the object is to improve task throughput while minimizing the cost. Throughput is limited by the most constrained component, so the designer must fully understand the trade-offs at that point. There is more flexibility in these designs, and correspondingly more options in determining the final design.

The purpose of this book is to provide an approach for determining the initial design by

(a) describing the range of components—processors, memories, and interconnects—that are available in building an SOC;

(b) providing examples of requirements for various domains of applications, such as data compression and encryption; and

(c) illustrating how an initial design, or a reported implementation, can show promise in meeting specific requirements.

We explain this approach in Chapters 3–5 on a component by component basis to cover (a), with Chapter 6 covering techniques for system configuration and customization. Chapter 7 contains application studies to cover (b) and (c).

As mentioned earlier, the designer must optimize each component for processing and storage. This optimization process requires extensive simulation. We provide access to basic simulation tools through our associated web site.

1.8   SYSTEM ARCHITECTURE AND COMPLEXITY

The basic difference between processor architecture and system architecture is that the system adds another layer of complexity, and the complexity of these systems limits the cost savings. Historically, the notion of a computer is a single processor plus a memory. As long as this notion is fixed (within broad tolerances), implementing that processor on one or more silicon die does not change the design complexity. Once die densities enable a scalar processor to fit on a chip, the complexity issue changes.

Suppose it takes about 100,000 transistors to implement a 32-bit pipelined processor with a small first-level cache. Let this be a processor unit of design complexity.

As long as we need to implement the 100,000 transistor processors, additional transistor density on the die does not much affect design complexity. More transistors per die, while increasing die complexity, simplify the problem of interconnecting multiple chips that make up the processor. Once the unit processor is implemented on a single die, the design complexity issue changes. As transistor densities significantly improve after this point, there are obvious processor extension strategies to improve performance:

1. *Additional Cache.* Here we add cache storage and, as large caches have slower access times, a second-level cache.

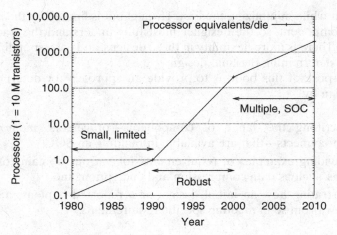

Figure 1.23   Complexity of design.

2. *A More Advanced Processor.* We implement a superscalar or a VLIW processor that executes more than one instruction each cycle. Additionally, we speed up the execution units that affect the critical path delay, especially the floating-point execution times.

3. *Multiple Processors.* Now we implement multiple (superscalar) processors and their associated multilevel caches. This leaves us limited only by the memory access times and bandwidth.

The result of the above is a significantly greater design complexity (see Figure 1.23). Instead of the 100,000 transistor processors, our advanced processor has millions of transistors; the multilevel caches are also complex, as is the need to coordinate (synchronize) the multiple processors, since they require a consistent image of the contents of memory.

The obvious way to manage this complexity is to reuse designs. So, reusing several simpler processor designs implemented on a die is preferable to a new, more advanced, single processor. This is especially true if we can select specific processor designs suited to particular parts of an application. For this to work, we also need a robust interconnection mechanism to access the various processors and memory.

So, when an application is well specified, the system-on-a-chip approach includes

1. multiple (usually) heterogeneous processors, each specialized for specific parts of the application;

2. the main memory with (often) ROM for partial program storage;

3. a relatively simple, small (single-level) cache structure or buffering schemes associated with each processor; and

4. a bus or switching mechanism for communications.

Even when the SOC approach is technically attractive, it has economic limitations and implications. Given the processor and interconnect complexity, if we limit the usefulness of an implementation to a particular application, we have to either (1) ensure that there is a large market for the product or (2) find methods for reducing the design cost through design reuse or similar techniques.

1.9 PRODUCT ECONOMICS AND IMPLICATIONS FOR SOC

1.9.1 Factors Affecting Product Costs

The basic cost and profitability of a product depend on many factors: its technical appeal, its cost, the market size, and the effect the product has on future products. The issue of cost goes well beyond the product's manufacturing cost.

There are fixed and variable costs, as shown in Figure 1.24. Indeed, the engineering costs, frequently the largest of the fixed costs, are expended before any revenue can be realized from sales (Figure 1.25).

Depending on the complexity, designing a new chip requires a development effort of anywhere between 12 and 30 months before the first manufactured unit can be shipped. Even a moderately sized project may require up to 30 or more hardware and software engineers, CAD design, and support personnel. For instance, the paper describing the Sony Emotion Engine has 22 authors [147, 187]. However, their salary and indirect costs might represent only a fraction of the total development cost.

Nonengineering fixed costs include manufacturing start-up costs, inventory costs, initial marketing and sales costs, and administrative overhead. The

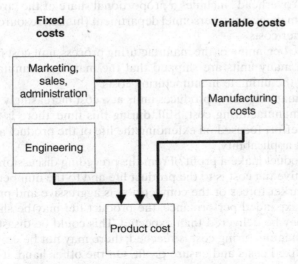

Figure 1.24 Project cost components.

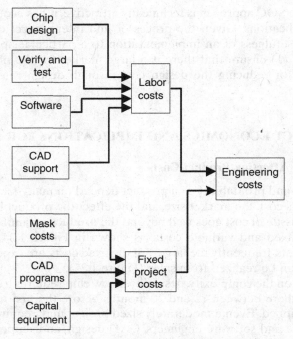

Figure 1.25 Engineering (development) costs.

marketing costs include obvious items such as market research, strategic market planning, pricing studies, and competitive analysis, and so on, as well as sales planning and advertising costs. The concept of general and administrative (G & A) "overhead" includes a proportional share of the "front office"—the executive management, personnel department (human resources), financial office, and other costs.

Later, in the beginning of the manufacturing process, unit cost remains high. It is not until many units are shipped that the marginal manufacturing cost can approach the ultimate manufacturing costs.

After this, manufacturing produces units at a cost increasingly approaching the ultimate manufacturing cost. Still, during this time, there is a continuing development effort focused on extending the life of the product and broadening its market applicability.

Will the product make a profit? From the preceding discussion, it is easy to see how sensitive the cost is to the product life and to the number of products shipped. If market forces or the competition is aggressive and produces rival systems with expanded performance, the product life may be shortened and fewer units may be delivered than expected. This could be disastrous even if the ultimate manufacturing cost is reached; there may not be enough units to amortize the fixed costs and ensure profit. On the other hand, if competition is not aggressive and the follow-on development team is successful in enhancing the product and continuing its appeal in the marketplace, the product can become one of those jewels in a company's repertoire, bringing fame to the designers and smiles to the stockholders.

1.9.2 Modeling Product Economics and Technology Complexity: The Lesson for SOC

To put all this into perspective, consider a general model of a product's *average* unit cost (as distinct from its ultimate manufactured cost):

$$\text{unit cost} = (\text{project cost}) / (\text{number of units}).$$

The product cost is simply the sum of all the fixed and variable costs. We represent the fixed cost as a constant, K_f. It is also clear that the variable costs are of the form $K_v \times n$, where n is the number of units. However, there are certain ongoing engineering, sales, and marketing costs that are related to n but are not necessarily linear.

Let us assume that we can represent this effect as a term that starts as 0.1 of K_f and then slowly increases with n, say, $\sqrt[3]{n}$. So, we get

$$\text{Product cost} = K_f + 0.1 \times K_f \times \sqrt[3]{n} + K_v \times n. \tag{1.1}$$

We can use Equation 1.1 to illustrate the effects of advancing technology on product design. We compare a design done in 1995 with a more complex 2005 design, which has a much lower production cost. With K_f fixed, Figure 1.26 shows the expected decrease in unit cost as the volume of 1995 products produced, n, increases. But the figure also shows that, if we increase the fixed costs

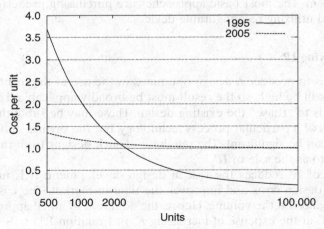

Figure 1.26 The effect of volume on unit cost.

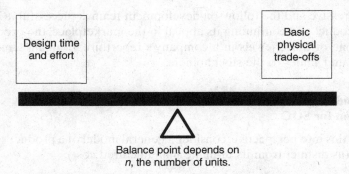

Figure 1.27   The design effort must balance volume.

(more complex designs) by 10-fold, even if we cut the unit costs (K_v) by the same amount, the 2005 unit product costs remain high until much larger volumes are reached. This might not be a problem for a "universal" processor design with a mass market, but it can be a challenge for those SOC designs targeted at specific applications, which may have limited production volume; a more specific design will be more efficient for a particular application, at the expense of generality, which affects volume.

1.10   DEALING WITH DESIGN COMPLEXITY

As design cost and complexity increase, there is a basic trade-off between the design optimization of the physical product and the cost of the design. This is shown in Figure 1.27. The balance point depends on n, the number of units expected to be produced. There are several approaches to the design productivity problem. The most basic approaches are purchasing predesigned components and utilizing reconfigurable devices.

1.10.1   Buying IP

If the goal is to produce a design optimized in the use of the technology, the fixed costs will be high, so the result must be broadly applicable. The alternative to this is to "reuse" the existing design. These may be suboptimal for all the nuances of a particular process technology, but the savings in design time and effort can be significant. The purchase of such designs from third parties is referred to as the sale of *IP*.

The use of IP reduces the risk in design development: It is intended to reduce the design costs and improves the time to market. The cost of an IP usually depends on the volume. Hence, the adoption of an IP approach tends to reduce K_f at the expense of increasing K_v in Equation 1.1.

TABLE 1.16   Types of Processor Cores Available as IP

Type of Design	Design Level	Description
Customized hard IP	Physical level	IP used in fixed process, optimized
Synthesized firm IP	Gate level	IP used in multiple processes but some optimization possible
Synthesizable soft IP	Register transfer level (RTL)	IP used in any process, nonoptimized

Specialized SOC designs often use several different types of processors. Noncritical and specialized processors are purchased as IP and are integrated into the design. For example, the ARM7TDMA is a popular licensed 32-bit processor or "core" design. Generally, processor cores can be designed and licensed in a number of ways as shown in Table 1.16.

Hard IPs are physical-level designs that use all features available in a process technology, including circuit design and physical layout. Many analog IPs and mixed-signal IPs (such as SRAM, phase-locked loop) are distributed in this format to ensure optimal timing and other design characteristics. Firm IPs are gate-level designs that include device sizing but are applicable to many fab facilities with different processor technologies. Soft IPs are logic-level designs in synthesizable format and are directly applicable to standard cell technologies. This approach allows users to adapt the source code to fit their design over a broad range of situations.

Clearly, the more optimized designs from the manufacturer are usually less customizable by the user, but they often have better physical, cost–performance trade-offs. There are potential performance–cost–power overheads in delaying the customization process, since the design procedure and even the product technology itself would have to support user customization. Moreover, customizing a design may also necessitate reverification to ensure its correctness. Current technologies, such as the reconfiguration technology described below, aim to maximize the advantages of late customization, such as risk reduction and improvement of time to market. At the same time, they aim to minimize the associated disadvantages, for instance, by introducing hardwired, nonprogrammable blocks to support common operations such as integer multiplication; such hardwired blocks are more efficient than reconfigurable resources, but they are not as flexible.

1.10.2   Reconfiguration

The term *reconfiguration* refers to a number of approaches that enable the same circuitry to be reused in many applications. A reconfigurable device can also be thought of as a type of purchased IP in which the cost and risk of fabrication are eliminated, while the support for user customization would

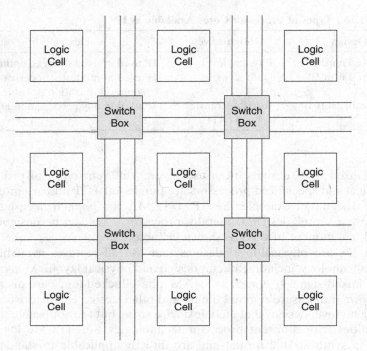

Figure 1.28   The FPGA array.

raise the unit cost. In other words, the adoption of reconfigurable devices would tend to reduce K_f at the expense of increasing K_v in Equation 1.1.

The best-known example of this approach is FPGA technology. An FPGA consists of a large array of cells. Each cell consists of a small lookup table, a flip-flop, and perhaps an output selector. The cells are interconnected by programmable connections, enabling flexible routing across the array (Figure 1.28). Any logic function can be implemented on the FPGA by configuring the lookup tables and the interconnections. Since an array can consist of over 100,000 cells, it can easily define a processor. An obvious disadvantage of the FPGA-based soft processor implementation is its performance–cost–power. The approach has many advantages, however:

1. Circuit fabrication costs increase exponentially with time; hence, it would not be economical to fabricate a circuit unless it can support a large volume. FPGAs themselves are general-purpose devices and are expected to be produced in large volume.
2. The design time for FPGA implementations is low compared to designing a chip for fabrication. There are extensive libraries of designs available for use. This is particularly important for designs for which a short time to market is critical.

3. FPGAs can be used for rapid prototyping of circuits that would be fabricated. In this approach, one or more FPGAs are configured according to the proposed design to emulate it, as a form of "in-circuit emulation." Programs are run and design errors can be detected.

4. The reconfigurability of FPGAs enables in-system upgrade, which helps to increase the time in market of a product; this capability is especially valuable for applications where new functions or new standards tend to emerge rapidly.

5. The FPGA can be configured to suit a portion of a task and then reconfigured for the remainder of the task (called "run-time reconfiguration"). This enables specialized functional units for certain computations to adapt to environmental changes.

6. In a number of compute-intensive applications, FPGAs can be configured as a very efficient systolic computational array. Since each FPGA cell has one or more storage elements, computations can be pipelined with very fine granularity. This can provide an enormous computational bandwidth, resulting in impressive speedup on selected applications. Some devices, such as the Stretch S5 software configurable processor, couple a conventional processor with an FPGA array [25].

Reconfiguration and FPGAs play an important part in efficient SOC design. We shall explore them in more detail in the next chapter.

1.11   CONCLUSIONS

Building modern processors or targeted application systems is a complex undertaking. The great advantages offered by the technology—hundreds of millions of transistors on a die—comes at a price, not the silicon itself, but the enormous design effort that is required to implement and support the product.

There are many aspects of SOC design, such as high-level descriptions, compilation technologies, and design flow, that are not mentioned in this chapter. Some of these will be covered later.

In the following chapters, we shall first take a closer look at basic trade-offs in the technology: time, area, power, and reconfigurability. Then, we shall look at some of the details that make up the system components: the processor, the cache, and the memory, and the bus or switch interconnecting them. Next, we cover design and implementation issues from the perspective of customization and configurability. This is followed by a discussion of SOC design flow and application studies. Finally, some challenges facing future SOC technology are presented.

The goal of the text is to help system designers identify the most efficient design choices, together with the mechanisms to manage the design complexity by exploiting the advances in technology.

1.12 PROBLEM SET

1. Suppose the TLB in Figure 1.18 had 256 entries (directly addressed). If the virtual address is 32 bits, the real memory is 512 MB and the page size is 4 KB, show the possible layout of a TLB entry. What is the purpose of the user ID in Figure 1.18 and what is the consequence of ignoring it?

2. Discuss possible arrangement of addressing the TLB.

3. Find an actual VLIW instruction format. Describe the layout and the constraints on the program in using the applications in a single instruction.

4. Find an actual vector instruction for vector ADD. Describe the instruction layout. Repeat for vector load and vector store. Is overlapping of vector instruction execution permitted? Explain.

5. For the pipelined processor in Figure 1.9, suppose instruction #3 sets the CC (condition code that can be tested by following a branch instruction) at the end of WB and instruction #4 is the condition branch. Without additional hardware support, what is the delay in executing instruction #5 if the branch is taken and if the branch is not taken?

6. Suppose we have four different processors; each does 25% of the application. If we improve two of the processors by 10 times, what would be the overall application speedup?

7. Suppose we have four different processors and all but one are totally limited by the bus. If we speed up the bus by three times and assume the processor performance also scales, what is the application speedup?

8. For the pipelined processor in Figure 1.9, assume the cache miss rate is 0.05 per instruction execution and the total cache miss delay is 20 cycles. For this processor, what is the achievable cycle per instruction (CPI)? Ignore other delays, such as branch delays.

9. Design validation is a very important SOC design consideration. Find several approaches specific to SOC designs. Evaluate each from the perspective of a small SOC vendor.

10. Find (from the Internet) two new VLIW DSPs. Determine the maximum number of operations issued in each cycle and the makeup of the operations (number of integer, floating point, branch, etc.). What is the stated maximum performance (operations per second)? Find out how this number was computed.

11. Find (from the Internet) two new, large FPGA parts. Determine the number of logic blocks (configurable logic blocks [CLBs]), the minimum cycle time, and the maximum allowable power consumption. What soft processors are supported?

2 Chip Basics: Time, Area, Power, Reliability, and Configurability

2.1 INTRODUCTION

The trade-off between cost and performance is fundamental to any system design. Different designs result either from the selection of different points on the cost–performance continuum or from differing assumptions about the nature of cost or performance.

The driving force in design innovation is the rapid advance in technology. The Semiconductor Industry Association (SIA) regularly makes projections, called the SIA road map, of technology advances, which become the basis and assumptions for new chip designs. While the projections change, the advance has been and is expected to continue to be formidable. Table 2.1 is a summary of the roadmap projections for the microprocessors with the highest performance introduced in a particular year [133]. With the advances in lithography, the transistors are getting smaller. The minimum width of the transistor gates is defined by the process technology. Table 2.1 refers to process technology generations in terms of nanometers; older generations are referred to in terms of microns (μm). So the previous generations are 65 and 90 nm, and 0.13 and 0.18 μm.

2.1.1 Design Trade-Offs

With increases in chip frequency and especially in transistor density, the designer must be able to find the best set of trade-offs in an environment of rapidly changing technology. Already the chip frequency projections have been called into question because of the resulting power requirements.

In making basic design trade-offs, we have five different considerations. The first is *time*, which includes partitioning instructions into events or cycles, basic pipelining mechanisms used in speeding up the instruction execution, and cycle time as a parameter for optimizing program execution. Second, we discuss *area*. The cost or area occupied by a particular feature is another important aspect of the architectural trade-off. Third, *power consumption*

Computer System Design: System-on-Chip, First Edition. Michael J. Flynn and Wayne Luk.
© 2011 John Wiley & Sons, Inc. Published 2011 by John Wiley & Sons, Inc.

TABLE 2.1   Technology Roadmap Projections

Year	2010	2013	2016
Technology generation (nm)	45	32	22
Wafer size, diameter (cm)	30	45	45
Defect density (per cm^2)	0.14	0.14	0.14
μP die size (cm^2)	1.9	2.6	2.6
Chip frequency (GHz)	5.9	7.3	9.2
Million transistors per square centimeter	1203	3403	6806
Max power (W) high performance	146	149	130

affects both performance and implementation. Instruction sets that require more implementation area are less valuable than instruction sets that use less—unless, of course, they can provide commensurately better performance. Long-term *cost–performance ratio* is the basis for most design decisions. Fourth, *reliability* comes into play to cope with deep submicron effects. Fifth, *configurability* provides an additional opportunity for designers to trade off recurring and nonrecurring design costs.

FIVE BIG ISSUES IN SYSTEM-ON-CHIP (SOC) DESIGN

Four of the issues are obvious. *Die area* (manufacturing cost) and *performance* (heavily influenced by cycle time) are important basic SOC design considerations. Power consumption has also come to the fore as a design limitation. As technology shrinks feature sizes, reliability will dominate as a design consideration.

The fifth issue, configurability, is less obvious as an immediate design consideration. However, as we saw in Chapter 1, in SOC design, the nonrecurring design costs can dominate the total project cost. Making a design flexible through reconfigurability is an important issue to broaden the market—and reduce the per part cost—for SOC design.

Configurability enables programmability in the field and can be seen to provide features that are "standardized in manufacturing while customized in application." The cyclical nature of the integrated circuit industry between standardization and customization has been observed by Makimoto [163] and is known as Makimoto's wave, as shown in Figure 2.1.

In terms of complexity, various trade-offs are possible. For instance, at a fixed feature size, area can be traded off for performance (expressed in term of execution time, T). Very large scale integration (VLSI) complexity theorists have shown that an A $\times$ T^n bound exists for processor designs, where n usually falls between 1 and 2 [247]. It is also possible to trade off time T for power P

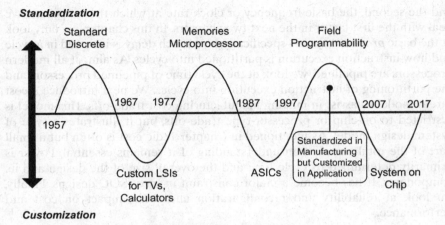

Figure 2.1 Makimoto's wave.

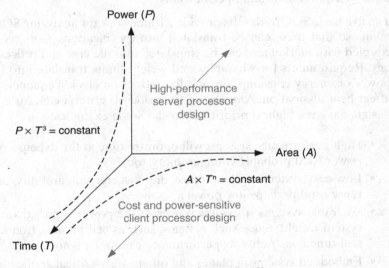

Figure 2.2 Processor design trade-offs.

with a $P \times T^3$ bound. Figure 2.2 shows the possible trade-off involving area, time, and power in a processor design [98]. Embedded and high-end processors operate in different design regions of this three-dimensional space. The power and area axes are typically optimized for embedded processors, whereas the time axis is typically for high-end processors.

This chapter deals with design issues in making these trade-offs. It begins with the issue of time. The ultimate measure of performance is the time required to complete required system tasks and functions. This depends on two factors: first, the organization and size of the processors and memories, and the second, the basic frequency or clock rate at which these operate. We deal with the first factor in the next two chapters. In this chapter, we only look at the basic *processor cycle*—specifically, how much delay is incurred in a cycle and how instruction execution is partitioned into cycles. As almost all modern processors are pipelined, we look at the cycle time of pipelined processors and the partitioning of instruction execution into cycles. We next introduce a cost (area) model to assist in making manufacturing cost trade-offs. This model is restricted to on-chip or processor-type trade-offs, but it illustrates a type of system design model. As mentioned in Chapter 1, die cost is often but a small part of the total cost, but an understanding of it remains essential. Power is primarily determined by cycle time and the overall size of the design and its components. It has become a major constraint in most SOC designs. Finally, we look at reliability and reconfiguration and their impact on cost and performance.

2.1.2   Requirements and Specifications

The five basic SOC trade-offs provide a framework for analyzing SOC require-ments so that these can be translated into specifications. Cost requirements coupled with market size can be translated into die cost and process technol-ogy. Requirements for wearables and weight limits translate into bounds on power or energy consumption, and limitations on clock frequency, which can affect heat dissipation. Any one of the trade-off criteria can, for a particular design, have the highest priority. Consider some examples:

- High-performance systems will optimize time at the expense of cost and power (and probably configurability, too).
- Low-cost systems will optimize die cost, reconfigurability, and design reuse (and perhaps low power).
- Wearable systems stress low power, as the power supply determines the system weight. Since such systems, such as cell phones, frequently have real-time constraints, its performance cannot be ignored.
- Embedded systems in planes and other safety-critical applications would stress reliability, with performance and design lifetime (configurability) being important secondary considerations.
- Gaming systems would stress cost—especially production cost—and, sec-ondarily, performance, with reliability being a lesser consideration.

In considering requirements, the SOC designer should carefully consider each trade-off item to derive corresponding specifications. This chapter, when coupled with the essential understanding of the system components, which we will see in later chapters, provides the elements for SOC requirements transla-tion into specifications and the beginning of the study of optimization of design alternatives.

2.2   CYCLE TIME

The notion of time receives considerable attention from processor designers. It is the basic measure of performance; however, breaking actions into cycles and reducing both cycle count and cycle times are important but inexact sciences.

The way actions are partitioned into cycles is important. A common problem is having unanticipated "extra" cycles required by a basic action such as a cache miss. Overall, there is only a limited theoretical basis for cycle selection and the resultant partitioning of instruction execution into cycles. Much design is done on a pragmatic basis.

In this section, we look at some techniques for instruction partitioning, that is, techniques for breaking up the instruction execution time into manageable and fixed time cycles. In a pipelined processor, data flow through stages much as items flow on an assembly line. At the end of each stage, a result is passed on to a subsequent stage and new data enter. Within limits, the shorter the cycle time, the more productive the pipeline. The partitioning process has its own overhead, however, and very short cycle times become dominated by this overhead. Simple cycle time models can optimize the number of pipeline stages.

THE PIPELINED PROCESSOR

At one time, the concept of *pipelining* in a processor was treated as an advanced processor design technique. For the past several decades, pipelining has been an integral part of any processor or, indeed, controller design. It is a technique that has become a basic consideration in defining cycle time and execution time in a processor or system.

The trade-off between cycle time and number of pipeline stages is treated in the section on *optimum pipeline*.

2.2.1   Defining a Cycle

A cycle (of the clock) is the basic time unit for processing information. In a synchronous system, the clock rate is a fixed value and the cycle time is determined by finding the maximum time to accomplish a frequent operation in the machine, such as an add or register data transfer. This time must be sufficient for data to be stored into a specified destination register (Figure 2.3). Less frequent operations that require more time to complete require multiple cycles.

A cycle begins when the instruction decoder (based on the current instruction opcode) specifies the values for the registers in the system. These control

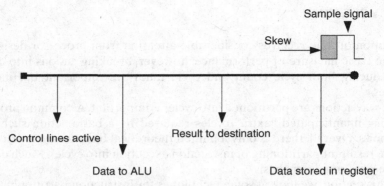

Figure 2.3   Possible sequence of actions within a cycle.

values connect the output of a specified register to another register or an adder or similar object. This allows data from source registers to propagate through designated combinatorial logic into the destination register. Finally, after a suitable setup time, all registers are sampled by an edge or pulse produced by the clocking system.

In a synchronous system, the cycle time is determined by the sum of the worst-case time for each step or action within the cycle. However, the clock itself may not arrive at the anticipated time (due to propagation or loading effects). We call the maximum deviation from the expected time of clock arrival the (uncontrolled) clock skew.

In an asynchronous system, the cycle time is simply determined by the completion of an event or operation. A completion signal is generated, which then allows the next operation to begin. Asynchronous design is not generally used within pipelined processors because of the completion signal overhead and pipeline timing constraints.

2.2.2 Optimum Pipeline

A basic optimization for the pipeline processor designer is the partitioning of the pipeline into concurrently operating segments. A greater number of segments allow a higher maximum speedup. However, each new segment carries clocking overhead with it, which can adversely affect performance.

If we ignore the problem of fitting actions into an integer number of cycles, we can derive an optimal cycle time, Δt, and hence the level of segmentation for a simple pipelined processor.

Assume that the total time to execute an instruction without pipeline segments is T nanoseconds (Figure 2.4a). The problem is to find the optimum number of segments S to allow clocking and pipelining. The ideal delay through a segment is $T/S = T_{\text{seg}}$. Associated with each segment is partitioning overhead. This clock overhead time C (in nanoseconds), includes clock skew and any register requirements for data setup and hold.

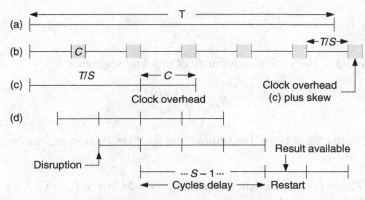

Figure 2.4 Optimal pipelining. (a) Unclocked instruction execution time, *T*. (b) *T* is partitioned into *S* segments. Each segment requires *C* clocking overhead. (c) Clocking overhead and its effect on cycle time, *T/S*. (d) Effect of a pipeline disruption (or a *stall* in the pipeline).

Now, the actual cycle time (Figure 2.4c) of the pipelined processor is the ideal cycle time *T/S* plus the overhead:

$$\Delta t = \frac{T}{S} + C.$$

In our idealized pipelined processor, if there are no code delays, it processes instructions at the rate of one per cycle, but delays can occur (primarily due to incorrectly guessed or unexpected branches). Suppose these interruptions occur with frequency *b* and have the effect of invalidating the *S* − 1 instructions prepared to enter, or already in, the pipeline (representing a "worst-case" disruption, Figure 2.4d). There are many different types of pipeline interruption, each with a different effect, but this simple model illustrates the effect of disruptions on performance.

Considering pipeline interruption, the performance of the processor is

$$\text{Performance} = \frac{1}{1 + (S-1)b} \text{ instructions per cycle.}$$

The throughput (*G*) can be defined as

$$G = \frac{\text{performance}}{\Delta t} \text{ instructions/ns}$$

$$= \left(\frac{1}{1 + (S-1)b} \right) \times \left(\frac{1}{(T/S) + C} \right).$$

If we find the *S* for which

$$\frac{dG}{dS} = 0,$$

we can find S_{opt}, the optimum number of pipeline segments:

$$S_{opt} = \sqrt{\frac{(1-b)T}{bC}}.$$

Once an initial S has been determined, the total instruction execution latency (T_{instr}) is

$$T_{instr} = T + S \times (\text{clocking overhead}) = T + SC, \text{ or } S(T_{seg} + C) = S\Delta t.$$

Finally, we compute the throughput performance G in (million) instructions per second.

Suppose $T = 12.0$ ns and $b = 0.2$, $C = 0.5$ ns. Then, $S_{opt} = 10$ stages.

This S_{opt} as determined is simplistic—functional units cannot be arbitrarily divided, integer cycle boundaries must be observed, and so on. Still, determining S_{opt} can serve as a design starting point or as an important check on an otherwise empirically optimized design.

The preceding discussion considers a number of pipeline segments, S, on the basis of performance. Each time a new pipeline segment is introduced, additional cost is added, which is not factored into the analysis. Each new segment requires additional registers and clocking hardware. Because of this, the optimum number of pipeline segments (S_{opt}) ought to be thought of as a probable upper limit to the number of useful pipeline segments that a particular processor can employ.

2.2.3 Performance

High clock rates with small pipeline segments may or may not produce better performance. Indeed, given problems in wire delay scaling, there is an immediate question of how projected clock rates are to be achieved. There are two basic factors enabling clock rate advances: (1) increased control over clock overhead and (2) an increased number of segments in the pipelines. Figure 2.5 shows that the length (in gate delays) of a pipeline segment has decreased significantly, probably by more than five times, measured in units of a standard gate delay. This standard gate has one input and drives four similar gates as output. Its delay is referred to as a fan-out of four (FO4) gate delay.

Low clock overhead (small C) may enable increased pipeline segmentation, but performance does not correspondingly improve unless we also decrease the probability of pipeline disruption, b. In order to accomplish this high clock rate, processors also employ large branch table buffers and branch vector prediction tables, significantly decreasing delays due to branching. However, disruptions can also come from cache misses, and this requires another strat-

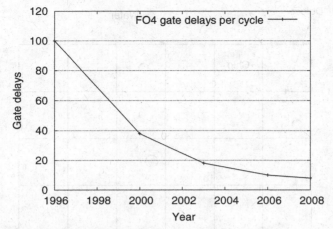

Figure 2.5 Number of gate delays (FO4) allowed in a cycle.

egy: multilevel, very large on-die caches. Often these cache structures occupy 80–90% of the die area. The underlying processor is actually less important than the efficiency of the cache memory system in achieving performance.

2.3   DIE AREA AND COST

Cycle time, machine organization, and memory configuration determine machine performance. Determining performance is relatively straightforward when compared to the determination of overall cost.

A good design achieves an optimum cost–performance trade-off at a particular target performance. This determines the *quality* of a processor design.

In this section, we look at the marginal cost to produce a system as determined by the die area component. Of course, the system designer must be aware of significant side effects that die area has on the fixed and other variable costs. For example, a significant increase in the complexity of a design may directly affect its serviceability or its documentation costs, or the hardware development effort and time to market. These effects must be kept in mind, even when it is not possible to accurately quantify their extent.

2.3.1   Processor Area

SOCs usually have die sizes of about 10–15 mm on a side. This die is produced in bulk from a larger wafer, perhaps 30 cm in diameter (about 12 in.). It might seem that one could simply expand the chip size and produce fewer chips from the wafer, and these larger chips could readily accommodate any function that the designer might wish to include. Unfortunately, neither the silicon wafers nor processing technologies are perfect. Defects randomly occur over the

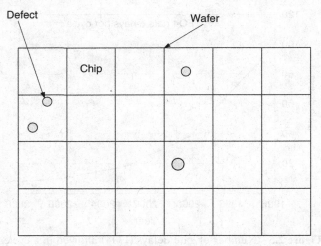

Figure 2.6   Defect distribution on a wafer.

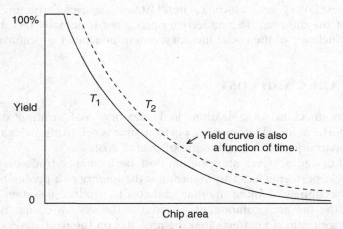

Figure 2.7   Yield versus chip area at various points in time.

wafer surface (Figure 2.6). Large chip areas require an absence of defects over that area. If chips are too large for a particular processing technology, there will be little or no yield. Figure 2.7 illustrates yield versus chip area.

A good design is not necessarily the one that has the maximum yield. Reducing the area of a design below a certain amount has only a marginal effect on yield. Additionally, small designs waste area because there is a required area for pins and for separation between the adjacent die on a wafer.

The area available to a designer is a function of the manufacturing processing technology. This includes the purity of the silicon crystals, the absence of dust and other impurities, and the overall control of the process technology. Improved manufacturing technology allows larger dice to be realized with higher yields. As photolithography and process technology improve, their

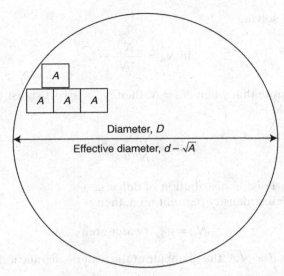

Figure 2.8 Number of die (of area A) on a wafer of diameter d.

design parameters do not scale uniformly. The successful designer must be aggressive enough in anticipating the movement of technology so that, although early designs may have low yield, with the advance of technology, the design life is extended and the yield greatly improves, thus allowing the design team to amortize fixed costs over a broad base of products.

Suppose a die with square aspect ratio has area A. About N of these dice can be realized in a wafer of diameter d (Figure 2.8):

$$N \approx \frac{\pi}{4A}\left(d - \sqrt{A}\right)^2.$$

This is the wafer area divided by the die area with diameter correction. Now suppose there are N_G good chips and N_D point defects on the wafer. Even if $N_D > N$, we might expect several good chips since the defects are randomly distributed and several defects would cluster on defective chips, sparing a few.

Following the analysis of Ghandi [109], suppose we add a random defect to a wafer; N_G/N is the probability that the defect ruins a good die. Note that if the defect hits an already bad die, it would cause no change to the number of good die. In other words, the change in the number of good die (N_G), with respect to the change in the number of defects (N_D), is

$$\frac{dN_G}{dN_D} = -\frac{N_G}{N}$$

$$\frac{1}{N_G}dN_G = -\frac{1}{N}dN_D.$$

Integrating and solving

$$\ln N_G = -\frac{N_D}{N} + C.$$

To evaluate C, note that when $N_G = N$, then $N_D = 0$; so, C must be $\ln(N)$.
    Then the yield is

$$\text{Yield} = \frac{N_G}{N} = e^{-N_D/N}.$$

This describes a Poisson distribution of defects.
    If ρ_D is the defect density per unit area, then

$$N_D = \rho_D \times (\text{wafer area}).$$

For large wafers $d \gg \sqrt{A}$, the diameter of the wafer is significantly larger than
the die side and

$$\left(d - \sqrt{A}\right)^2 \approx d^2$$

and

$$\frac{N_D}{N} = \rho_D A,$$

so that

$$\text{Yield} = e^{-\rho_D A}.$$

Figure 2.9 shows the projected number of good die as a function of die area
for several defect densities. Currently, a modern fab facility would have ρ_D
between 0.15–0.5, depending on the maturity of the process and the expense
of the facility.
    Large die sizes are very costly. Doubling the die area has a significant effect
on yield for an already large $\rho_D \times A$ (≈ 5–10 or more). Thus, the large die
designer gambles that technology will lower ρ_D in time to provide a sufficient
yield for a profitable product.

2.3.2   Processor Subunits

Within a system or processor, the amount of area that a particular subunit of
a design occupies is a primary measure of its cost. In making design choices
or in evaluating the relative merits of a particular design choice, it is frequently
useful to use the principle of marginal utility: Assume we have a complete base
design and some additional pins/area available to enhance the design. We

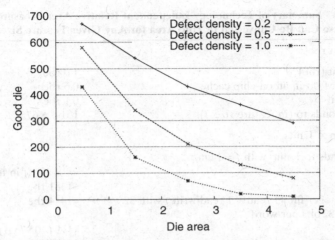

Figure 2.9 Number of good die versus die area for several defect densities.

select the design enhancement that best uses the available pins and area. In the absence of pinout information, we assume that area is a dominant factor in a particular trade-off.

The obvious unit of area is *millimeter square*, but since photolithography and geometries' resulting minimum feature sizes are constantly shifting, a dimensionless unit is preferred. Among others, Mead and Conway [170] used the unit λ, the fundamental resolution, which is the distance from which a geometric feature on any one layer of mask may be positioned from another. The minimum size for a diffusion region would be 2λ with a necessary allowance of 3λ between adjacent diffusion regions.

If we start with a device $2\lambda \times 2\lambda$, then a device of nominal $2\lambda \times 2\lambda$ can extend to $4\lambda \times 4\lambda$. We need at least 1λ isolation from any other device or $25\lambda^2$ for the overall device area. Thus, a single transistor is $4\lambda^2$, positioned in a minimum region of $25\lambda^2$.

The minimum feature size (f) is the length of one polysilicon gate, or the length of one transistor, $f = 2\lambda$. Clearly, we could define our design in terms of λ^2, and any other processor feature (gate, register size, etc.) can be expressed as a number of transistors. Thus, the selection of the area unit is somewhat arbitrary. However, a better unit represents primary architectural trade-offs. One useful unit is the register bit equivalent (rbe). This is defined to be a six-transistor register cell and represents about $2700\lambda^2$. This is significantly more than six times the area of a single transistor, since it includes larger transistors, their interconnections, and necessary inter-bit isolating spaces.

A staticRAM (SRAM) cell with lower bandwidth would use less area than an rbe, and a DRAM bit cell would use still less. Empirically, they would have the relationship shown in Table 2.2.

In the table, the area for the register file is determined by the number of register bits and the number of ports (P) available to access the file:

TABLE 2.2 Summary of Technology-Independent Relative Area Measures, rbe and A (These Can Be Converted to True Area for Any Given Feature Size, f)

Item: Size in rbe	
1 register bit (rbe)	1.0 rbe
1 static RAM bit in an on-chip cache	0.6 rbe
1 DRAM bit	0.1 rbe
rbe corresponds to (in feature size: f)	1 rbe = $675f^2$
Item: Size in A Units	
A corresponds to $1\,mm^2$ with $f = 1\,\mu m$.	
$1\,A$	$=f^2 \times 10^6$ (f in μm)
or about	≈ 1481 rbe
A simple integer file (1 read + 1 read/write) with 32 words of 32 bits per word	=1444 rbe
or about	$\approx 1\,A$ ($=0.975\,A$)
A 4-KB direct mapped cache	=23,542 rbe
or about	$\approx 16\,A$
Generally a simple cache (whose tag and control bits are less than one-fifth the data bits) uses	$=4\,A/KB$
Simple Processors (Approximation)	
A 32-bit processor (no cache and no floating point)	$=50\,A$
A 32-bit processor (no cache but includes 64-bit floating point)	$=100\,A$
A 32-bit (signal) processor, as above, with vector facilities but no cache or vector memory	$=200\,A$
Area for interunit latches, buses, control, and clocking	Allow an additional 50% of the processor area.
Xilinx FPGA	
A slice (2 LUTs + 2 FFs + MUX)	=700 rbe
A configurable logic block (4 slices) Virtex 4	=2800 rbe $\approx 1.9\,A$
A 18-KB block RAM	=12,600 rbe $\approx 8.7\,A$
An embedded PPC405 core	$\approx 250\,A$

$$\text{Area of register file} = (\text{number of regs} + 3P)(\text{bits per reg} + 3P) \text{ rbe.}$$

The cache area uses the SRAM bit model and is determined by the total number of cache bits, including the array, directory, and control bits.

The number of rbe on a die or die section rapidly becomes very large, so it is frequently easier to use a still larger unit. We refer to this unit simply as A and define it as $1\,mm^2$ of die area at $f = 1\,\mu m$. This is also the area occupied by a 32×32 bit three-ported register file or 1481 rbe.

Transistor density, rbe, and A all scale as the square of the feature size. As seen from Table 2.3, for feature size f, the number of A in $1\,mm^2$ is simply $(1/f)^2$. There are almost 500 times as many transistors of rbe in $1\,mm^2$ of a technology with a feature size of 45 nm as there are with the reference 1-μm feature size.

TABLE 2.3   Density in *A* Units for Various Feature Sizes

Feature Size (μm)	Number of *A* per mm^2
1.000	1.00
0.350	8.16
0.130	59.17
0.090	123.46
0.065	236.69
0.045	493.93

One *A* is 1481 rbe.

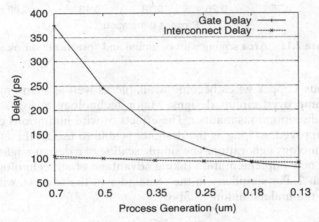

Figure 2.10   The dominance of wire delay over gate delay.

2.4   IDEAL AND PRACTICAL SCALING

As feature sizes shrink and transistors get smaller, one expects the transistor density to improve with the square of the change in feature size. Similarly, transistor delay (or gate delay) should decrease linearly with feature size (corresponding to the decrease in capacitance). Practical scaling is different as wire delay, and wire density does not scale at the same rate as transistors scale. Wire delay remains almost constant as feature sizes shrink since the increase in resistance offsets the decrease in length and capacitance. Figure 2.10 illustrates the increasing dominance of wire delay over gate delay especially in feature sizes less than 0.10 μm. Similarly for feature sizes below 0.20 μm, transistor density improves at somewhat less than the square of the feature size. A suggested scaling factor of 1.5 is commonly considered more accurate, as shown in Figure 2.11; that is, scaling occurs at $(f_1/f_2)^{1.5}$ rather than at $(f_1/f_2)^2$. What actually happens during scaling is more complex. Not only does the feature size shrink but other aspects of a technology also change and usually

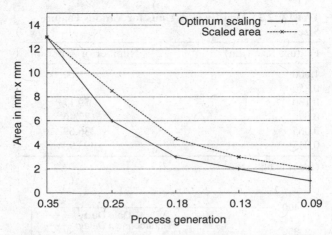

Figure 2.11   Area scaling with optimum and "practical" shrinkage.

improve. Thus, copper wires become available as well as many more wiring layers and improved circuit designs. Major technology changes can affect scaling in a discontinuous manner. The effects of wire limitations can be dramatically improved, so long as the designer is able to use all the attributes of the new technology generation. The simple scaling of a design might only scale as 1.5, but a new implementation taking advantage of all technology features could scale at 2. For simplicity in the remainder of the text, we will use ideal scaling with the understanding as above.

Study 2.1   A Baseline SOC Area Model

The key to efficient system design is chip floor planning. The process of chip floor planning is not much different from the process of floor-planning a residence. Each functional area of the processor must be allocated sufficient room for its implementation. Functional units that frequently communicate must be placed close together. Sufficient room must be allocated for connection paths.

To illustrate possible trade-offs that can be made in optimizing the chip floor plan, we introduce a baseline system with designated areas for various functions. The area model is based upon empirical observations made of existing chips, design experience, and, in some cases, logical deduction (e.g., the relationship between a floating-point adder and an integer ALU). The chip described here ought not to be considered optimal in any particular sense, but rather a typical example of a number of designs in the marketplace today.

The Starting Point. The design process begins with an understanding of the parameters of the semiconductor process. Suppose we expect to be able to use a manufacturing process that has a defect density of 0.2 defect per square centimeter; for economic reasons, we target an initial yield of about 95%:

$$Y = e^{-\rho_D A},$$

where $\rho_D = 0.2$ defect per square centimeter, $Y = 0.95$. Then,

$$A = 25 \text{ mm}^2$$

or approximately 0.25 cm^2.

So the chip area available to us is 25 mm^2. This is the total die area of the chip, but such things as pads for the wire bonds that connect the chip to the external world, drivers for these connections, and power supply lines all act to decrease the amount of chip area available to the designer. Suppose we allow 12% of the chip area—usually around the periphery of the chip—to accommodate these functions, then the net area will be 22 mm^2 (Figure 2.12).

Feature Size. The smaller the feature size, the more logic that can be accommodated within a fixed area. At $f = 65 \text{ nm}$, we have about $5200 A$ or area units in 22 mm^2.

The Architecture. Almost by definition, each system is different with different objectives. For our example, assume that we need the following:

- a small 32-bit core processor with an $8 KB$ I-cache and a $16 KB$ D-cache;
- two 32-bit vector processors, each with 16 banks of $1K \times 32b$ vector memory; an $8 KB$ I-cache and a $16 KB$ D-cache for scalar data;
- a bus control unit;
- directly addressed application memory of $128 KB$; and
- a shared L2 cache.

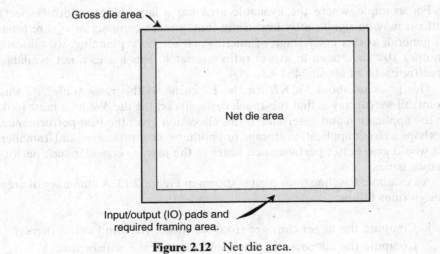

Figure 2.12 Net die area.

An Area Model. The following is a breakdown of the area required for various units used in the system.

Unit	Area (A)
Core processor (32^b)	100
Core cache ($24\,KB$)	96
Vector processor #1	200
Vector registers and cache #1	256 + 96
Vector processor #2	200
Vector registers and cache #2	352
Bus and bus control (50%)	See below 650
Application memory (128 KB)	512
Subtotal	2462

Latches, Buses, and (Interunit) Control. For each of the functional units, there is a certain amount of overhead to accommodate nonspecific storage (latches), interunit communications (buses), and interunit control. This is allocated as 10% overhead for latches and 40% overhead for buses, routing, clocking, and overall control.

Total System Area. The designated processor elements and storage occupy $2462\,A$. This leaves a net of $5200 - 2462 = 2738\,A$ available for cache. Note that the die is highly storage oriented. The remaining area will be dedicated to the L2 cache.

Cache Area. The net area available for cache is $2738\,A$. However, bits and pieces that may be unoccupied on the chip are not always useful to the cache designer. These pieces must be collected into a reasonably compact area that accommodates efficient cache designs.

For example, where the available area has a large height/width (aspect) ratio, it may be significantly less useful than a more compact or square area. In general, at this early stage of microprocessor floor planning, we allocate another 10% overhead to aspect ratio mismatch. This leaves a net available area for cache of about $2464\,A$.

This gives us about $512\,KB$ for the L2 cache. Is this reasonable? At this point, all we can say is that this much cache fits on the die. We now must look to the application and determine if this allocation gives the best performance. Perhaps a larger application storage or another vector processor and a smaller L2 would give better performance. Later in the text we consider such performance issues.

An example baseline floor plan is shown in Figure 2.13. A summary of area design rules follow:

1. Compute the target chip size from the target yield and defect density.
2. Compute the die cost and determine whether it is satisfactory.

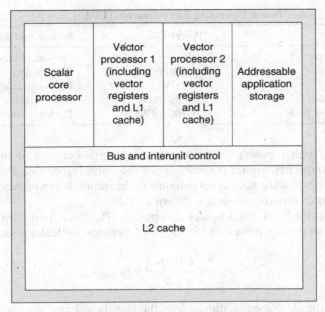

Figure 2.13   A baseline die floor plan.

3. Compute the net available area. Allow 10–20% (or other appropriate factor) for pins, guard ring, power supplies, and so on.
4. Determine the **rbe** size from the minimum feature size.
5. Allocate the area based on a trial system architecture until the basic system size is determined.
6. Subtract the basic system size (5) from the net available area (3). This is the die area available for cache and storage optimization.

Note that in this study (and more surely with much small feature sizes), most of the die area is dedicated to storage of one type or another. The basic processor area is around 20%, allowing for a partial allocation of bus and control area. Thus, however rough our estimate of processor core and vector processor area, it is likely to have little effect on the accuracy of the die allocation so long as our storage estimates are accurate. There are a number of commercial tools available for chip floor planning in specific design situations.

2.5 POWER

Growing demands for wireless and portable electronic appliances have focused much attention recently on power consumption. The SIA road map points to

TABLE 2.4   Some Power Operating Environments [133]

Type	Power/Die	Source and Environment
Cooled high power	70.0 W	Plug-in, chilled
High power	10.0–50.0 W	Plug-in, fan
Low power	0.1–2.0 W	Rechargeable battery
Very low power	1.0–100.0 mW	AA batteries
Extremely low power	1.0–100.0 μW	Button battery

increasingly higher power for microprocessor chips because of their higher operating frequency, higher overall capacitance, and larger size. Power scales indirectly with feature size, as its primary determinate is frequency.

Some power environments are shown in Table 2.4.

At the device level, total power dissipation (P_{total}) has two major sources: dynamic or switching power and static power caused by leakage current:

$$P_{total} = \frac{CV^2 \text{freq}}{2} + I_{leakage}V,$$

where C is the device capacitance; V is the supply voltage; freq is the device switching frequency; and $I_{leakage}$ is the leakage current. Until recently, switching loss was the dominant factor in dissipation, but now static power is increasing. On the other hand, gate delays are roughly proportional to $CV/(V - V_{th})^2$, where V_{th} is the threshold voltage (for logic-level switching) of the transistors.

As feature sizes decrease, so do device sizes. Smaller device sizes result in reduced capacitance. Decreasing the capacitance decreases both the dynamic power consumption and the gate delays. As device sizes decrease, the electric field applied to them becomes destructively large. To increase the device reliability, we need to reduce the supply voltage V. Reducing V effectively reduces the dynamic power consumption but results in an increase in the gate delays. We can avoid this loss by reducing V_{th}. On the other hand, reducing V_{th} increases the leakage current and, therefore, the static power consumption. This has an important effect on design and production; there are two device designs that must be accommodated in production:

1. the high-speed device with low V_{th} and high static power; and
2. the slower device maintaining V_{th} and V at the expense of circuit density and low static power.

In either case, we can reduce switching loss by lowering the supply voltage, V. Chen et al. [55] showed that the drain current is proportional to

$$I = (V - V_{th})^{1.25},$$

where again V is the supply voltage.

From our discussion above, we can see that the signal transition time and frequency scale with the charging current. So, the maximum operating frequency is also proportional to $(V - V_{th})^{1.25}/V$. For values of V and V_{th} of interest, this means that frequency scales with the supply voltage, V.

Assume V_{th} is 0.6V; suppose we reduce the supply voltage by one-half, say, from 3.0 to 1.5V, the operating frequency is also reduced by about one-half. So, reducing the supply voltage by half also reduces the operating frequency by half.

Now by the power equation (since the voltage and frequency were halved), the total power consumption is one-eighth of the original. Thus, if we take an existing design optimized for frequency and modify that design to operate at a lower voltage, the frequency is reduced by approximately the cube root of the original (dynamic) power:

$$\frac{freq_1}{freq_2} = \sqrt[3]{\frac{P_2}{P_1}}.$$

It is important to understand the distinction between scaling the frequency of an existing design and that of a power-optimized implementation. Power-optimized implementations differ from performance-optimized implementations in several ways.

Power-optimized implementations use less chip area not only because of reduced requirements for power supply and clock distributions but also, and more importantly, because of reduced performance targets. Performance-oriented designs use a great deal of area to achieve marginally improved performance, as in very large floating-point units, minimum-skew clock distribution networks, or maximally sized caches. Power dissipation, not performance, is the most critical issue for applications such as portable and wireless processors running on batteries. Some battery capacities are shown in Table 2.5.

For SOC designs to run on battery power for an extended period, the entire system power consumption must remain very small (in the order of a milliwatt). As a result, power management must be implemented from the system architecture and operating system down to the logic gate level.

There is another power constraint, *peak power*, which the designer cannot ignore. In any design, the power source can only provide a certain current at the specified voltage; going beyond this, even as a transient, can cause logic errors or worse (damaging the power source).

TABLE 2.5   Battery Capacity and Duty Cycle

Type	Energy Capacity (mAh)	Duty Cycle/Lifetime	At Power
Rechargeable	10,000	50h (10–20% duty)	400mW–4W
2 × AA	4000	0.5 year (10–20% duty)	1–10mW
Button	40	5 years (always on)	1 μW

2.6 AREA–TIME–POWER TRADE-OFFS IN PROCESSOR DESIGN

Processor design trade-offs are quite different for our two general classes of processors:

1. *Workstation Processor.* These designs are oriented to high clock frequency and AC power sources (excluding laptops). Since they are not area limited as the cache occupies most die area, the designs are highly elaborated (superscalar with multithreading).

2. *Embedded Processor Used in SOC.* Processors here are generally simpler in control structure but may be quite elaborate in execution facilities (e.g., digital signal processor [DSP]). Area is a factor as is design time and power.

2.6.1 Workstation Processor

To achieve a general-purpose performance, the designer assumes ample power. The most basic trade-off is between high clock rates and the resulting power consumption. Up until the early 1990s, emitter coupled logic (ECL) using bipolar technology was dominant in high-performance applications (mainframes and supercomputers). At power densities of 80W/cm^2, the module package required some form of liquid cooling. An example from this period is the Hitachi M-880 (Figure 2.14). A $10 \times 10 \text{cm}$ module consumed 800 W. The

Figure 2.14 Hitachi processor module. The Hitachi M-880 was introduced about 1991 [143]. Module is $10.6 \times 10.6 \text{cm}$, water-cooled and dissipated at 800 W.

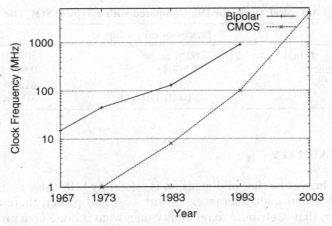

Figure 2.15 Processor frequency for bipolar and CMOS over time. Generally, CMOS frequency scaling ceased in around 2003 at around 3.5 GHz due to power limitations.

module contained 40 dice, sealed in helium gas with chilled water pumped across a water jacket at the top of the module. As CMOS performance approached bipolar's, the extraordinary cost of such a cooling system could no longer be sustained, and the bipolar era ended (see Figure 2.15). Now CMOS has reached the same power densities, and similar cooling techniques would have to be reconsidered if chip frequencies were to continue to increase. In fact, after 2003 the useful chip frequency stabilized at about 3.5 GHz.

2.6.2   Embedded Processor

System-on-a-chip-type implementations have a number of advantages. The requirements are generally known. So, memory sizes and real-time delay constraints can be anticipated. Processors can be specialized to a particular function. In doing so, usually clock frequency (and power) can be reduced as performance can be regained by straightforward concurrency in the architecture (e.g., use of a simple very long instruction word [VLIW] for DSP applications). The disadvantages of SOC compared to processor chips are available design time/effort and intra-die communications between functional units. In SOC, the market for any specific system is relatively small; hence, the extensive custom optimization used in processor dies is difficult to sustain, so off-the-shelf core processor designs are commonly used. As the storage size for programs and data may be known at design time, specific storage structures can be included on-chip. These are either SRAM or a specially designed DRAM (as ordinary DRAM uses an incompatible process technology). With multiple storage units, multiple processors (some specialized, some generic), and specialized controllers, the problem is designing a robust bus hierarchy to ensure timely communications. A comparison between the two design classes is shown in Table 2.6.

TABLE 2.6   A Typical Processor Die Compared with a Typical SOC Die

	Processor on a Chip	SOC
Area used by storage	80% cache	50% ROM/RAM
Clock frequency	3.5 GHz	0.5 GHz
Power	≥50 W	≤10 W
Memory	≥1-GB DRAM	Mostly on-die

2.7   RELIABILITY

The fourth important design dimension is reliability [218], also referred to as dependability and fault tolerance. As with cost and power, there are many more factors that contribute to reliability than what is done on a processor or SOC die.

Reliability is related to die area, clock frequency, and power. Die area increases the amount of circuitry and the probability of a fault, but it also allows the use of error correction and detection techniques. Higher clock frequencies increase electrical noise and noise sensitivity. Faster circuits are smaller and more susceptible to radiation.

Not all failures or errors produce faults, and indeed not all faults result in incorrect program execution. Faults, if detected, can be masked by error-correcting codes (ECCs), instruction retry, or functional reconfiguration.

First, some definitions:

1. A *failure* is a deviation from a design specification.
2. An *error* is a failure that results in an incorrect signal value
3. A *fault* is an error that manifests itself as an incorrect logical result.
4. A *physical fault* is a failure caused by the environment, such as aging, radiation, temperature, or temperature cycling. The probability of physical faults increases with time.
5. A *design fault* is a failure caused by a design implementation that is inconsistent with the design specification. Usually, design faults occur early in the lifetime of a design and are reduced or eliminated over time.

2.7.1   Dealing with Physical Faults

From a system point of view, we need to create processor and subunit configurations that are robust over time.

Let the probability of a fault occurrence be $P(t)$, and let T be the *mean time between faults* (MTBF). So, if λ is the fault rate, then

$$\lambda = \frac{1}{T}.$$

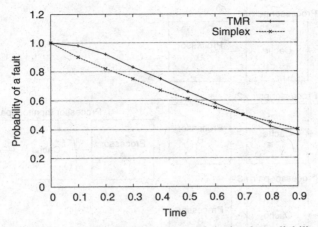

Figure 2.16   TMR reliability compared to simplex reliability.

Now imagine that faults occur on the time axis in particular time units, separated with mean, T. Using the same reasoning that we used to develop the Poisson yield equation, we can get the Poisson fault equation:

$$P(t) = e^{\frac{-t}{T}} = e^{-t\lambda}.$$

Redundancy is an obvious approach to improved reliability (lower $P(t)$). A well-known technique is *triple modular redundancy* (TMR). Three processors execute the same computation and compare results. A voting mechanism selects the output on which at least two processors agree. TMR works but only up to a point. Beyond the obvious problem of the reliability of the voting mechanism, there is a problem with the sheer amount of hardware. Clearly, as time t approaches T, we expect to have more faults in the TMR system than in a simple simplex system (Figure 2.16). Indeed, the probability of a TMR fault (any two out of three processor faults) exceeds the simplex system when

$$t = T \times \log_e 2.$$

Most fault-tolerant designs involve simpler hardware built around the following:

- *Error Detection.* The use of parity, residue, and other codes are essential to reliable system configurations.
- *Instruction (Action) Retry.* Once a fault is detected, the action can be retried to overcome transient errors.

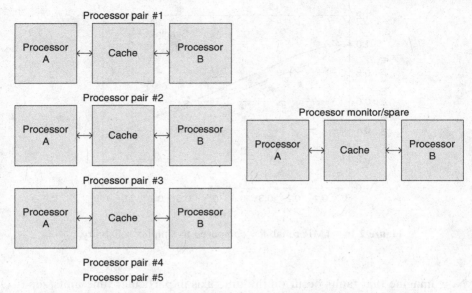

Figure 2.17 A duplex approach to fault tolerance using error detection.

- *Error Correction.* Since most of the system is storage and memory, an ECC can be effective in overcoming storage faults.
- *Reconfiguration.* Once a fault is detected, it may be possible to reconfigure parts of the system so that the failing subsystem is isolated from further computation.

Note that with error detection, efficient, reliable system configurations are limited. As a minimum, most systems should incorporate error detection on all parts of essential system components and should selectively use ECC and other techniques to improve reliability.

The IBM mainframe S/390 (Figure 2.17) is an example of a system oriented to reliability. One model provides a module of 12 processors. Five pairs in duplex configuration (5×2) run five independent tasks, and two processors are used as monitor and spare. Within a duplex, the processor pairs share a common cache and storage system. The processor pairs run the same task and compare results. The processors use error detection wherever possible. The cache and storage uses ECC, usually single error correction, double error detection (SECDED).

Recent research addresses reliability for multiprocessor SOC technology. For instance, to improve reliability due to single-event upsets due to cosmic rays, techniques involving voltage scaling and application task mapping can be applied [214].

2.7.2   Error Detection and Correction

The simplest type of error detection is parity. A bit is added (a check bit) to every stored word or data transfer, which ensures that the sum of the number of 1's in the word is even (or odd, by predetermined convention). If a single error occurs to any bit in the word, the sum modulo two of the number of 1's in the word is inconsistent with the parity assumption, and the memory word is known to have been corrupted.

Knowing that there is an error in the retrieved word is valuable. Often, a simple reaccessing of the word may retrieve the correct contents. However, often the data in a particular storage cell have been lost and no amount of reaccessing can restore the true value of the data. Since such errors are likely to occur in a large system, most systems incorporate hardware to automatically correct single errors by making use of ECCs.

The simplest code of this type consists of a geometric block code. The message bits to be checked are arranged in a roughly square pattern, and the message is augmented by a parity bit for each row and for each column. If a row and a column indicate a flaw when the message is decoded at the receiver, the intersection is the damaged bit, which may be simply inverted for correction. If only a single row or a column or multiple rows or columns indicate a parity failure, a multiple-bit error is detected and a noncorrectable state is entered.

For 64 message bits, we need to add 17 parity bits: eight for each of the rows and columns and one additional parity bit to compute parity on the parity row and column (Figure 2.18).

It is more efficient to consider the message bits as forming a hypercube, for each message combination forms a particular point in this hypercube. If the

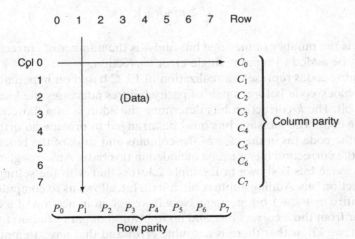

Figure 2.18   Two-dimensional error-correcting codes (ECCs).

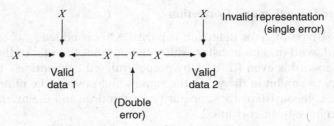

Figure 2.19 ECC code distance.

hypercube can be enlarged so that each valid data point is surrounded by associated invalid data points that are caused by a single-bit corruption in the message, the decoder will recognize that the invalid data point belongs to the valid point and will be able to restore the message to its original intended form. This can be extended one more step by adding yet another invalid point between two valid data combinations (Figure 2.19). The minimum number of bits by which valid representations may differ is the code distance. This third point indicates that two errors have occurred. Hence, either of two valid code data points is equally likely, and the message is detectably flawed but noncorrectable. For a message of 64 bits, and for single-bit error correction, each of the 2^{64} combinations must be surrounded by, or must accommodate, a failure of any of the 64 constituent bits ($2^6 = 64$). Thus, we need 2^{64+6} total code combinations to be able to identify the invalid states associated with each valid state, or a total of 2^{64+6+1} total data states. We can express this in another way:

$$2^k \geq m + k + 1,$$

where m is the number of message bits and k is the number of correction bits that must be added to support single error correction.

Hamming codes represent a realization of ECC based on hypercubes. Just as in the block code before, a pair of parity failures addresses the location of a flawed bit. The k correction bits determine the address of a flawed bit in a Hamming code. The message bits must be arranged to provide an orthogonal basis for the code (as in the case of the columns and rows of the block code). Further, the correction bits must be included in this basis. An orthogonal basis for 16 message bits is shown in Example 2.1, together with the setting of the five correction bits. Adding another bit, a sixth bit, allows us to compute parity on the entire $m + k + 1$ bit message. Now if we get an indication of a correctable error from the k correct bits, and no indication of parity failure from this new d bit, we know that there is a double error and that any attempt at correction may be incorrect and should not be attempted. These codes are commonly called SECDED.

EXAMPLE 2.1   A HAMMING CODE EXAMPLE

Suppose we have a 16-bit message, $m = 16$.

$2^k \geq 16 + k + 1$; therefore, $k = 5$.

Thus, the message has $16 + 5 = 21$ bits. The five correction bits will be defined by parity on the following groups, defined by base 2 hypercubes:

k_5 bits 16–21.

k_4 bits 8–15.

k_3 bits 4–7, 12–15, and 20–21.

k_2 bits 2–3, 6–7, 10–11, 14–15, and 18–19.

k_1 bits 1, 3, 5, 7, 9 . . . , 19, 21.

In other words, the 21-bit formatted message bits $f_1 - f_{21}$ consist of original message bits $m_1 - m_{16}$ and correction bits $k_1 - k_5$. Each correction bit is sited in a location within the group it checks.

Suppose the message consists of $f_1 - f_{21}$ and $m_1 - m_{16} = 0101010101010101$. For simplicity of decoding, let us site the correction bits at locations that are covered only by the designated correction bit (e.g., only k_5 covers bit 16):

$$k_1 = f_1.$$
$$k_2 = f_2.$$
$$k_3 = f_4.$$
$$k_4 = f_8.$$
$$k_5 = f_{16}.$$

Now we have (m_1 is at f_3, m_2 at f_5, etc.)

$$f_1 \, f_2 \, f_3 \, f_4 \, f_5 \, f_6 \, f_7 \, f_8 \, f_9 \, f_{10} \, f_{11} \, f_{12} \, f_{13} \, f_{14} \, f_{15} \, f_{16} \, f_{17} \, f_{18} \, f_{19} \, f_{20} \, f_{21}$$
$$k_1 \, k_2 \, 0 \, k_3 \, 1 \, 0 \, 1 \, k_4 \, 0 \, 1 \, 0 \, 1 \, 0 \, 1 \, 0 \, k_5 \, 1 \, 0 \, 1 \, 0 \, 1.$$

Thus, with even parity,

$$k_5 = 1.$$
$$k_4 = 1.$$
$$k_3 = 1.$$
$$k_2 = 0.$$
$$k_1 = 1.$$

Suppose this message is sent but received with $f_8 = 0$ (when it should be $f_8 = k_4 = 1$). When parity is recomputed at the receiver for each of the five correction groups, only one group covers f_8.

In recomputing parity across the groups, we get

$$k'_5 = 0 \text{ (i.e., there is no error in bits 16–21).}$$
$$k'_4 = 1.$$
$$k'_3 = 0.$$
$$k'_2 = 0.$$
$$k'_1 = 0.$$

The failure pattern 01000 is the binary representation for the incorrect bit (bit 8), which must be changed to correct the message.

2.7.3 Dealing with Manufacturing Faults

The traditional way of dealing with manufacturing faults is through testing. As transistor density increases and the overall die transistor count increases proportionally, the problem of testing increases even faster. The testable combinations increase exponentially with transistor count. Without a testing breakthrough, it is estimated that within a few years, the cost of die testing will exceed the remaining cost of manufacturing.

Assuring the integrity of a design a priori is a difficult, if not impossible, task. Depending on the level at which the design is validated, various design automation tools can be helpful. When a design is complete, the logical model of the design can, in some cases, be *validated*. Design validation consists of comparing the logical output of a design with the logical assertions specifying the design. In areas such as storage (cache) or even floating-point arithmetic, it is possible to have a reasonably comprehensive validation. More generalized validation is a subject of ongoing research.

Of course, the hardware designer can help the testing and validation effort, through a process called *design for testability* [104]. Error detection hardware, where applicable, is an obvious test assist. A technique to give testing access to interior (not accessible from the instruction set) storage cells is called *scan*. A scan chain in its simplest form consists of a separate entry and exit point from each storage cell. Each of these points is MUXed (multiplexed) onto a serial bus, which can be loaded from/to storage independent of the rest of the system. Scan allows predetermined data configurations to be entered into storage, and the output of particular configurations can be compared with known correct output configurations. Scan techniques were originally developed in the 1960s as part of mainframe technology. They were largely abandoned later only to be rediscovered with the advent of high-density dice.

Scan chains require numerous test configurations to cover large design; hence, even scan is limited in its potential for design validation. Newer techniques extend scan by compressing the number of patterns required and by incorporating various *built-in self-test* features.

2.7.4   Memory and Function Scrubbing

Scrubbing is a technique that tests a unit by exercising it when it would otherwise be idle or unavailable (such as on startup). It is most often used with memory. When memory is idle, the memory cells are cycled with write and read operations. This potentially detects damaged portions of memory, which are then declared unavailable, and processes are relocated to avoid it.

In principle, the same technique can be applied to functional units (such as floating-point units). Clearly, it is most effective if there is a possibility of reconfiguring units so that system operation can continue (at reduced performance).

2.8   CONFIGURABILITY

This section covers two topics involving configurability, focusing on designs that are reconfigurable. First, we provide a number of motivations for reconfigurable designs and include a simple example illustrating the basic ideas. Second, we estimate the area cost of current reconfigurable devices based on the rbe model developed earlier in this chapter.

2.8.1   Why Reconfigurable Design?

In Chapter 1, we describe the motivation for adopting reconfigurable designs, mainly from the point of view of managing complexity based on high-performance intellectual properties (IPs) and avoiding the risks and delays associated with fabrication. In this section, we provide three more reasons for using reconfigurable devices, such as FPGAs, based on the topics introduced in the previous sections of this chapter: time, area, and reliability:

Time. Since FPGAs, particularly the fine-grained ones, contain an abundance of registers, they support highly pipelined designs. Another consideration is parallelism: Instead of running a sequential processor at a high clock rate, an FPGA-based processor at a lower clock rate can have similar or even superior performance by having customized circuits executing in parallel. In contrast, the instruction set and the pipeline structure of a microprocessor may not always fit a given application. We shall illustrate this point by a simple example later.

Area. While it is true that the programmability of FPGAs would incur area overheads, the regularity of FPGAs simplifies the adoption of more aggressive manufacturing process technologies than the ones for application-specific integrated circuits (ASICs). Hence, FPGAs tend to be able to exploit advances in process technologies more readily than other forms of circuits. Furthermore, a small FPGA can support a large design by time-division multiplex and run-time reconfiguration, enabling trade-off in execution time and the amount of resources required. In the next section, we shall estimate the size of some FPGA designs based on the rbe model that we introduced earlier this chapter.

Reliability. The regularity and homogeneity of FPGAs enable the introduction of redundant cells and interconnections into their architecture. Various strategies have been developed to avoid manufacturing or runtime faults by means of such redundant structures. Moreover, the reconfigurability of FPGAs has been proposed as a way to improve their circuit yield and timing due to variations in the semiconductor fabrication process [212].

To illustrate the opportunity of using FPGAs for accelerating a demanding application, lets us consider a simplified example comparing HDTV processing for microprocessors and for FPGAs. The resolution of HDTV is 1920×1080 pixels, or around 2 million pixels. At 30 Hz, it corresponds to 60 million pixels per second. A particular application involves 100 operations, so the amount of processing required is 6000 million operations per second.

Consider a 3-GHz microprocessor that takes, on average, five cycles to complete an operation. It can support 0.2 operation per cycle and, in aggregate, only 600 million operations per second, 10 times slower than the required processing rate.

In contrast, consider a 100-MHz FPGA design that can cover 60 operations in parallel per cycle. This design meets the required processing rate of 6000 million operations per second, 10 times more than the 3 GHz microprocessor, although its clock rate is only 1/30th of that of the microprocessor. The design can exploit reconfigurability in various ways, such as making use of instance-specific optimization to improve area, speed, or power consumption for specific execution data, or reconfiguring the design to adapt to run-time conditions. Further discussions on configurability can be found in Chapter 6.

2.8.2   Area Estimate of Reconfigurable Devices

To estimate the area of reconfigurable devices, we use the rbe, discussed earlier as the basic measure. Recall, for instance, that in practical designs, the six-transistor register cell takes about $2700\lambda^2$.

There are around 7000 transistors required for configuration, routing, and logic for a "slice" in a Xilinx FPGA, and around 12,000 transistors in a logic element (LE) of an Altera device. Empirically, each rbe contains around 10 logic transistors, so each slice contains 700 rbe. A large Virtex XC2V6000 device contains 33,792 slices, or 23.65 million rbe or 16,400 A.

An 8×8 multiplier in this technology would take about 35 slices, or 24,500 rbe or 17 A. In contrast, given that a 1-bit multiplier unit containing a full adder and an AND gate has around 60 transistors in VLSI technology, the same multiplier would have $64 \times 60 = 3840$ transistors, or around 384 rbe, which is around 60 times smaller than the reconfigurable version.

Given that multipliers are used often in designs, many FPGAs now have dedicated resources for supporting multipliers. This technique frees up reconfigurable resources to implement other functions rather than multipliers, at the expense of making the device less regular and wasting area when the design cannot use them.

2.9 CONCLUSION

Cycle time is of paramount importance in processor design. It is largely determined by technology but is significantly influenced by secondary considerations, such as clocking philosophy and pipeline segmentation.

Once cycle time has been determined, the designer's next challenge is to optimize the cost–performance of a design by making maximum use of chip area—using chip area to the best possible advantage of performance. A technology-independent measure of area called the rbe provides the basis for storage hierarchy trade-offs among a number of important architectural considerations.

While efficient use of die area can be important, the power that a chip consumes is equally (and sometime more) important. The performance–power trade-off heavily favors designs that minimize the required clock frequency, as power is a cubic function of frequency. As power enables many environmental applications, particularly those wearable or sensor based, careful optimization determines the success of a design, especially an SOC design.

Reliability is usually an assumed requirement, but the ever smaller feature sizes in the technology make designs increasingly sensitive to radiation and similar hazards.

Depending on the application, the designer must anticipate hazards and incorporate features to preserve the integrity of the computation.

The great conundrum in SOC design is how to use the advantages the technology provides within a restricted design budget. Configurability is surely one useful approach that has been emerging, especially the selected use of FPGA technology.

2.10 PROBLEM SET

1. A four-segment pipeline implements a function and has the following delays for each segment ($b = 0.2$):

Segment #	Maximum delay*
1	1.7 ns
2	1.5 ns
3	1.9 ns
4	1.4 ns

*Excludes clock overhead of 0.2 ns.

(a) What is the cycle time that maximizes performance without allocating multiple cycles to a segment?

(b) What is the total time to execute the function (through all stages)?

(c) What is the cycle time that maximizes performance if each segment can be partitioned into sub-segments?

2. Repeat problem 1 if there is a 0.1 ns clock skew (uncertainty of ±0.1 ns) in the arrival of each clock pulse.

3. We can generalize the equation for S_{opt} by allowing for pipeline interruption delay of $S - a$ cycles (rather than $S - 1$), where $S > a \geq 1$. Find the new expression for S_{opt}.

4. A certain pipeline has the following functions and functional unit delays (without clocking overhead):

Function	Delay
A	0.6
B	0.8
C	0.3
D	0.7
E	0.9
F	0.5

Function units B, D, and E can be subdivided into two equal delay stages. If the expected occurrence of pipeline breaks is $b = 0.25$ and clocking overhead is 0.1 ns:

(a) What is the optimum number of pipeline segments (round down to integer value)?

(b) What cycle time does this give?

(c) Compute the pipeline performance with this cycle time.

5. A processor die (1.4 cm × 1.4 cm) will be produced for five years. Over this period, defect densities are expected to drop linearly from 0.5 defects/cm² to 0.1 defects/cm². The cost of 20 cm wafer production will fall linearly from $5,000 to $3,000, and the cost of 30 cm wafer production will fall linearly from $10,000 to $6,000. Assume production of good devices is constant in each year. Which production process should be chosen?

6. DRAM chip design is a specialized art where extensive optimizations are made to reduce cell size and data storage overhead. For a cell size of $135\lambda^2$, find the capacity of a DRAM chip. Process parameters are: yield = 80%, $\rho_D = 0.3$ defects/cm², feature size = $0.1 \, \mu m$, overhead consists of 10% for drivers and sense amps. Overhead for pads, drivers, guard ring, etc., is 20%. There are no buses or latches.

Since memory must be sized as an even power of 2, find the capacity and resize the die to the *actual gross area* (eliminating wasted space) and find the corresponding yield.

7. Compute the cost of a $512^M \times 1^b$ die, using the assumptions of problem 6. Assume a 30 cm diameter wafer costs $15,000.

8. Suppose a 2.3 cm^2 die can be fabricated on a 20 cm wafer at a cost of $5,000, or on a 30 cm wafer at a cost of $8,000. Compare the effective cost per die for defect densities of 0.2 defects/cm^2 and 0.5 defects/cm^2.

9. Following the reasoning of the yield equation derivation, show

$$P(t) = e^{\frac{-t}{T}}$$

10. Show that, for the triple modular system the expected time, t, for 2 modules failure is

$$t = T \times \log_e 2$$

   Hint: there are 3 modules, if any 2 (3 combinations) or all 3 fail, the system fails.

11. Design a Hamming code for a 32 bit message. Place the check bits in the resulting message.

12. Suppose we want to design a Hamming code for double error correct for a 64-bit message. How many correct bits are required? Explain.

3 Processors

3.1 INTRODUCTION

Processors come in many types and with many intended uses. While much attention is focused on high-performance processors in servers and workstations, by actual count, they are a small percentage of processors produced in any year. Figure 3.1 shows the processor production profile by annual production count (not by dollar volume).

THIS CHAPTER AND PROCESSOR DETAILS

This chapter contains details about processor design issues, especially for advanced processors in high-performance applications. Readers selecting processors from established alternatives may choose to skip some of the details, such as sections about branch prediction and superscalar processor control. We indicate such sections with an asterisk (*) in the section title.

Such details are important, even for those selecting a processor, for two reasons:

1. Year by year, SOC processors and systems are becoming more complex. The SOC designer will be dealing with increasingly complex processors.
2. Processor performance evaluation tool sets (such as SimpleScalar [51]) provide options to specify issues such as branch prediction and related parameters.

Readers interested in application-specific instruction processors, introduced in Section 1.3, can find relevant material in Sections 6.3, 6.4, and 6.8.

Computer System Design: System-on-Chip, First Edition. Michael J. Flynn and Wayne Luk.
© 2011 John Wiley & Sons, Inc. Published 2011 by John Wiley & Sons, Inc.

Clearly, controllers, embedded controllers, digital signal processors (DSPs), and so forth, are the dominant processor types, providing the focus for much of the processor design effort. If we look at the market growth, the same data show that the demand for SOC and larger microcontrollers is growing at almost three times that of microprocessor units (MPUs in Figure 3.2).

Especially in SOC type applications, the processor itself is a small component occupying just a few percent of the die. SOC designs often use many different types of processors suiting the application. Often, noncritical processors are acquired (purchased) as design files (IP) and are integrated into the

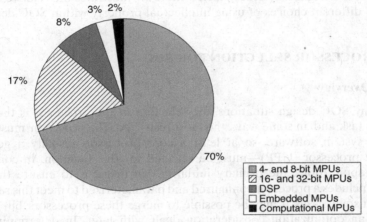

Figure 3.1   Worldwide production of microprocessors and controllers [227].

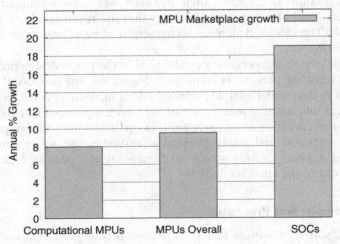

Figure 3.2   Annual growth in demand for microprocessors and controllers [227].

TABLE 3.1 Optimized Designs Provide Better Area–Time Performance at the Expense of Design Time

Type of Design	Design Level	Relative Expected Area × Time
Customized hard IP	Complete physical	1.0
Synthesized firm IP	Generic physical	3.0–10.0
Soft IP	RTL or ASIC	10.0–100.0

SOC design. Therefore, a specialized SOC design may integrate generic processor cores designed by other parties. Table 3.1 illustrates the relative advantages of different choices of using intellectual property within SOC designs.

3.2 PROCESSOR SELECTION FOR SOC

3.2.1 Overview

For many SOC design situations, the selection of the processor is the most obvious task and, in some ways, the most restricted. The processor must run a specific system software, so at least a core processor—usually a general-purpose processor (GPP)—must be selected for this function. In compute-limited applications, the primary initial design thrust is to ensure that the system includes a processor configured and parameterized to meet this requirement. In some cases, it may be possible to merge these processors, but that is usually an optimization consideration dealt with later. In determining the processor performance and the system performance, we treat memory and interconnect components as simple delay elements. These are referred to here as idealized components since their behavior has been simplified, but the idealization should be done in such a way that the resulting characterization is realizable. The idealized element is characterized by a conservative estimate of its performance.

Figure 3.3 shows the processor model used in the initial design process. The process of selecting processors is shown in Figure 3.4. The process of selection is different in the case of compute-limited selection, as there can be a real-time requirement that must be met by one of the selected processors. This becomes a primary consideration at an early point in the initial SOC design phase. The processor selection and parameterization should result in an initial SOC design that appears to fully satisfy all functional and performance requirements set out in the specifications.

3.2.2 Example: Soft Processors

The term "soft core" refers to an instruction processor design in bitstream format that can be used to program a field programmable gate array (FPGA)

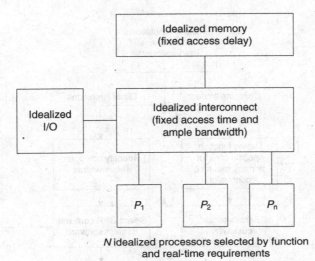

Figure 3.3   Processors in the SOC model.

device. The 4 main reasons for using such designs, despite their large area–power–time cost, are

1. cost reduction in terms of system-level integration,
2. design reuse in cases where multiple designs are really just variations on one,
3. creating an exact fit for a microcontroller/peripheral combination, and
4. providing future protection against discontinued microcontroller variants.

The main instruction processor soft cores include the following:

- *Nios II* [12]. Developed by Altera for use on their range of FPGAs and application-specific integrated circuits (ASICs).
- *MicroBlaze* [258]. Developed by Xilinx for use on their range of FPGAs and ASICs.
- *OpenRISC* [190]. A free and open-source soft-core processor.
- *Leon* [106]. Another free and open-source soft-core processor that implements a complete SPARC v8 compliant instruction set architecture (ISA). It also has an optional high-speed floating-point unit called GRFPU, which is free for download but is not open source and is only for evaluation/research purposes.
- *OpenSPARC* [235]. This SPARC T1 core supports single- and four-thread options on FPGAs.

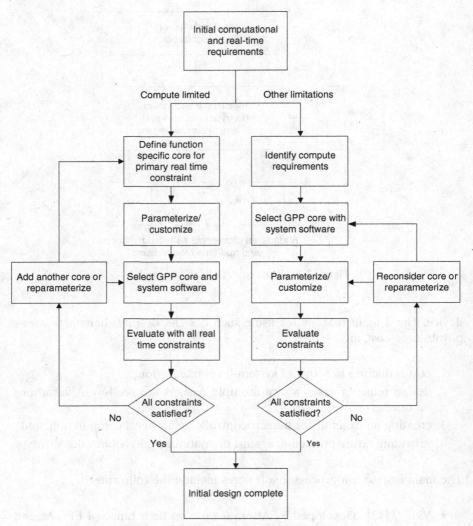

Figure 3.4 Process of processor core selection.

There are many distinguishing features among all of these, but in essence, they support a 32-bit reduced instruction set computer (RISC) architecture (except OpenSPARC, which is 64 bits) with single-issue five-stage pipelines, have configurable data/instruction caches, and have support for the Gnu compiler collection (GCC) compiler tool chain. They also feature bus architectures suitable for adding extra processing units as slaves or masters that could be used to accelerate the algorithm, although some go further and allow the addition of custom instructions/coprocessors.

TABLE 3.2 Some Features of Soft-Core Processors

	Nios II (fast) [13]	MicroBlaze [260]	OpenRISC [190]	Leon4 [106]
Open source	No	No	Yes	Yes
Hardware FPU	Yes	Yes	No	Yes
Bus standard	Avalon	CoreConnect	WISHBONE	AMBA
Integer division unit	Yes	Yes	No	Yes
Custom coprocessors/ instructions	Yes	Yes	Yes	Yes
Maximum frequency on FPGA (MHz)	290	200	47	125
Max MIPS on FPGA	340	280	47	210
Resources	1800 LE	1650 slices	2900 slices	4000 slices
Area estimate	1500 A	800 A	1400 A	1900 A

Table 3.2 contains a brief comparison of some of the distinguishing features of these different SOCs. It should be noted that the measurements for MIPS (million instructions per second) are mostly taken from marketing material and are likely to fluctuate wildly, depending on the specific configuration of a particular processor.

Now a simple comparison, we estimated in an earlier section that a 32-bit processor, without the floating-point unit, is around 60 A. We can see from Table 3.2 that such a processor is around 15–30 times smaller than soft processors.

3.2.3 Examples: Processor Core Selection

Let us consider two examples that illustrate the steps shown in Figure 3.4.

Example 1: Processor Core Selection, General Core Path Consider the "other limitation" path in Figure 3.4 and look at some of the trade-offs. For this simple analysis, we shall ignore the processor details and just assume that the processor possibilities follow the AT^2 rule discussed in Chapter 2. Assume that an initial design had performance of 1 using 100K rbe (register bit equivalent) of area, and we would like to have additional speed and functionality. So we double the performance (half the T for the processor). This increases the area to 400K rbe and the power by a factor of 8. Each rbe is now dissipating twice the power as before. All this performance is modulated by the memory system. Doubling the performance (instruction execution rate) doubles the number of cache misses per unit time. The effect of this on realized system performance depends significantly on the average cache miss time; we will see more of this in Chapter 4.

Suppose the effect of cache misses significantly reduces the realized performance; to recover this performance, we now need to increase the cache size. The general rule cited in Chapter 4 is to half the miss rate, we need to double the cache size. If the initial cache size was also 100K rbe, the new design now has 600K rbe and probably dissipates about 10 times the power of the initial design.

Is it worth it? If there is plenty of area while power is not a significant constraint, then perhaps it is worth it. The faster processor cache combination may provide important functionality, such as additional security checking or input/output (I/O) capability. At this point, the system designer refers back to the design specification for guidance.

Example 2: Processor Core Selection, Compute Core Path Again refer to Figure 3.4, only now consider some trade-offs for the compute-limited path. Suppose the application is generally parallelizable, and we have several different design approaches. One is a 10-stage pipelined vector processor; the other is multiple simpler processors. The application has performance of 1 with the vector processor (area is 300K rbe) and half of that performance with a single simpler processor (area is 100K rbe). In order to satisfy the real-time compute requirements, we need to increase the performance to 1.5.

Now we must evaluate the various ways of achieving the target performance. Approach 1 is to increase the pipeline depth and double the number of vector pipelines; this satisfies the performance target. This increases the area to 600K rbe and doubles the power, while the clock rate remains unchanged. Approach 2 is to use an "array" of simpler interconnected processors. The multiprocessor array is limited by memory and interconnect contention (we will see more of these effects in Chapter 5). In order to achieve the target performance, we need to have at least four processors: three for the basic target and one to account for the overhead. The area is now 400K rbe plus the interconnect area and the added memory sharing circuitry; this could also add another 200K rbe. So we still have two approaches undifferentiated by area or power considerations.

So how do we pick one of these two alternatives? There are usually many more than two. Now all depends on the secondary design targets, which we only begin to list here:

1. Can the application be easily partitioned to support both approaches?
2. What support software (compilers, operating systems, etc.) exists for each approach?
3. Can we use the multiprocessor approach to gain at least some fault tolerance?
4. Can the multiprocessor approach be integrated with the other compute path?
5. Is there a significant design effort to realize either of the enhanced approaches?

Clearly, there are many questions the system designer must answer. Tools and analysis only eliminate the unsatisfactory approaches; after that, the real system analysis begins.

The remainder of this chapter is concerned with understanding the processor, especially at the microarchitecture level, and how that affects performance. This is essential in evaluating performance and in using simulation tools.

WAYS TO ACHIEVE PERFORMANCE

The examples used in Section 3.2 are quite simplistic. How does one create designs that match the AT^2 design rule, or do even better? The secret is in understanding design possibilities, the freedom to choose among design alternatives. In order to do this, one must understand the complexity of the modern processor and all of its ramifications. This chapter presents a number of these alternatives, but it only touches the most important, and many other techniques can serve the designer well in specific situations. There is no substitute for understanding.

3.3   BASIC CONCEPTS IN PROCESSOR ARCHITECTURE

The processor architecture consists of the *instruction set* of the processor. While the instruction set implies many implementation (microarchitecture) details, the resulting implementation is a great deal more than the instruction set. It is the synthesis of the physical device limitations with area–time–power trade-offs to optimize specified user requirements.

3.3.1   Instruction Set

The instruction set for most processors is based upon a register set to hold operands and addresses. The register set size varies from 8 to 64 words or more, each word consisting of 32–64 bits. An additional set of floating-point registers (32–128 bits) is usually also available. A typical instruction set specifies a program status word, which consists of various types of control status information, including condition codes (CCs) set by the instruction. Common instruction sets can be classified by format differences into two basic types, the load–store (*L/S*) architecture and the register–memory (*R/M*) architecture:

- The L/S instruction set includes the RISC microprocessors. Arguments must be in registers before execution. An ALU instruction has both source operands and result specified as registers. The advantages of the L/S architecture are regularity of execution and ease of instruction decode. A simple instruction set with straightforward timing is easily implemented.
- The R/M architectures include instructions that operate on operands in registers or with one of the operands in memory. In the R/M architecture, an ADD instruction might sum a register value and a value contained in

memory, with the result going to a register. The R/M instruction sets trace their evolution to the IBM mainframes and the Intel x86 series (now called the Intel IA32).

The trade-off in instruction sets is an area–time compromise. The R/M approach offers a more concise program representation using fewer instructions of variable size compared with L/S. Programs occupy less space in memory and require smaller instruction caches. The variable instruction size makes decoding more difficult. The decoding of multiple instructions requires predicting the starting point of each. The R/M processors require more circuitry (and area) to be devoted to instruction fetch and decode. Generally, the success of Intel-type x86 implementations in achieving high clock rates has shown that there is no decisive advantage of one approach over the other.

Figure 3.5 shows a general outline of some instruction layouts for typical machine instruction sets. RISC machines use a fixed 32-bit instruction size or a 32-bit format with 64-bit instruction extensions. Intel IA32 and the IBM System 390 (now called zSeries) mainframes use variable-size instructions. Intel uses 8-, 16-, and 32-bit instructions, while IBM uses 16-, 32-, and 48-bit instructions. Intel's byte-sized instructions are possible because of the limited register set size. The size variability and the R/M format gave good code density, at the expense of decode complexity. The RISC-based ARM format is an interesting compromise. It offers a 32-bit instruction set with a built-in conditional field, so every instruction can be conditionally executed. It also offers a 16-bit instruction set (called the thumb instructions). The result offers both decode efficiency and code density.

Recent developments in instruction set extension will be covered in Chapter 6.

3.3.2 Some Instruction Set Conventions

Table 3.3 is a list of basic instruction operations and commonly used mnemonic representations. Frequently, there are different instructions for differing data types (integer and floating point). To indicate the data type that the operation specifies, the operation mnemonic is extended by a data-type indicator, so OP.W might indicate an OP for integers, while OP.F indicates a floating-point operation. Typical data-type modifiers are shown in Table 3.4. A typical instruction has the form OP.M destination, source 1, source 2. The source and destination specification has the form of either a register or a memory location (which is typically specified as a base register plus an offset)

3.3.3 Branches

Branches (or *jumps*) manage program control flow. They typically consist of unconditional BR, conditional BC, and subroutine call and return (link). The BC tests the state of the CC, which usually consists of 4 bits in a program status

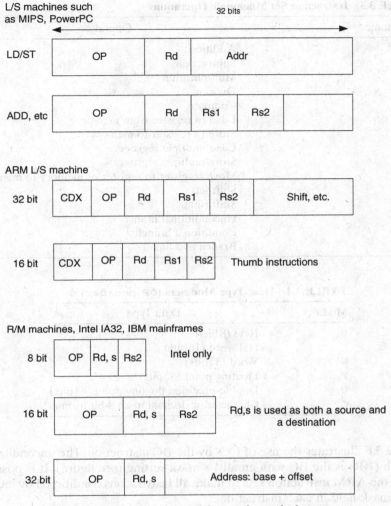

Figure 3.5 Instruction size and format for typical processors.

or control register. Typically, the CC is set by an ALU instruction to record one of several results (encoded in 2 or 4 bits), for example, specifying whether the instruction has generated

1. a positive result,
2. a negative result,
3. a zero result, or
4. an overflow.

TABLE 3.3   Instruction Set Mnemonic Operations

Mnemonic	Operation
ADD	Addition
SUB	Subtraction
MPY	Multiplication
DIV	Division
CMP	Compare
LD	Load (a register from memory)
ST	Store (a register to memory)
LDM	Load multiple registers
STM	Store multiple registers
MOVE	Move (register to register or memory to memory)
SHL	Shift left
SHR	Shift right
BR	Unconditional branch
BC	Conditional branch
BAL	Branch and link

TABLE 3.4   Data-Type Modifiers (`OP.modifier`)

Modifier	Data Type
B	Byte (8 bits)
H	Halfword (16 bits)
W	Word (32 bits)
F	Floating point (32 bits)
D	Double-precision floating point (64 bits)
C	Character or decimal in an 8-bit format

Figure 3.6 illustrates the use of CCs by the BC instruction. The unconditional branch (BR) is the BC with an all 1's mask setting (see figure). It is possible (as in the ARM instruction set) to make all instructions conditional by including a mask field in each instruction.

3.3.4   Interrupts and Exceptions

Many embedded SOC controllers have external interrupts and internal exceptions, which indicate the need for attention by an interrupt manager (or handler) program. These facilities can be managed and supported in various ways:

1. *User Requested versus Coerced.* The former often covers erroneous execution, such as divide by zero, while the latter is usually triggered by external events, such as device failure.
2. *Maskable versus Nonmaskable.* The former type of event can be ignored by setting a bit in an interrupt mask, while the latter cannot be ignored.

Setting the condition code

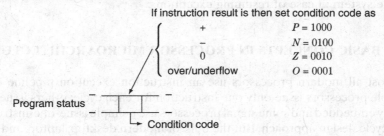

If instruction result is then set condition code as

$$+ \qquad P = 1000$$
$$- \qquad N = 0100$$
$$0 \qquad Z = 0010$$
over/underflow $\qquad O = 0001$

Program status

Condition code

Using the condition code

Mask

BC

A BC instruction tests for a particular condition or combination of conditions. The 4-bit mask is ANDed with the four condition code states, *PNZO*; these result bits are then ORed to determine the outcome. If the result is "1," the branch is taken (i.e., is successful); if the result is "0," the branch is not taken and execution conditions in line.

Mask = 0000 is no op, since all conditions are masked out—producing 0s from the ANDing operation.
Mask = 1111 is unconditional branch, since the previous computation produced *some* result (*P*, *N*, *Z*, *O*), and at least one mask AND condition will be true.
Mask = 1010 selects the condition *P* or *Z*, and branch is taken if result is ≥0 (e.g., BC.GE).
Mask = 0110 Similarly, the condition selected is *N* or *Z*, and branch is taken if result is ≤0 (e.g., BC.LE).

Figure 3.6 Examples of BC instruction using the condition code.

3. *Terminate versus Resume.* An event such as divide by zero would terminate ordinary processing, while a processor resumes operation.

4. *Asynchronous versus Synchronous.* Interrupt events can occur in asynchrony with the processor clock by an external agent or not, as when caused by a program's execution.

5. *Between versus Within Instructions.* Interrupt events can be recognized only between instructions or within an instruction execution.

In general, the first alternative of most of these pairs is easier to implement and may be handled after the completion of the current instruction. Whether the designer chooses to constrain the design only to precise exceptions, an exception is precise if all the instructions before the exception finish correctly, and all those after it do not change the state. Once the exception is handled, the latter instructions are restarted from scratch.

Moreover, some of these events may occur simultaneously and may even be nested. There is a need to prioritize them. Controllers and general-purpose processors have special units to handle these problems and preserve the state of the system in case of resuming exceptions.

3.4 BASIC CONCEPTS IN PROCESSOR MICROARCHITECTURE

Almost all modern processors use an instruction execution pipeline design. Simple processors issue only one instruction for each cycle; others issue many. Many embedded and some signal processors use a simple issue-one-instruction-per-cycle design approach. But the bulk of modern desktop, laptop, and server systems issue multiple instructions for each cycle.

Every processor (Figure 3.7) has a memory system, execution unit (data paths), and instruction unit. The faster the cache and memory, the smaller the number of cycles required for fetching instructions and data (IF and DF). The more extensive the execution unit, the smaller the number of execution cycles (EX). The control of the cache and execution unit is done by the instruction unit.

The pipeline mechanism or control has many possibilities. Potentially, it can execute one or more instructions for each cycle. Instructions may or may not be decoded and/or executed in program order. Indeed, instructions from several *different* programs can be executed in the same cycle in multithreaded pipelines. Table 3.5 illustrates some of the possibilities.

Regardless of the type of pipeline, "breaks" or delays are the major limit on performance.

Pipeline delays or *breaks* generally arise from one of three causes:

1. *Data Conflicts—Unavailability of a Source Operand.* This can occur for several reasons; typically, the current instruction requires an operand that is the result of a preceding uncompleted instruction. Extensive buffering of operands can minimize this effect.
2. *Resource Contention.* Multiple successive instructions use the same resource or an instruction with a long execution time delays a successor instruction's execution. Additional resources (floating-point units, register ports, and out-of-order execution) contribute to reducing contention.

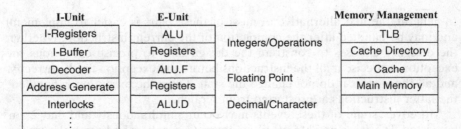

Figure 3.7 Processor units.

TABLE 3.5   Types of Pipelined Processors

Type	n Instructions Decoded per Cycle	Comment	Typical Relative Performance
Partial or static pipeline	1 or less	All actions in order	0.5–0.9
Typical pipeline	1	All D and all WB in order	1.0
O.O.O.* pipeline	1	All D in order WB unordered	1.2
Multiple-issue superscalar	$n = 4$	No order restriction†	2.5
Multiple-issue VLIW	$n = 8$	Ordered by compiler	3.0
Superscalar with multithreading	$n = 4$	Two threads typically	3.0

*Out of order (execution).
†Ordered only by dependencies.

TABLE 3.6   Processor Characteristics of Some SOC Designs

SOC	ISA	Type	Instruction Size	Extension
Freescale e600 [101]	PowerPC	Load/store	32 bits	Vector extension
ClearSpeed CSX600 [59]	Proprietary	Load/store	32 bits	SIMD 96 PEs
PlayStation 2 [147, 187]	MIPS	Load/store	32 bits	Vector extension
AMD Geode [18]	IA32	Register/ memory	One byte or more	MMX, 3DNow!

3. *Run-On Delays (in Order Execution Only).* When instructions must complete the WB (writeback) in program order, any delay in execution (as in the case of multiply or divide) necessarily delays the instruction execution in the pipeline.

4. *Branches.* The pipeline is delayed because of branch resolution and/or delay in the fetching of the branch target instruction before the pipeline can resume execution. Branch prediction, branch tables, and buffers all can be used to minimize the effect of branches.

In the next section, we look at simple pipeline control and the operation of a basic pipeline. These simple processors have minimum complexity but suffer the most from (mostly branch) disruptions. Next, we consider the buffers that are required to manage data movement both through the pipeline and between units. Since the optimum pipeline layout (number of stages) is a strong function of the frequency of breaks, we look at branches and techniques for minimizing the effects of branch pipeline delays. Then, we look at multiple instruction execution and more robust pipeline control. Table 3.6 describes the architecture of some SOC processors.

3.5 BASIC ELEMENTS IN INSTRUCTION HANDLING

An instruction unit consists of the state registers as defined by the instruction set—the instruction register—plus the instruction buffer, decoder, and an interlock unit. The instruction buffer's function is to fetch instructions into registers so that instructions can be rapidly brought into a position to be decoded. The decoder has the responsibility for controlling the cache, ALU, registers, and so on. Frequently, in pipelined systems, the instruction unit sequencing is managed strictly by hardware, but the execution unit may be microprogrammed so that each instruction that enters the execution phase will have its own microinstruction associated with it. The interlock unit's responsibility is to ensure that the concurrent execution of multiple instructions has the same result as if the instructions were executed completely serially.

With instructions in various stages of execution, there are many design considerations and trade-offs in even simple pipelined processors.

Figure 3.8 shows the processor control or I-unit and basic communications paths to memory.

3.5.1 The Instruction Decoder and Interlocks

When an instruction is decoded, the decoder must provide more than control and sequencing information for that instruction. Proper execution of the

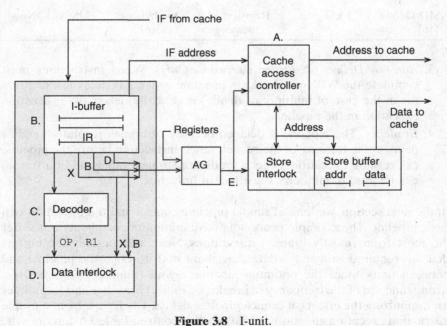

Figure 3.8 I-unit.

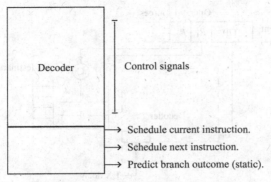

Figure 3.9 Decoder functions.

current instruction *depends* on the other instructions in the pipeline. The decoder (Figure 3.9)

1. schedules the current instruction; the current instruction may be delayed if a data dependency (e.g., at the address generate or AG cycle) occurs or if an exception arises—for example, *not in translation lookaside buffer (TLB)* and cache miss;
2. schedules subsequent instructions; later instructions may be delayed to preserve in-order completion if, for example, the current instruction has multiple cycle execution; and
3. selects (or predicts) the path on branch instruction.

The data interlocks (subunit D in Figure 3.8) may be part of the decoder. This determines *register* dependencies and schedules the AG and EX units. The interlocks ensure that the current instruction does not *use* (depend on) a result of a previous instruction until that result is available.

The execution controller performs a similar function on *subsequent* instructions, ensuring that they do not enter the pipeline until the execution unit is scheduled to complete the current instruction, and, if required, preserve the execution order.

The effect of the interlocks (Figure 3.10) is that for each instruction as it is decoded, its source registers (for operands or addresses) must be compared (indicated by "C" in Figure 3.10) against the destination registers of previously issued but uncompleted instructions to determine dependencies. The opcode itself usually establishes the number of EX cycles required (indicated by the EX box in the figure). If this exceeds the number specified by the timing template, subsequent instructions must be delayed by that amount to preserve in-order execution.

The store interlocks (E) perform the same function as the data interlocks for storage addresses. On STORE instructions, the address is sent to the store interlocks so that subsequent reads either from the AG (data reads) or the IB

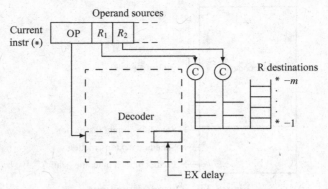

Figure 3.10   Interlocks.

TABLE 3.7   Characteristics of Some Floating-Point Implementations

Implementation	Word Size (bit)	Register Set	Execution Time Add–Mul–Div	Pipelined	Area A Units
Minimal	32	4	3–8–30	No	25
Typical	64	8–16	3–3–15	No	50
Extended arithmetic	80	32	3–5–15	No	60
Multiple issue	64–80	40+	2–3–8	Yes	200+

(instruction reads) can be compared with pending stores and dependencies detected.

3.5.2   Bypassing

Bypassing or forwarding is a data path that routes a result—usually from an ALU—to a user (perhaps also the ALU), bypassing a destination register (which is subsequently updated). This allows a result produced by the ALU to be used at an earlier stage in the pipeline than would otherwise be possible.

3.5.3   Execution Unit

As with the cache, the execution unit (especially the floating-point unit) can represent a significant factor in both performance and area. Indeed, even a straightforward floating-point unit can occupy as much or more area than a basic integer core processor (without cache). In simple in-order pipelines, the execution delay (run-on) can be a significant factor in determining performance. More robust pipelines use corresponding better arithmetic algorithms for both integer and floating-point operations. Some typical area–time trade-offs in floating-point units are shown in Table 3.7.

In the table, word size refers to the operand size (exponent and mantissa), and the IEEE standard 754 format is assumed. The execution time is the estimated total execution time in cycles. The pipelined column indicates the throughput: whether the implementation supports the execution of a new operation for each cycle. The final column is an estimate of the units of area needed for the implementation.

The minimal implementation would probably only support specialized applications and 32-bit operands. The typical implementation refers to the floating-point unit of a simple pipelined processor with 64-bit operands. Advanced processors support the extended IEEE format (80 bits), which protects the accuracy of intermediate computations. The multiple-issue implementation is a typical straightforward implementation. If the implementation is to support issue rates greater than four, the size could easily double.

3.6   BUFFERS: MINIMIZING PIPELINE DELAYS

Buffers change the way instruction timing events occur by decoupling the time at which an event occurs from the time at which the input data are used. It allows the processor to tolerate some delay without affecting the performance. Buffers enable latency tolerance as they hold the data awaiting entry into a stage.

Buffers can be designed for a *mean* request rate [115] or for a *maximum* request rate. In the former case, knowing the expected number of requests, we can trade off buffer size against the probability of an overflow. Overflows per se (where an action is lost) do not happen in internal CPU buffers, but an "overflow" condition—full buffer and a new request—will force the processor to slow down to bring the buffer entries down below buffer capacity. Thus, each time an overflow condition occurs, the processor pipeline stalls to allow the overflowing buffer to access memory (or other resources). The store buffer, for example, is usually designed for a mean request rate.

Maximum request rate buffers are used for request sources that dominate performance, such as in-line instruction requests or data entry in a video buffer. In this case, the buffer size should be sufficient to match the processor request rate with the cache or other storage service rate. A properly sized buffer allows the processor to continue accessing instructions or data at its maximum rate without the buffer running out of information.

3.6.1   Mean Request Rate Buffers

We assume that q is a random variable describing the request size (number of pending requests) for a resource; Q is the mean of this distribution; and σ is the standard deviation.

Little's Theorem   The mean request size is equal to the mean request rate (requests per cycle), multiplied by the mean time to service a request [142].

We assume a buffer size of BF, and we define the probability of a buffer overflow as p. There are two upper bounds for p based on Markov's and Chebyshev's inequalities.

Markov's Inequality

$$\text{Prob}\{q \geq BF\} \leq \frac{Q}{BF}$$

Chebyshev's Inequality

$$\text{Prob}\{q \geq BF\} \leq \frac{\sigma^2}{(BF - Q)^2}$$

Using these two inequalities, for a given probability of overflow (p), we can conservatively select BF, since either term provides an upper bound, as

$$BF = \min\left(\frac{Q}{p}, Q + \frac{\sigma}{\sqrt{p}}\right).$$

EXAMPLE 3.1

Suppose we wish to determine the effectiveness of a two-entry write buffer. Assume the write request rate is 0.15 per cycle, and the expected number of cycles to complete a store is two. The mean request size is $0.15 \times 2 = 0.3$, using Little's theorem. Assuming $\sigma^2 = 0.3$ for the request size, we can calculate an upper bound on the probability of overflow as

$$p = \max\left(\frac{Q}{BF}, \frac{\sigma^2}{(BF - Q)^2}\right) = 0.10.$$

3.6.2   Buffers Designed for a Fixed or Maximum Request Rate

A buffer designed to supply a fixed rate is conceptually easy to design. The primary consideration is masking the access latency. If we process one item per cycle and it takes three cycles to access an item, then we need to have a buffer space of at least three, or four, if we count the item being processed.

In general, the maximum rate buffer supplies a fixed rate of data or instructions for processing. There are many examples of such buffers, including the instruction buffer, video buffers, graphics, and multimedia buffers.

In the general case where s items are processed for each cycle, and p items are fetched from a storage with a fixed access time, the buffer size, BF is

$$BF = 1 + \left[s \cdot \frac{\text{access time (cycles)}}{p} \right].$$

The initial "1" is an allowance for a single entry buffer used for processing during the current cycle. In some cases, it may not be necessary. The buffer described here is designed to buffer entry into a functional unit or decoder (as an I decoder); it is not exactly the same as the frame buffer or the image buffer that manages transfers between the processor and a media device. However, the same principles apply in the design to these media buffers.

3.7 BRANCHES: REDUCING THE COST OF BRANCHES

Branches represent one of the difficult issues in optimizing processor performance. Typically, branches can significantly reduce performance. For example, the conditional branch instruction (BC) tests the CC set by a preceding instruction. There may be a number of cycles between the decoding of the branch and the setting of the CC (see Figure 3.11). The simplest strategy is for the processor to do nothing but simply to await the outcome of the CC set and to defer the decoding of the instruction following the BC until the CC is known. In case the branch is taken, the target is fetched during the time allocated to a data fetch in an arithmetic instruction. This policy is simple to implement and minimizes the amount of excess memory traffic created by branch instructions. More complicated strategies that attempt to guess a particular path will occasionally be wrong and will cause additional or excess instruction fetches from memory.

In Figure 3.11, the actual decode is five cycles late (i.e., a five-cycle branch penalty). This is not the whole effect, however. The timing of NEXT + 1 is delayed an additional cycle when the target path is taken, as this instruction has not been prefetched.

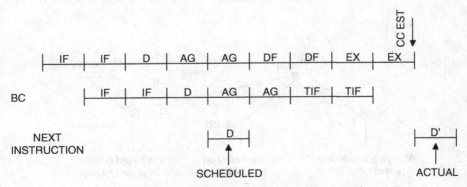

Figure 3.11 The delay caused by a branch (BC).

Since branches are a major limitation to processor performance [75, 222], there has been a great deal of effort to reduce the effect. There are two simple and two substantial approaches to the branch problem. The simple approaches are the following:

1. *Branch Elimination*. For certain code sequences, we can replace the branch with another operation.
2. *Simple Branch Speedup*. This reduces the time required for target instruction fetch and CC determination.

The two more complex approaches are generalizations of the simple approaches:

1. *Branch Target Capture*. After a branch has been executed, we can keep its target instruction (and its address) in a table for later use to avoid the branch delay. If we could predict the branch path outcome and had the target instruction in the buffer, there would be no branch delay.
2. *Branch Prediction*. Using available information about the branch, one can predict the branch outcome and can begin processing on the predicted program path. If the strategy is simple or trivial, for example, always fetch in-line on true conditional branches, it is called a fixed strategy. If the strategy varies by opcode type or target direction, it is called a static strategy. If the strategy varies according to current program behavior, it is called a dynamic strategy (see Figure 3.12).

Table 3.8 summarizes these techniques. In the following sections, we look at two general approaches.

3.7.1   Branch Target Capture: Branch Target Buffers (BTBs)

The BTB (Figure 3.13) stores the target instruction of the previous execution of the branch. Each BTB entry has the current instruction address (needed

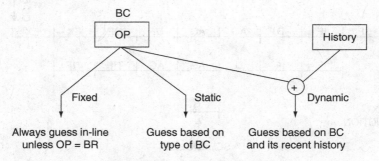

Figure 3.12   Branch prediction.

TABLE 3.8 Branch Management Techniques

Approach	What It Does	Hardware Cost	Effect on Branch Delay (Taken Branch)	Effect on Branch Prediction
Branch Resolution				
Early CC set	Determines the outcome of the tested condition early	Nil	Can save a cycle	None
Delayed branch	Determines the outcome of the tested condition early	Nil	"	None
Branch adder	Determines the target address early	Nil	Generally saves a cycle	None
Reducing Branch Target Delay				
Branch table buffer	Stores the last target instruction for each branch in a special table (BTB)	Tables can be large	Reduce to zero	80–90+% hit rate, depends on size and application
Improving Branch Prediction Rate				
Static	Uses branch opcode or test to predict the outcome	Small	None	70–80% accurate
Three Dynamic Techniques				
1. Bimodal	Records outcome of each branch	Small table	None	80–90% accurate
2. Two-level adaptive	Creates vector of branch outcomes	Can be 16KB+	Enables path speculation	95+% accuracy
3. Combined bimodal and two-level	Uses best outcome	As above	As above	As above

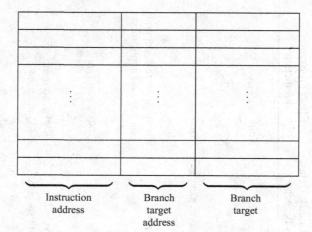

Instruction   Branch   Branch
address   target   target
                  address

Figure 3.13   Branch target buffer (BTB) organization. The BTB is indexed by instruction bits. The particular branch can be confirmed (avoiding an alias) by referencing an
instruction address field in the table.

only if branch aliasing is a problem), the branch target address, and the most
recent target instruction. (The target address enables the initiation of the
target fetch earlier in the pipeline, since it is not necessary to wait for the
address generation to complete.) The BTB functions as follows: Each instruction fetch indexes the BTB. If the instruction address matches the instruction
addresses in the BTB, then a prediction is made as to whether the branch
located at that address is likely to be taken. If the prediction is that the branch
will occur, then the target instruction is used as the next instruction. When the
branch is actually resolved, at the execute stage, the BTB can be updated with
the corrected target information if the actual target differs from the stored
target.

The BTB's effectiveness depends on its hit ratio—the probability that a
branch is found in the BTB at the time it is fetched. The hit rate for a 512-entry
BTB varies from about 70% to over 98%, depending on the application.

BTBs can be used in conjunction with the I-cache. Suppose we have a configuration as shown in Figure 3.14. The IF is made to both the BTB and I-cache.
If the IF "hits" in the BTB, the target instruction that was previously stored
in the BTB is now fetched and forwarded to the processor at its regularly
scheduled time. The processor will begin the execution of the target instruction
with no branch delay.

The BTB provides both the target instruction and the new PC. There is now
no delay on a taken branch *so long as the branch prediction is correct*. Note
that the branch itself must still be fetched from the I-cache and must be fully
executed. If either the AG outcome or the CC outcome is not as expected, all
instructions in the target fetch path must be aborted. Clearly, no conditionally

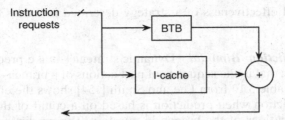

Figure 3.14 Typical BTB structure. If "hit" in the BTB, then the BTB returns the target instruction to the processor; CPU guesses the target. If "miss" in the BTB, then the cache returns the branch and in-line path; CPU guesses in-line.

TABLE 3.9   A Static Branch Prediction Strategy

Instruction Class	Instruction	Guessed Successful (S)	Guessed Unsuccessful (U)
Unconditional branch	BR	Always	Never
Branch on condition	BC	Guess S on backward*	Guess U on forward*
Loop control	BCT	Always	Never
Call/return	BAL	Always	Never

*When the branch target is less than the current PC, assume a loop and take the target. Otherwise, guess in-line.

executed (target path) instruction can do a final result write, as this would make it impossible to recover in case of a misprediction.

3.7.2   Branch Prediction

Beyond the trivial fixed prediction, there are two classes of strategies for guessing whether or not a branch will be taken: a static strategy, which is based upon the type of branch instruction, and a dynamic strategy, which is based upon the recent history of branch activity.

Even perfect prediction does not eliminate branch delay. Perfect prediction simply converts the delay for the conditional branch into that for the unconditional branch (branch taken). So, it is important to have BTB support before using a more robust (and expensive) predictor.

Static Prediction   Static prediction is based on the particular branch opcode and/or the relative direction of the branch target. When a branch is decoded, a guess is made on the outcome of the branch, and if it is determined that the branch will be successful, the pipeline fetches the target instruction stream and begins decoding from it. A simple approach is shown in Table 3.9.

The general effectiveness of a strategy described in Table 3.9 is typically 70–80%.

Dynamic Prediction: Bimodal   Dynamic strategies make predictions based on past history; that is, the sequence of past actions of a branch—was it or was it not taken? Table 3.10 from Lee and Smith [154] shows the effectiveness of a branch prediction when prediction is based on a count of the outcome of preceding executions of the branch in question. The prediction algorithm is quite simple. In implementing this scheme, a small up/down saturating counter is used. If the branch is taken, the counter is incremented up to a maximum value (n). An unsuccessful branch decrements the counter. In a 2-bit counter, the values 00 and 01 would predict a branch not taken, while 10 and 11 predicts a branch taken. The table can be separate or integrated into a cache is shown in Figure 3.15.

Depending on the table organization, two branches can map into the same history, creating an aliasing problem.

A number of observations can be made from Table 3.10. First, the predictive accuracy very closely approaches its maximum with just a few bits. Second, the predictive accuracy for a two bit counter varies from 83.4% to 96.5%, which

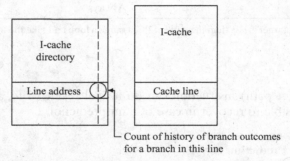

Figure 3.15 Branch history counter can be kept in I-cache (above) or in a separate table.

TABLE 3.10   Percentage Correct Guess Using History with n-bit Counters [154]

	Mix Definition			
n	Compiler	Business	Scientific	Supervisor
0	64.1	64.4	70.4	54.0
1	91.9	95.2	86.6	79.7
2	93.3	96.5	90.8	83.4
3	93.7	96.6	91.0	83.5
4	94.5	96.8	91.8	83.7
5	94.7	97.0	92.0	83.9

is much higher than the accuracy using only the branch opcode prediction strategy of Table 3.9. Third, the effectiveness of prediction in a standard test suite (SPECmarks) is reported to be 93.5% using a very large table.

Dynamic Prediction: Two-Level Adaptive   Bimodal prediction is generally limited to prediction rates around 90% across multiple environments. Yeh and Patt [267, 268] have looked at adaptive branch prediction as a method of raising prediction rates to 95%. The basic method consists of associating a shift register with each branch in, for example, a branch table buffer. The shift register records branch history. A branch twice taken and twice not taken, for example, would be recorded as "1100." Each pattern acts as an address into an array of counters, such as the 2-bit saturating counters. Each time the pattern 1100 is encountered, the outcome is recorded in the saturating counter. If the branch is taken, the counter is incremented; if the branch is not taken, it is decremented.

Adaptive techniques can require a good deal of support hardware. Not only must we have history bits associated with the possible branch entries but we must also have a table of counters to store outcomes. The approach is more effective in large programs where it is possible to establish a stable history pattern.

The average trace data from Yeh and Patt indicates that an adaptive strategy using a 6-bit entry provided a 92% correct prediction rate increasing to 95% with a 24-bit entry. Notice that the published SPECmark performance is significantly higher than other data.

The 2-bit saturating counter achieves 89.3% averaged over all programs. However, the data in Figure 3.16 is based on a different set of programs than those presented in Table 3.10.

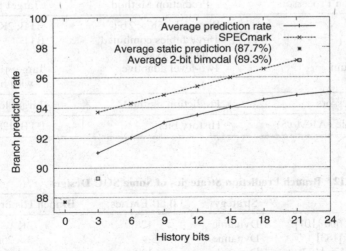

Figure 3.16   Branch prediction rates for a two-level adaptive predictor.

The adaptive results are shown for the prediction rate averaged over all programs [267]. Differences between 89% and 95% may not seem significant, but overall execution delay is often dominated by mispredicted branches.

Dynamic Prediction: Combined Methods The bimodal and the adaptive approaches provide rather different information about the likelihood of a branch path. Therefore, it is possible to combine these approaches by adding another (vote) table of (2-bit saturating) counters. When the outcomes differ, the vote table selects between the two, and the final result updates the count in the vote table. This is referred to as *combined prediction* method and offers an additional percent or so improvement in the prediction rate. Of course, one can conceive of combining more than two predictions for an even more robust predictor.

The disadvantage of the two-level approach includes the hardware requirement for control and two serial table accesses. An approximation to it is called the global adaptive predictor. It uses only one shift register for all branches (global) to index into a single history table. While faster than the two-level in prediction, its prediction accuracy is only comparable to the bimodal predictor. But one can combine the bimodal predictor with the global adaptive predictor to create an *approximate combined* method. This gives results comparable to the two-level adaptive predictor.

Some processor branch strategies are shown in Table 3.11. Some SOC type processor branch strategies are shown in Table 3.12; they are notably simpler than workstation processors.

TABLE 3.11 Some Typical Branch Strategies

Workstation Processors	Prediction Method	Target Location
AMD	Bimodal: $16K \times 2\,bit$	BTB: 2K entries
IBM G5	Three tables combined method	BTB
Intel Itanium	Two-level adaptive	Targets in I-cache with branch
SOC processors	Prediction method	Target location
Intel XScale (ARM v5)	History bits	BTB: 128 entries

TABLE 3.12 Branch Prediction Strategies of Some SOC Designs

SOC	Strategy	BTB Entries	Branch History Entries
Freescale e600 [101]	Dynamic	128	2K
MIPS 74K [183]	Dynamic	—	3×256
Intel PXA27x [132]	Dynamic	128	—
ARC 600 [19]	Static	—	—

3.8 MORE ROBUST PROCESSORS: VECTOR, VERY LONG INSTRUCTION WORD (VLIW), AND SUPERSCALAR

To go beyond one cycle per instruction (CPI), the processor must be able to execute multiple instructions at the same time. Concurrent processors must be able to make simultaneous accesses to instruction and data memory and to simultaneously execute multiple operations. Processors that achieve a higher degree of concurrency are called concurrent processors, short for processors with instruction-level concurrency.

For the moment, we restrict our attention to those processors that execute only from one program stream. They are *uniprocessors* in that they have a single instruction counter, but the instructions may have been significantly rearranged from the original program order so that concurrent instruction execution can be achieved.

Concurrent processors are more complex than simple pipelined processors. In these processors, performance depends in greater measure on compiler ability, execution resources, and memory system design. Concurrent processors depend on sophisticated compilers to detect the instruction-level parallelism that exists within a program. The compiler must restructure the code into a form that allows the processor to use the available concurrency. Concurrent processors require additional execution resources, such as adders and multipliers, as well as an advanced memory system to supply the operand and instruction bandwidth required to execute programs at the desired rate [208, 250].

3.9 VECTOR PROCESSORS AND VECTOR INSTRUCTION EXTENSIONS

Vector instructions boost performance by

1. reducing the number of instructions required to execute a program (they reduce the I-bandwidth);
2. organizing data into regular sequences that can be efficiently handled by the hardware; and
3. representing simple loop constructs, thus removing the control overhead for loop execution.

Vector processing requires extensions to the instruction set, together with (for best performance) extensions to the functional units, the register sets, and particularly to the memory of the system.

Vectors, as they are usually derived from large data arrays, are the one data structure that is not well managed by a conventional data cache. Accessing array elements, separated by an addressing distance (called the stride), can fill a smaller- to intermediate-sized data cache with data of little temporal locality; hence, there is no reuse of the localities before the items must be replaced (Figure 3.17).

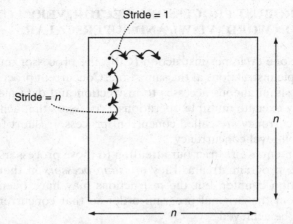

Figure 3.17 For an array in memory, different accessing patterns use different strides in accessing memory.

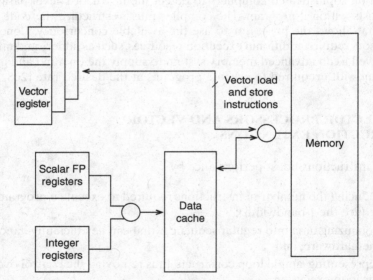

Figure 3.18 The primary storage facilities in a vector processor. Vector LD/ST usually bypasses the data cache.

Vector processors usually include vector register (VR) hardware to decouple arithmetic processing from memory. The VR set is the source and destination for all vector operands. In many implementations, accesses bypass the cache. The cache then contains only scalar data objects—objects not used in the VRs (Figure 3.18).

3.9.1 Vector Functional Units

The VRs typically consist of eight or more register sets, each consisting of 16–64 vector elements, where each vector element is a floating-point word.

The VRs access memory with special load and store instructions. The vector execution units are usually arranged as an independent functional unit for each instruction class. These might include

- add/subtract,
- multiplication,
- division or reciprocal, and
- logical operations, including compare.

Since the purpose of the vector vocabulary is to manage operations over a vector of operands, once the vector operation is begun, it can continue at the cycle rate of the system. Figure 3.19 shows timing for a sample four-stage functional pipeline. A vector add (VADD) sequence passes through various stages in the adder. The sum of the first elements of VR1 and VR2 (labeled VR1.1 and VR2.1) are stored in VR3 (actually, VR3.1) after the fourth adder stage.

Pipelining of the functional units is more important for vector functional units than for scalar functional units, where latency is of primary importance.

The advantage of vector processing is that fewer instructions are required to execute the vector operations. A single (overlapped) vector load places the information into the VRs. The vector operation executes at the clock rate of

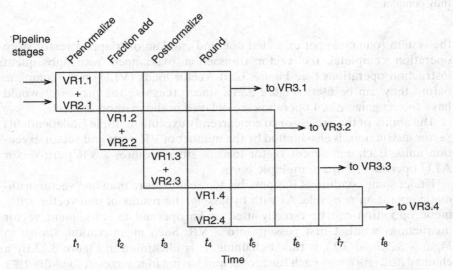

Figure 3.19 Approximate timing for a sample four-stage functional pipeline.

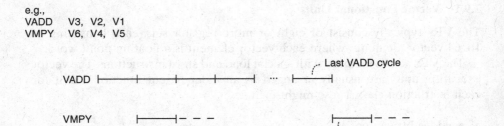

e.g.,
VADD   V3, V2, V1
VMPY   V6, V4, V5

Figure 3.20 For logically independent vector instructions, the number of access paths to the vector register (VR) set and vector units may limit performance. If there are four read ports, the vector multiply (VMPY) can start on the second cycle. Otherwise, with two ports, the VMPY must wait until the VADD completes use of the read ports.

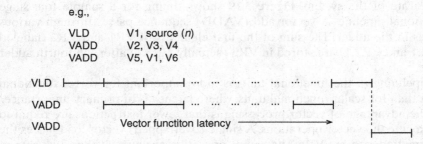

e.g.,

VLD   V1, source (n)
VADD   V2, V3, V4
VADD   V5, V1, V6

Figure 3.21 While independent VLD and VADD may proceed concurrently (with sufficient VR ports), operations that use the results of VLD do not begin until the VLD is fully complete.

the system (one cycle per executed operand), and an overlapped vector store operation completes the vector transaction overlapped with subsequent instruction operations (see Figure 3.20). Vector loads (VLD) must complete before they can be used (Figure 3.21), since otherwise the processor would have to recognize when operands are delayed in the memory system.

The ability of the processor to concurrently execute multiple (independent) vector instructions is also limited by the number of VR ports and vector execution units. Each concurrent vector load or store requires a VR port; vector ALU operations require multiple ports.

Under some conditions, it is possible to execute more than one vector arithmetic operation per cycle. As with bypassing, the results of one vector arithmetic operation can be directly used as an operand in subsequent vector instructions without first passing into a VR. Such an operation, shown in Figures 3.22 and 3.23, is called chaining. It is illustrated in Figure 3.22 by a chained ADD-MPY with each functional unit having four stages. If the ADD-MPY were unchained, it would take 4 (startup) + 64 (elements/VR) = 68 cycles for

For these two instructions,

    VADD   VR3, VR1, VR2

    VMPY   VR5, VR3, VR4

the timing would be

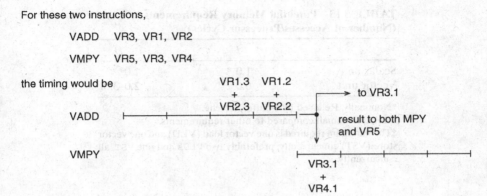

Figure 3.22   Effect of vector chaining.

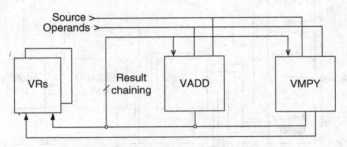

Figure 3.23   Vector chaining path.

each instruction—a total of 136 cycles. With chaining, this is reduced to 4 (add startup) + 4 (multiply startup) + 64 (elements/VR) = 72 cycles.

One of the crucial aspects in achieving the performance potential of the vector processor is the management of references to memory. Since arithmetic operations complete one per cycle, a vector code makes repeated references to memory to introduce new vectors in the VRs and to write out old results. Thus, on the average, memory must have sufficient bandwidth to support at least a two-words-per-cycle execution rate (one read and one write), and preferably three references per cycle (two reads and one write). This bandwidth allows for two vector reads and one vector write to be initiated and executed concurrently with the execution of a vector arithmetic operation. If there is insufficient memory bandwidth from memory to the VRs, the processor necessarily goes idle after the vector operation until the vector loads and stores are complete. It is a significant challenge to the designer of a processor not to simply graft a vector processing extension onto a scalar processor design but rather to adapt the scalar design—especially the memory system—to accommodate the requirements of fast vector execution (Table 3.13). If the memory

TABLE 3.13 Potential Memory Requirements (Number of Accesses/Processor Cycles)

	I	D
Scalar unit	1.0^-*	1.0*
Vector unit	0.0^+†	2.0–3.0‡

*Nominally. Reduced by I-buffer, I-cache.
†Relatively small compared to other requirements.
‡The minimum required is one vector load (VLD) and one vector store (VST) concurrently; preferably two VLDs and one VST, all concurrently.

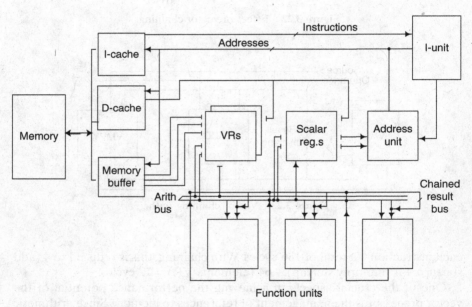

Figure 3.24 Major data paths in a generic vector processor.

system bandwidth is insufficient, there is correspondingly less performance improvement from the vector processing hardware.

The major elements of the vector processor are shown in (Figure 3.24). The functional units (add, multiply, etc.) and the two register sets (vector and scalar, or general) are connected by one or more bus sets. If chaining (Figure 3.23) is allowed, then three (or more) source operands are simultaneously accessed from the VRs and a result is transmitted back to the VRs. Another bus couples the VRs and the memory buffer. The remaining parts of the system—I-cache, D-cache, general registers, and so on—are typical of pipelined processors.

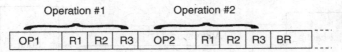

Figure 3.25   A partial VLIW format. Each fragment concurrently accesses a single centralized register set.

3.10   VLIW PROCESSORS

There are two broad classes of multiple-issue machines: statically scheduled and dynamically scheduled. In principle, these two classes are quite similar. Dependencies among groups of instructions are evaluated, and groups found to be independent are simultaneously dispatched to multiple execution units. For statically scheduled processors, this detection process is done by the compiler, and instructions are assembled into instruction packets, which are decoded and executed at run time. For dynamically scheduled processors, the detection of independent instructions may also be done at compile time and the code can be suitably arranged to optimize execution patterns, but the ultimate selection of instructions (to be executed or dispatched) is done by the hardware in the decoder at run time. In principle, the dynamically scheduled processor may have an instruction representation and form that is indistinguishable from slower pipeline processors. Statically scheduled processors must have some additional information either implicitly or explicitly indicating instruction packet boundaries.

As mentioned in Chapter 1, early VLIW machines [92] are typified by processors from Multiflow and Cydrome. These machines use an instruction word that consists of 10 instruction fragments. Each fragment controls a designated execution unit; thus, the register set is extensively multiported to support simultaneous access to the multiplicity of execution units. In order to accommodate the multiple instruction fragments, the instruction word is typically over 200 bits long (see Figure 3.25). In order to avoid the obvious performance limitations imposed by the occurrence of branches, a novel compiler technology called trace scheduling was developed. By use of trace scheduling, the dynamic frequency of branching is greatly reduced. Branches are predicted where possible, and on the basis of the probable success rate, the predicted path is incorporated into a larger basic block. This process continues until a suitably sized basic block (code without branches) can be efficiently scheduled. If an unanticipated (or unpredicted) branch occurs during the execution of the code, at the end of the basic block, the proper result is fixed up for use by a target basic block.

More recent attempts at multiple-issue processors have been directed at rather lower amounts of concurrency. However there has been increasing use of simultaneous multithreading (SMT). In SMT, multiple programs (threads) use the same processor execution hardware (adders, decoders, etc.) but have their own register sets and instruction counter and register. Two processors

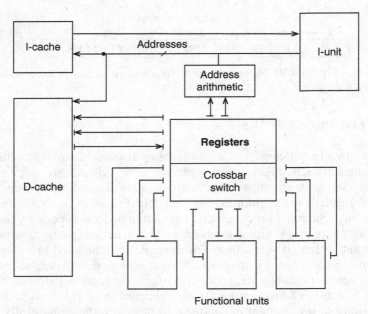

Figure 3.26 Major data paths in a generic VLIW processor.

(or cores) on the same die each using two-way SMT allows four programs to be in simultaneous execution.

Figure 3.26 shows the data paths for a generic VLIW machine. The extensive use of register ports provides simultaneous access to data as required by a VLIW processor. This suggests the register set may be a processor bottleneck.

3.11 SUPERSCALAR PROCESSORS

Superscalar processors can also be implemented by the data paths shown in Figure 3.26. Usually, such processors use multiple buses connecting the register set and functional units, and each bus services multiple functional units. This may limit the maximum degree of concurrency but can correspondingly reduce the required number of register ports.

The issue of detection of independence within or among instructions is theoretically the same regardless of whether the detection process is done statically or dynamically (although the realized effect is quite different). In the next sections, we review the theory of instruction independence. In superscalar processors, detection of independence must be done in hardware. This necessarily complicates both the control hardware and the options in realizing the processor. The remaining discussion in this section is somewhat more detailed and complex than the discussion of other approaches.

3.11.1 Data Dependencies

With out-of-order execution, three types of dependencies are possible between two instructions, I_i and I_j (i precedes j in execution sequence). The first, variously called a read-after-write (RAW) dependency or an essential dependency, arises when the destination of I_i is the same as the source of I_j:

$$D_i = S_{1j} \text{ or}$$

$$D_i = S_{2j}$$

This is a data or address dependency.

Another condition that causes a dependency occurs when the destination of instruction I_j is the same as the source of a preceding instruction I_i. This occurs when

$$D_j = S_{1i} \text{ or}$$

$$D_j = S_{2i}.$$

This arises when an instruction in sequence is delayed and a following instruction is allowed to precede in execution order and to change the contents of one of the original instruction's source registers; as in the following example (R3 is the destination),

I_1	DIV	R3,	R1,	R2
I_2	ADD	R5,	R3,	R4
I_3	ADD	R3,	R6,	R7.

Instruction 2 is delayed by a divide operation in instruction 1. If instruction 3 is allowed to execute as soon as its operands are available, this might change the register (R3) used in the computation of instruction 2. A dependency of this type is called a write-after-read (WAR) dependency or an ordering dependency, since it only happens when out-of-order execution is allowed.

In the final type of dependency, the destination of instruction I_i, is the same as the destination of instruction I_j, or

$$D_i = D_j.$$

In this case, instruction I_i could complete after instruction I_j, and the result in the register is that of instruction I_i when it ought to be that of I_j. This dependency, called a write-after-write (WAW) dependency or an output dependency, is somewhat debatable. If instruction I_i produces a result that is not used by an instruction that follows it until instruction I_j produces a new result for the same destination, then instruction I_i was unnecessary in the first place

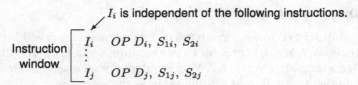

Figure 3.27   Detecting independent instructions.

Figure 3.27. As this type of dependency is generally eliminated by an optimizing compiler, it can be largely ignored in our discussions. We illustrate this with two examples:

Example #1

DIV	R3,	R1,	R2
ADD	R3,	R4,	R5.

Example #2

DIV	R3,	R1,	R2
ADD	R5,	R3,	R4
ADD	R3,	R6,	R7.

The first example is a case of a redundant instruction (the DIV), whereas the second has an output dependency, but also has an essential dependency; once this essential dependency is dealt with, the output dependency is also covered. The fewer the dependencies that arise in the code, the more concurrency available in the code and the faster the overall program execution.

3.11.2   Detecting Instruction Concurrency

Detection of instruction concurrency can be done at compile time, at run time (by the hardware), or both. It is clearly best to use both the compiler and the run-time hardware to support concurrent instruction execution. The compiler can unroll loops and generally create larger basic block sizes, reducing branches. However, it is only at run time that the complete machine state is known. For example, an apparent resource dependency created by a sequence of divide, load, divide instructions may not exist if, say, the intervening load instruction created a cache miss.

Instructions are checked for dependencies during decode. If an instruction is found to be independent of other, earlier instructions, and if there are available resources, the instruction is issued to the functional unit. The total number of instructions checked determines the size of the instruction window (Figure 3.28). Suppose the instruction window has N instructions, and at any given cycle M instructions are issued. In the next cycle, the successor M instructions

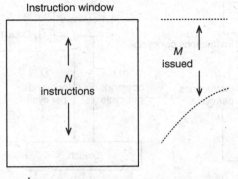

Instruction window

N instructions

M issued

The next *M* instructions are added to the window for issue in the following cycle.

Figure 3.28   Instruction window.

TABLE 3.14   Renaming Characteristics of Some SOC Designs

SOC	Renaming Buffer Size	Reservation Station Number
Freescale e600	16 GPR, 16 FPR, 16 VR	8
MIPS 74K	32 CB	—

GPR, general-purpose register; FPR, floating-point register; VR, vector register; CB, completion buffer.

are brought into the buffer, and again *N* instructions are checked. Up to *M* instructions may be issued in a single cycle.

Ordering and output dependencies can be eliminated with sufficient registers. When either of these dependencies is detected it is possible to rename the dependent register to another register usually not available to the instruction set. This type of renaming requires that the register set be extended to include *rename registers*. A typical processor may extend a 32-register set specified by the instruction set to a set of 45–60 total registers, including the rename registers (for SOC processor usage see Table 3.14).

Figure 3.29 illustrates the overall layout of an *M* pipelined processor inspecting *N* instructions and issuing *M* instructions.

Any of the *N* instructions in the window are candidates for issue, depending on whether they are independent and whether there are execution resources available.

If the processor, for example, can only accommodate two L/S instructions, a floating-point instruction, and a fixed-point instruction, then the decoder in the instruction window must select these types of instructions for issue. So three L/S instructions could not be issued even if they were all independent.

Scheduling is the process of assigning specific instructions and their operand values to designated resources at designated times. Scheduling can be done either centrally or in a distributed manner by the functional units themselves

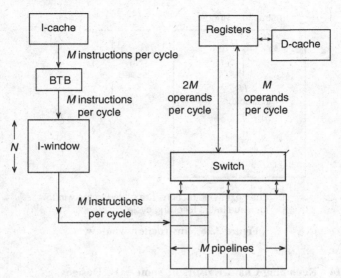

Figure 3.29   An M pipelined processor.

at execution time. The former approach is called control flow scheduling; the latter is called dataflow scheduling. In control flow scheduling, dependencies are resolved during the decode cycle and the instructions are held (not issued) until the dependencies have been resolved. In a dataflow scheduling system, the instructions leave the decode stage when they are decoded and are held in buffers at the functional units until their operands and the functional unit are available.

Early machines used either control flow or dataflow to ensure correct operation of out-of-order instructions. The CDC 6600 [242] used a control flow approach. The IBM 360 Model 91 [246] was the first system to use dataflow scheduling.

3.11.3   A Simple Implementation

In this section, we look at a simple scheduling implementation. While it uses $N = 1$ and $M = 1$, it allows out-of-order execution and illustrates a basic strategy in managing dependencies.

Consider a system with multiple functional units, each of whose executions may involve multiple cycles. Using the L/S architecture as our model, we assume that there is a centralized single set of registers that provide operands for the functional units.

Suppose there are up to N instructions already dispatched for execution, and we must determine how to issue an instruction currently at the decoder. Issuing a single instruction in the presence of up to $N - 1$ unissued previous instructions is equivalent to issuing that instruction as the last of N instructions issued at one time.

Functional unit

ADD

OP	D	S_1	S_2

MPY

OP	D	S_1	S_2

DIV

OP	D	S_1	S_2

Figure 3.30 Reservation stations are associated with function units. They contain instruction opcode and data values or a tag corresponding to a data value pending entry into a functional unit. They perform the function of a rename register.

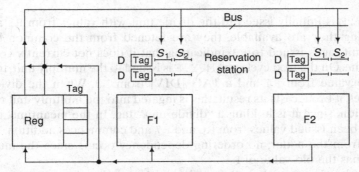

Figure 3.31 Dataflow. Each reservation station consists of registers to hold S_1 and S_2 values (if available), or tags to identify where the values come from.

We use an approach sometimes referred to as the dataflow approach or a tag-forwarding approach. It was first suggested by Tomasulo [246], and it is also known by his name.

Each register in the central register set is extended to include a tag that identifies the functional unit that produces a result to be placed in a particular register. Similarly, each of the multiple functional units has one or more reservation stations (Figure 3.30).

The reservation station contains either a tag identifying another functional unit or register, *or it can contain the value needed*. Operand values for a particular instruction need not be available for the instruction to be issued to the reservation station; the tag of a particular register may be substituted for a value, in which case the reservation station waits until the value is available. Since the reservation station holds the current *value* of the available data, it acts as a rename register, and thus the scheme avoids ordering and output dependencies.

Control is distributed within the functional units. Each reservation station effectively defines its own functional unit; thus, two reservations for a floating-point multiplier are two functional unit tags: multiplier 1 and multiplier 2 (Figure 3.31). If operands can go directly into the multiplier, then there is another tag: multiplier 3. Once a pair of operands has a designated functional unit tag, that tag remains with that operand pair until the completion of the operation. Any unit (or register) that depends on that result has a copy of the functional unit tag and ingates the result that is broadcast on the bus.

For the preceding example,

DIV.F	R3,	R1,	R2
MPY.F	R5,	R3,	R4
ADD.F	R4,	R6,	R7.

The DIV.F is initially issued to the divide unit with values from R1 and R2. (Assuming they are available, they are fetched from the common bus.) A divide unit tag is issued to R3, indicating that it does not currently contain a valid value. On the next cycle, the MPY.F is issued to the multiply unit, together with the value from R4 and a TAG [DIV] from R3. When the divide unit completes, it broadcasts its result; this is ingated into the multiply unit reservation station, since it is holding a "divide unit" tag. In the meantime, the add unit has been issued values from R6 and R7 and commences addition. R4 gets the tag from the adder; no ordering dependency occurs since the multiplier already has the old value of R4.

In the dataflow approach, the results to a targeted register may never actually go to that register; in fact, the computation based on the load of a particular register may be continually forwarded to various functional units, so that before the value is stored, a new value based upon a new computational sequence (a new load instruction) is able to use the targeted register. This approach partially avoids the use of a central register set, thereby avoiding the register ordering and output dependencies.

Whether the ordering and output dependencies are a serious problem or not is the subject of some debate [228]. With a larger register set, an optimizing compiler can distribute the usage of the registers across the set and avoid the register–resource dependencies. Of course, all schemes are left with the essential (type 1) dependency. Large register sets may have their own disadvantages, however, especially if save and restore traffic due to interrupts becomes a significant consideration.

Study 3.1 Sample Timing

For the code sequence

I_1	DIV.F	R3,	R1,	R2
I_2	MPY.F	R5,	R3,	R4
I_3	ADD.F	R4,	R6,	R7,

assume three separate floating-point units with execution times:

Divide	Eight cycles
Multiply	Four cycles
Add	Three cycles

and show the timing for a dataflow.

For this approach, we might have the following:

Cycle 1	Decoder issues $I_1 \rightarrow$ DIV unit
	R1 $\rightarrow$ DIV Res Stn
	R2 $\rightarrow$ DIV Res Stn
	TAG_DIV $\rightarrow$ R3
Cycle 2	Begin DIV.F
	Decoder issues $I_2 \rightarrow$ MPY unit
	TAG_DIV $\rightarrow$ MPY unit
	R4 $\rightarrow$ MPY Res Stn
	TAG_MPY $\rightarrow$ R5
Cycle 3	Multiplier waits
	Decoder issues $I_3 \rightarrow$ ADD unit
	R6 $\rightarrow$ ADD Res Stn
	R7 $\rightarrow$ ADD Res Stn
	TAG_ADD $\rightarrow$ R4
Cycle 4	Begin ADD.F
Cycle 6	ADD unit requests broadcast next cycle (granted).
	ADD unit completes this cycle.
Cycle 7	ADD unit result $\rightarrow$ R4
Cycle 9	DIV unit requests broadcast next cycle (granted).
	DIV unit completes this cycle.
Cycle 10	DIV unit $\rightarrow$ R3
	DIV unit $\rightarrow$ MPY unit
Cycle 11	Begin MPY.F
Cycle 14	Multiply completes and requests data broadcast (granted).
Cycle 15	MPY unit result $\rightarrow$ R5.

As far as implementation is concerned, the issue logic is distributed in the reservation stations. When multiple instructions are to be issued in the same cycle, then there must be multiple separate buses to transmit the information: operation, tag/value #1, tag/value #2, and destination. We assume that the reservation stations are associated with the functional units. If we centralize the reservation stations for implementation convenience, the design would be generally similar to an improved control flow, or *scoreboard*.

Action Summary   We can summarize the basic rules:

1. The decoder issues instructions to a functional unit reservation station with data values if available otherwise with register tag.
2. The destination register (specified by instruction) gets the functional unit tag.
3. Continue issue until a type of reservation station is FULL. Unissued instructions are held PENDING.
4. Any instruction that depends on an unissued or pending instruction must also be held in a pending state.

3.11.4   Preserving State with Out-of-Order Execution

Out-of-order execution leads to an apparently ill-defined machine state, even as the code is executing correctly. If an interrupt arises or some sort of an exception is taken (perhaps even a misguessed branch outcome), there can be a general ambiguity as to the exact source of the exception or how the machine state should be saved and restored for further instruction processing. There are two basic approaches to this problem:

1. Restrict the programmer's model. This applies only to interrupts and involves the use of a device called an imprecise interrupt, which simply indicates that an exception has occurred someplace in some region of code without trying to isolate it further. This simple approach may be satisfactory for signal or embedded processors that use only real (no virtual) memory but is generally unacceptable for virtual memory processors.

   A load instruction that accesses a page not currently in memory can have disastrous consequences if several instructions that followed it are already in execution. When control returns to the process after the missing page is loaded, the load can execute together with instructions that depended upon it, but other instructions that were previously executed should not be re-executed. The control for all this can be formidable. The only acceptable alternative would be to require that all pages used by a particular process be resident in memory before execution begins. In programming environments where this is feasible and practical, such as in large scientific applications, this may be a solution.
2. Create a write-back that preserves the ordered use of the register set or at least allows the reconstruction of such an ordered register set.

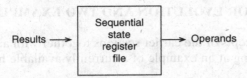

Figure 3.32   Simple register file organization.

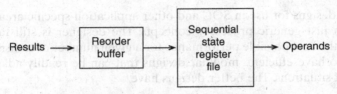

Figure 3.33   Centralized reorder buffer method.

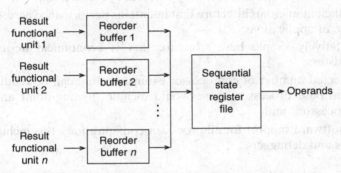

Figure 3.34   Distributed reorder buffer method.

In order to provide a sequential model of program execution, some mechanism must be provided that properly manages the register file state. The key to any successful scheme [135, 221] is the efficient management of the register set and its state. If instructions execute in order, then results are stored in the register file (Figure 3.32). Instructions that can complete early must be held pending the completion of previously issued but incomplete instructions. This sacrifices performance.

Another approach uses a reorder buffer (Figure 3.33). The results arrive at the reorder buffer out of program sequence, but they are written back to the sequential register file in program order, thus preserving the register file state. In order to avoid conflicts at the reorder buffer, we can distribute the buffer across the various functional units as shown in Figure 3.34. Either of these techniques allows out-of-order instruction execution but preserves in-order write-back to the register set.

3.12   PROCESSOR EVOLUTION AND TWO EXAMPLES

We bring the concepts of the earlier sections together with a few observations and then by looking at an example of a currently available high-performance processor.

3.12.1   Soft and Firm Processor Designs: The Processor as IP

Processor designs for use in SOC and other application-specific areas require more than just generic processor concepts. The designer is still faced with achieving the best possible performance for a given number of transistors. The object is to have efficient, modular designs that can be readily adapted to a number of situations. The better designs have

1. an instruction set that makes efficient use of both instruction memory (code density) and data memory (several operand sizes);
2. an efficient microarchitecture that maintains performance across a broad range of applications;
3. a relatively simple base structure that is economical in its use of transistors;
4. a selected number of coprocessor extensions that can be readily added to the base processor; these would include floating-point and vector coprocessors; and
5. full software support for all processor configurations; this includes compilers and debuggers.

A classic example of this type of processor design is the ARM 1020. It uses an instruction set with both 16- and 32-bit instructions for improved code density. The data paths for the 1020T are shown in Figure 3.35. A debug and system control coprocessor and/or a vector and floating-point coprocessor can be added directly for enhanced performance. The ARM bus is also a standard for SOC use.

The instruction timing is a quite simple six-stage pipeline as shown in Figure 3.36. Because of its simplicity, it can achieve close to its peak performance of one instruction for each cycle (ignoring cache misses).

3.12.2   High-Performance, Custom-Designed Processors

When the target is high-performance workstations, design effort is a secondary issue to performance (but not to time-to-market). The result is that large teams of designers focus on custom circuitry, clocking, algorithms and microarchitecture to achieve performance on a schedule. An example is the Freescale e600 (Figure 3.37). Such processors use all the design techniques discussed in this chapter plus others:

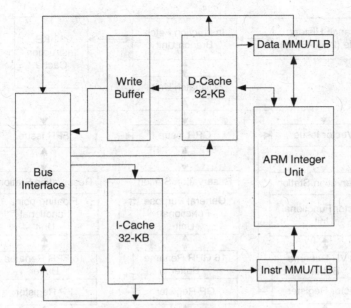

Figure 3.35 ARM 1020 data paths [20].

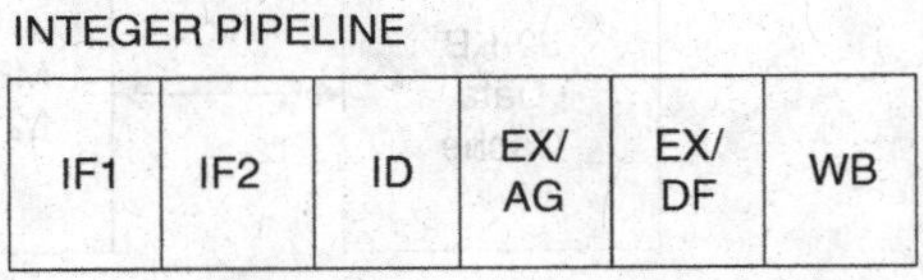

INTEGER PIPELINE

IF1	IF2	ID	EX/ AG	EX/ DF	WB

Figure 3.36 The ARM pipeline.

1. With lots of area (transistors) available, we would expect to see large branch tables, multiple execution units, multiple instruction issue, and out-of-order instruction completion.
2. With increased clock rates and a shorter cycle time, we would expect to see some basic operations (e.g., I fetch) to take more than one cycle. Overall, with shorter clocks and a much more elaborate pipeline, the timing template is significantly longer (a larger number of steps).
3. Since large caches have a long access time, we would expect to see small first-level caches supported by a hierarchy of one or more levels of increasing larger caches.

3.13 CONCLUSIONS

Pipelined processors have become the implementation of choice for almost all machines from mainframes to microprocessors. High-density VLSI logic

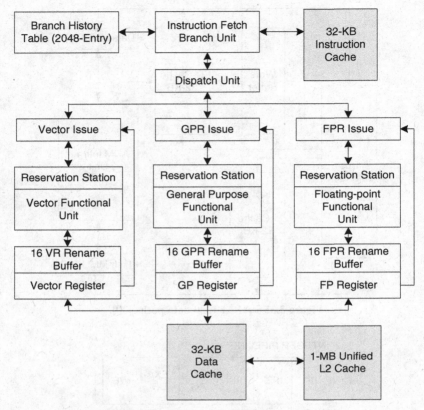

Figure 3.37   Freescale e600 data paths [101].

technology, coupled with high-density memory, has made possible this movement to increasingly complex processor implementations.

In modeling the performance of pipelined processors, we generally allocate a basic quantum of time for each instruction and then add to that the expected delays due to dependencies that arise in code execution. These dependencies usually arise from branches, dependent data, or limited execution resources. For each type of dependency, there are implementation strategies that mitigate the effect of the dependency. Implementing branch prediction strategies, for example, mitigates the effect of branch delays. Dependency detection comes at the expense of interlocks, however. The interlocks consist of logic associated with the decoder to detect dependencies and to ensure proper logical operation of the machine in executing code sequences.

3.14   PROBLEM SET

1. Following Study 3.1, show the timing for the following three instruction sequences:

ADD.F	R1,	R2,	R3
SUB.F	R3,	R4,	R5
MPY.F	R3,	R1,	R7

2. From the Internet, find three recent processor offerings and their corresponding parameters.

3. Suppose a vector processor achieves a speedup of 2.5 on vector code. In an application whose code is 50% vectorizable, what is the overall speedup over a nonvector machine? Contrast the expected speedup with a VLIW machine that can execute a maximum of four arithmetic operations per cycle (cycle time for VLIW and vector processor are the same).

4. A certain store buffer has a size of four entries. The mean number used is two entries.

   (a) Without knowing the variance, what is the probability of a "buffer full or overflow" delay?

   (b) Now suppose the variance is known to be $\sigma^2 = 0.5$; what is the probability of such a delay?

5. **(a)** Suppose a certain processor has the following BC behavior: a three-cycle penalty on correct guess of target, and a six-cycle penalty when it incorrectly guesses the target and the code actually goes in-line. Similarly, it has a zero-cycle penalty on correct in-line guess, but a six-cycle penalty when it incorrectly guesses in-line and the target path is taken. The target path should be guessed when the probability of going to the target is known to exceed what percent?

   (b) For an L/S machine that has a three-cycle cache access and an 8-byte physical word, how many words (each 8 bytes) are required for the in-line (primary) path of an I-buffer to avoid runout?

6. **(a)** A branch table buffer (BTB) can be accessed while the branch is decoded so that the target address (only) is available at the end of the branch decode cycle.

   IF   IF   D   AG   AG   DF   DF   EX   EX

   For an R/M machine with BTB and timing template as shown in the above chart (one decode each cycle), what is the BR penalty and the BC penalty in cycles? (Assume that all of the BRs and 50% of the BCs hit in the BTB, that 80% of those BCs that hit are actually taken, and that 20% of those BCs that did not hit were actually taken.)

   (b) If target instructions are placed directly in the BTB, what is the penalty for BR and for BC in cycles (same assumptions as [a])?

7. A BTB can be used together with history bits to determine when to place a target in the BTB. This might make small BTBs more effective. Below

what size BTB would a 2-bit branch history approach be attractive (for the scientific environment)?

8. Find a commercial VLIW machine and its instruction layout. Describe it and then write an instruction sequence that could compute $A^2 + 7 \times B + A \times C - D/(A \times B)$. Load values into registers, then compute.

9. Rename registers can take the place of a register set specified by the instruction set. Compare the approach of having no register set (as in a single accumulator instruction set) and having no rename registers but having a large register set in the instruction set.

10. Find an SOC configuration that uses a vector processor and describe the architecture of the vector processor—number of register sets, register per set, instruction format, and so on.

11. Find an SOC configuration that uses a superscalar processor and describe the architecture of the processor—register sets, number of rename registers, control flow or dataflow, instruction format, and so on.

4 Memory Design: System-on-Chip and Board-Based Systems

4.1 INTRODUCTION

Memory design is the key to system design. The memory system is often the most costly (in terms of area or number of die) part of the system and it largely determines the performance. Regardless of the processors and the interconnect, the application cannot be executed any faster than the memory system, which provides the instructions and the operands.

Memory design involves a number of considerations. The primary consideration is the application requirements: the operating system, the size, and the variability of the application processes. This largely determines the size of memory and how the memory will be addressed: real or virtual. Figure 4.1 is an outline for memory design, while Table 4.1 compares the relative area required for different memory technologies.

We start by looking at issues in SOC external and internal memories. We then examine scratchpad and cache memory to understand how they operate and how they are designed. After that, we consider the main memory problem, first the on-die memory and then the conventional dynamic RAM (DRAM) design. As part of the design of large memory systems, we look at multiple memory modules, interleaving, and memory system performance. Figure 4.2 presents the SOC memory design issues. In this chapter the interconnect, processors, and I/O are idealized so that the memory design trade-offs can be characterized.

Table 4.2 shows the types of memory that can be integrated into an SOC design.

Example. Required functionality can play a big role in achieving performance. Consider the differences between the two paths of Figure 4.1: the maximum functionality path and the restricted functionality path. The difference seems slight, whether the memory is off-die or on-die. The resulting performance difference can be great because of the long off-die access time. If the memory (application data and program) can be contained in an on-die memory, the access time will be 3–10 cycles.

Computer System Design: System-on-Chip, First Edition. Michael J. Flynn and Wayne Luk.
© 2011 John Wiley & Sons, Inc. Published 2011 by John Wiley & Sons, Inc.

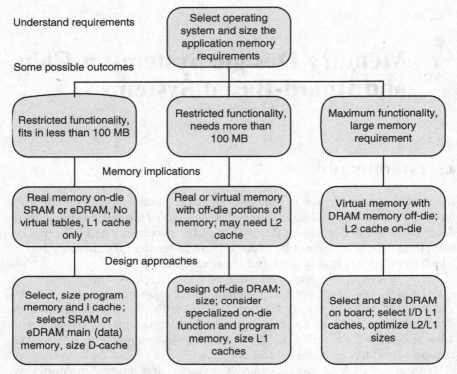

Figure 4.1   An outline for memory design.

TABLE 4.1   Area Comparison for Different Memory Technologies

Memory Technology	rbe	KB per Unit A
DRAM	0.05–0.1	1800–3600
SRAM	0.6	300
ROM/PROM	0.2–0.8+	225–900
eDRAM	0.15	1200
Flash: NAND	0.02	10,000

Off-die access times are an order of magnitude greater (30–100 cycles). To achieve the same performance, the off-die memory design must have an order of magnitude more cache, often split into multiple levels to meet access time requirements. Indeed, a cache bit can be 50 times larger than an on-die embedded DRAM (eDRAM) bit (see Chapter 2 and Section 4.13). So the true cost of the larger cache required for off-die memory support may be 10 by 50 or 500 DRAM bits. If a memory system uses 10K rbe for cache to support an on-die memory, the die would require 100K rbe to support off-die memory. That 90K rbe difference could possibly accommodate 450K eDRAM bits.

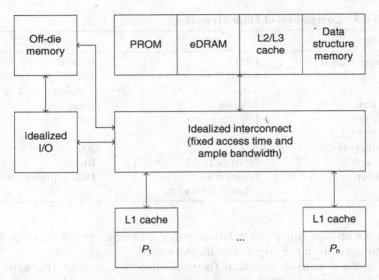

Figure 4.2 The SOC memory model.

n selected processors with idealized execution time

TABLE 4.2 Some Flash Memory (NAND) Package Formats (2- to 128-GB Size)

Format	(Approx.) Size (mm)	Weight (g)	Speed (Read/ Write) (MBps)	Typical Applications
Compact flash (CF)	$36 \times 43 \times 3.3$	11.4	22/18	Digital camera
Secure digital (SD)	$32 \times 24 \times 2.1$	2.0	22/18	Digital/video camera
Mini SD	$20 \times 20 \times 1.2$	1.0	22/18	Cell phone, GPS
Micro SD	$15 \times 11 \times 0.7$	0.5	22/15	Mini cell phone

4.2 OVERVIEW

4.2.1 SOC External Memory: Flash

Flash technology is a rapidly developing technology with improvements announced regularly. Flash is not really a memory replacement but is probably better viewed as a disk replacement. However, in some circumstances and configurations, it can serve the dual purpose of memory and nonvolatile backup storage.

Flash memory consists of an array of floating gate transistors. These transistors are similar to MOS transistors but with a two-gate structure: a control gate and an insulated floating gate. Charge stored on the floating gate is trapped there, providing a nonvolatile storage. While the data can be rewritten, the current technology has a limited number of reliable rewrite cycles, usually

TABLE 4.3 Comparison of Flash Memories

Technology	NOR	NAND
Bit density (KB/A)	1000	10,000
Typical capacity	64 MB	16 GB (dice can be stacked by 4 or more)
Access time	20–70 ns	10 μs
Transfer rate (MB per sec.)	150	300
Write time(μs)	300	200
Addressability	Word or block	Block
Application	Program storage and limited data store	Disk replacement

less than a million. Since degradation with use can be a problem, error detection and correction are frequently implemented.

While the density is excellent for semiconductor devices, the write cycle limitation generally restricts the usage to storing infrequently modified data, such as programs and large files.

There are two types of flash implementations: NOR and NAND. The NOR implementation is more flexible, but the NAND provides a significantly better bit density. Hybrid NOR/NAND implementations are also possible with the NOR array acting as a buffer to the larger NAND array. Table 4.3 provides a comparison of these implementations.

Flash memory cards come in various package formats; larger sizes are usually older (see Table 4.2). Small flash dice can be "stacked" with an SOC chip to present a single system/memory package. A flash die can also be stacked to create large (64–256 GB) single memory packages.

In current technology, flash usually is found in off-die implementations. However, there are a number of flash variants that are specifically designed to be compatible with ordinary SOC technology. SONOS [201] is a nonvolatile example, and Z-RAM [91] is a DRAM replacement example. Neither seems to suffer from rewrite cycle limitations. Z-RAM seems otherwise compatible with DRAM speeds while offering improved density. SONOS offers density but with slower access time than eDRAM.

4.2.2 SOC Internal Memory: Placement

The most important and obvious factor in memory system design is the placement of the main memory: on-die (the same die as the processor) or off-die (on its own die or on a module with multiple dice). As pointed out in Chapter 1, this factor distinguishes conventional workstation processors and application-oriented board designs from SOC designs.

The design of the memory system is limited by two basic parameters that determine memory systems performance. The first is the access time. This is the

TABLE 4.4 Comparing System Design Environments

Item	Workstation Type	SOC Single Die	SOC Board Based
Processor	Fastest available	Smaller, perhaps four to six times slower	As with SOC
Cache	Two to three levels, very large (4–64 MB)	Simple, single level (256 KB)	Single level, multielement
Memory bus	Complex, slow pin limited	Internal, wide, high bandwidth	Mix
Bus control	Complex timing and control	Simple, internal	Mix
Memory	Very large (16+ GB), limited bandwidth	Limited size (256 MB), relatively fast	Specialized on board
Memory access time	20–30 ns	3–5 ns	Mix

time for a processor request to be transmitted to the memory system, access a datum, and return it back to the processor. Access time is largely a function of the physical parameters of the memory system—the physical distance between the processor and the memory system, or the bus delay, the chip delay, and so on. The second parameter is *memory bandwidth*, the ability of the memory to respond to requests per unit time. Bandwidth is primarily determined by the way the physical memory system is organized—the number of independent memory arrays and the use of special sequential accessing modes.

The cache system must compensate for limits on memory access time and bandwidth.

The workstation processor, targeting high performance, requires a very efficient memory system, a task made difficult by memory placement off-die. Table 4.4 compares the memory system design environments.

The workstation and board-based memory design is clearly a greater challenge for designers. Special attention must be paid to the cache, which must make up for the memory placement difficulties.

4.2.3 The Size of Memory

As it will become obvious in this chapter, designing for large off-die memory is the key problem in system board designs. So why not limit memory to sizes that could be incorporated on a die? In a virtual memory system, we can still access large address spaces for applications. For workstations, the application environment (represented by the operating system) has grown considerably (see Figure 4.3). As the environment continues to grow, so too does the working set or the active pages of storage. This requires more real (physical) memory to hold a sufficient number of pages to avoid excessive page swapping,

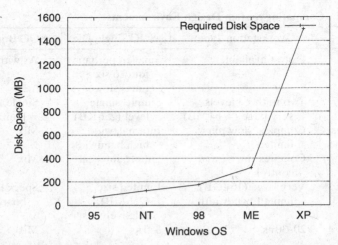

Figure 4.3 Required disk space for several generations of Microsoft's Windows operating system. The newer Vista operating system requires 6 GB.

which can destroy performance. Board-based systems face a slightly different problem. Here, the media-based data sets are naturally very large and require large bandwidths from memory and substantial processing ability from the media processor. Board-based systems have an advantage, however, as the access time is rarely a problem so long as the bandwidth requirements are met. How much memory can we put on a die? Well, that depends on the technology (feature size) and the required performance. Table 4.1 shows the area occupied for various technologies. The eDRAM size assumes a relatively large memory array (see later in this chapter). So, for example, in a 45-nm technology, we might expect to have about $49.2\,\text{kA/cm}^2$ or about 8 MB of eDRAM. Advancing circuit design and technology could significantly improve that, but it does seem that about 64 MB would be a limit, unless a compatible flash technology becomes available.

4.3 SCRATCHPADS AND CACHE MEMORY

Smaller memories are almost always faster than larger memory, so it is useful to keep frequently used (or anticipated) instructions and data in a small, easily accessible (one cycle access) memory. If this memory is managed directly by the programmer, it is called a scratchpad memory; if it is managed by the hardware, it is called a cache.

Since management is a cumbersome process, most general-purpose computers use only cache memory. SOC, however, offers the potential of having the scratchpad alternative. Assuming that the application is well-known, the programmer can explicitly control data transfers in anticipation of use.

Eliminating the cache control hardware offers additional area for larger scratchpad size, again improving performance.

SOC implements scratchpads usually for data and not for instructions, as simple caches work well for instructions. Furthermore, it is not worth the programming effort to directly manage instruction transfers.

The rest of this section treats the theory and experience of cache memory. Because there has been so much written about cache, it is easy to forget the simpler and older scratchpad approach, but with SOC, sometimes the simple approach is best.

Caches work on the basis of the locality of program behavior [113]. There are three principles involved:

1. *Spatial Locality*. Given an access to a particular location in memory, there is a high probability that other accesses will be made to either that or neighboring locations within the lifetime of the program.
2. *Temporal Locality*. Given a sequence of references to n locations, there will be references into the same locations with high probability.
3. *Sequentiality*. Given that a reference has been made to location s, it is likely that within the next few references, there will be a reference to the location of $s + 1$. This is a special case of spatial locality.

The cache designer must deal with the processor's accessing requirements on the one hand, and the memory system's requirements on the other. Effective cache designs balance these within cost constraints.

4.4 BASIC NOTIONS

Processor references contained in the cache are called cache hits. References not found in the cache are called cache misses. On a cache miss, the cache fetches the missing data from memory and places it in the cache. Usually, the cache fetches an associated region of memory called the line. The line consists of one or more physical words accessed from a higher-level cache or main memory. The physical word is the basic unit of access to the memory.

The processor–cache interface has a number of parameters. Those that directly affect processor performance (Figure 4.4) include the following:

1. Physical word—unit of transfer between processor and cache.
   Typical physical word sizes:
   2–4 bytes—minimum, used in small core-type processors
   8 bytes and larger—multiple instruction issue processors (superscalar)
2. Block size (sometimes called *line*)—usually the basic unit of transfer between cache and memory. It consists of n physical words transferred from the main memory via the bus.

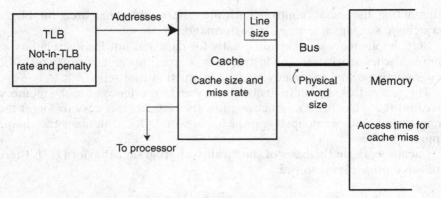

Figure 4.4   Parameters affecting processor performance.

3. Access time for a cache hit—this is a property of the cache size and organization.
4. Access time for a cache miss—property of the memory and bus.
5. Time to compute a real address given a virtual address (not-in-translation lookaside buffer [TLB] time)—property of the address translation facility.
6. Number of processor requests per cycle.

Cache performance is measured by the miss rate or the probability that a reference made to the cache is not found. The miss rate times the miss time is the delay penalty due to the cache miss. In simple processors, the processor stalls on a cache miss.

IS CACHE A PART OF THE PROCESSOR?

For many IP designs, the first-level cache is integrated into the processor design, so what and why do we need to know cache details? The most obvious answer is that an SOC consists of multiple processors that must share memory, usually through a second-level cache. Moreover, the details of the first-level cache may be essential in achieving memory consistency and proper program operation. So for our purpose, the cache is a separate, important piece of the SOC. We design the SOC memory hierarchy, not an isolated cache.

4.5   CACHE ORGANIZATION

A cache uses either a fetch-on-demand or a prefetch strategy. The former organization is widely used with simple processors. A demand fetch cache

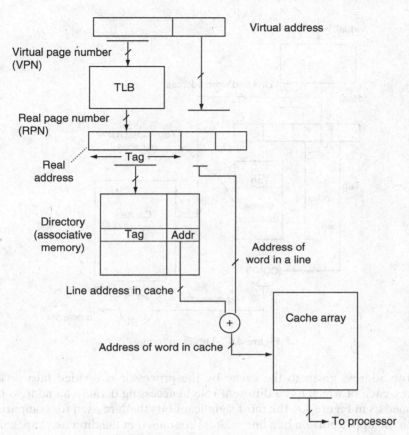

Figure 4.5 Fully associative mapping.

brings a new memory locality into the cache only when a miss occurs. The prefetch cache attempts to anticipate the locality about to be requested and *prefetches* it. It is commonly used in I-caches.

There are three basic types of cache organization: fully associative (FA) mapping (Figure 4.5), direct mapping (Figure 4.6), and set associative mapping (Figure 4.7, which is really a combination of the other two). In an FA cache, when a request is made, the address is compared (COMP) to the addresses of all entries in the directory. If the requested address is found (a directory hit), the corresponding location in the cache is fetched; otherwise, a *miss* occurs.

In a direct-mapped cache, the lower-order line address bits access the directory (index bits in Figure 4.8). Since multiple line addresses map into the same location in the cache directory, the upper line address bits (tag bits) must be compared to the directory address to validate a hit. If a comparison is not valid, the result is a miss. The advantage of the direct-mapped cache is that a reference to the cache array itself can be made *simultaneously with the access to the directory.*

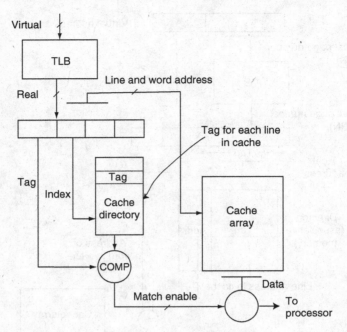

Figure 4.6   Direct mapping.

The address given to the cache by the processor is divided into several pieces, each of which has a different role in accessing data. In an address partitioned as in Figure 4.8, the most significant bits that are used for comparison (with the upper portion of a line address contained in the directory) are called the tag.

The next field is called the *index*, and it contains the bits used to address a line in the cache directory. The *tag* plus the *index* is the line address in memory.

The next field is the *offset*, and it is the address of a physical word within a line.

Finally, the least significant address field specifies a *byte in a word*. These bits are not usually used by the cache since the cache references a word. (An exception arises in the case of a *write* that modifies only a part of a word.)

The set associative cache is similar to the direct-mapped cache. Bits from the line address are used to address a cache directory. However, now there are multiple choices: Two, four, or more complete line addresses may be present in the directory. Each address corresponds to a location in a subcache. The collection of these subcaches forms the total cache array. These subarrays can be accessed simultaneously, together with the cache directory. If any of the entries in the cache directory match the reference address, then there is a hit, and the matched subcache array is sent back to the processor. While selection in the matching process increases the cache access time, the set associative cache access time is usually better than that of the fully associative mapped cache. But

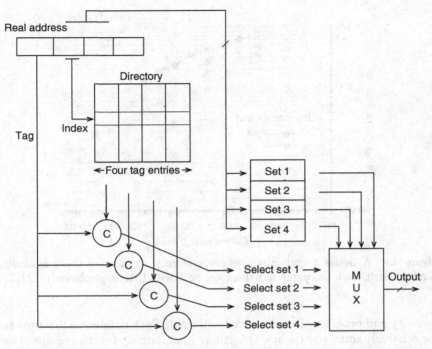

Figure 4.7 Set associative (multiple direct-mapped caches) mapping.

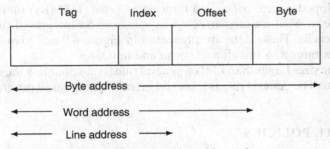

Figure 4.8 Address partitioned by cache usage.

the direct-mapped cache provides the fastest processor access to cache data for any given cache size.

4.6 CACHE DATA

Cache size largely determines cache performance (miss rate). The larger the cache, the lower the miss rate. Almost all cache miss rate data are empirical and, as such, have certain limitations. Cache data are strongly program dependent. Also, data are frequently based upon older machines, where the

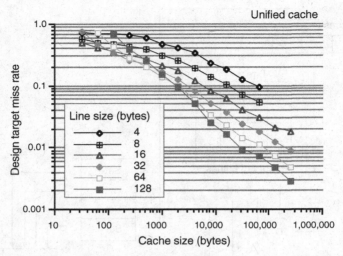

Figure 4.9 A design target miss rate per reference to memory (fully associative, demand fetch, fetch [allocate] on write, copy-back with LRU replacement) [223, 224].

memory and program size were fixed and small. Such data show low miss rate for relatively small size caches. Thus, there is a tendency for the measured miss rate of a particular cache size to increase over time. This is simply the result of measurements made on programs of increasing size. Some time ago, Smith [224] developed a series of design target miss rates (DTMRs) that represent an estimate of what a designer could expect from an integrated (instruction and data) cache. These data are presented in Figure 4.9 and give an idea of typical miss rates as a function of cache and line sizes.

For cache sizes larger than 1 MB, a general rule is that doubling the size halves the miss rate. The general rule is less valid in transaction-based programs.

4.7 WRITE POLICIES

How is memory updated on a write? One could write to both .cache and memory (write-through or WT), or write only to the cache (copy-back or CB—sometimes called write-back), updating memory when the line is replaced. These two strategies are the basic cache write policies (Figure 4.10).

The write-through cache (Figure 4.10a) stores into both cache and main memory on each CPU store.

Advantage: This retains a consistent (up-to-date) image of program activity in memory.

Disadvantage: Memory bandwidth may be high—dominated by write traffic.

In the copy-back cache (Figure 4.10b), the new data are written to memory when the line is replaced. This requires keeping track of modified (or "dirty") lines, but results in reduced memory traffic for writes:

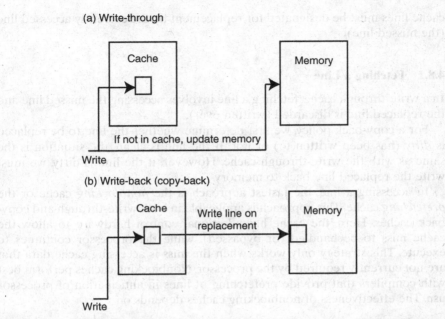

Figure 4.10   Write policies: (a) write-through cache (no allocate on write) and (b) copy-back cache (allocate on write).

1. Dirty bit is set if a write occurs anywhere in line.
2. From various traces [223], the probability that a line to be replaced is dirty is 47% on average (ranging from 22% to 80%).
3. Rule of thumb: Half of the data lines replaced are dirty. So, for a data cache, assume 50% are dirty lines, and for an integrated cache, assume 30% are dirty lines.

Most larger caches use copy-back; write-through is usually restricted to either small caches or special-purpose caches that provide an up-to-date image of memory. Finally, what should we do when a write (or store) instruction misses in the cache? We can fetch that line from memory (write allocate or WA) or just write into memory (no write allocate or NWA). Most write-through caches do not allocate on writes (WTNWA) and most copy back caches do allocate (CBWA).

4.8   STRATEGIES FOR LINE REPLACEMENT AT MISS TIME

What happens on a cache miss? If the reference address is not found in the directory, a *cache miss* occurs. Two actions must promptly be taken: (1) The missed line must be fetched from the main memory, and (2) one of the current cache lines must be designated for replacement by the currently accessed line (the missed line).

4.8.1 Fetching a Line

In a write-through cache, fetching a line involves accessing the missed line and the replaced line is discarded (written over).

For a copy-back policy, we first determine whether the line to be replaced is *dirty* (has been written to) or not. If the line is clean, the situation is the same as with the write-through cache. However, if the line is dirty, we must write the replaced line back to memory.

In accessing a line, the fastest approach is the *nonblocking* cache or the *prefetching* cache. This approach is applicable in both write-through and copy-back caches. Here, the cache has additional control hardware to allow the cache miss to be handled (or bypassed), while the processor continues to execute. This strategy only works when the miss is accessing cache data that are not currently required by the processor. Nonblocking caches perform best with compilers that provide prefetching of lines in anticipation of processor use. The effectiveness of nonblocking caches depends on

1. the number of misses that can be bypassed while the processor continues to execute; and
2. the effectiveness of the prefetch and the adequateness of the buffers to hold the prefetch information; the longer the prefetch is made before expected use, the less the miss delay, but this also means that the buffers or registers are occupied and hence are not available for (possible) current use.

4.8.2 Line Replacement

The replacement policy selects a line for replacement when the cache is full. There are three replacement policies that are widely used:

1. *Least Recently Used (LRU).* The line that was least recently accessed (by a read or write) is replaced.
2. *First In–First Out (FIFO).* The line that had been in the cache the longest is replaced.
3. *Random Replacement (RAND).* Replacement is determined randomly.

Since the LRU policy corresponds to the concept of temporal locality, it is generally the preferred policy. It is also the most complex to implement. Each line has a counter that is updated on a read (or write). Since these counters could be large, it is common to create an approximation to the true LRU with smaller counters.

While LRU performs better than either FIFO or RAND, the use of the simpler RAND or FIFO only amplifies the LRU miss rate (DTMR) by about 1.10 (i.e., 10%) [223].

4.8.3 Cache Environment: Effects of System, Transactions, and Multiprogramming

Most available cache data are based upon trace studies of user applications. Actual applications are run in the context of the system. The operating system tends to slightly increase (20% or so) the miss rate experienced by a user program [7].

Multiprogramming environments create special demands on a cache. In such environments, the cache miss rates may not be affected by increasing cache size. There are two environments:

1. *A Multiprogrammed Environment.* The system, together with several programs, is resident in memory. Control is passed from program to program after a number of instructions, Q, have been executed, and eventually returns to the first program. This kind of environment results in what is called a *warm* cache. When a process returns for continuing execution, it finds some, but not all, of its most recently used lines in the cache, increasing the expected miss rate (Figure 4.11 illustrates the effect).

2. *Transaction Processing.* While the system is resident in memory together with a number of support programs, short applications (transactions) run

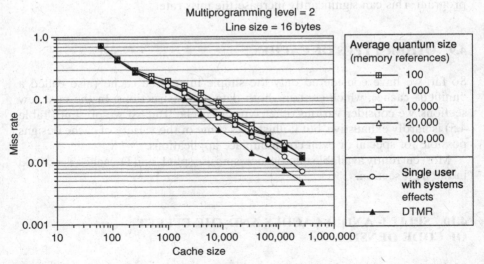

Figure 4.11 Warm cache: cache miss rates for a multiprogrammed environment switching processes after Q instructions.

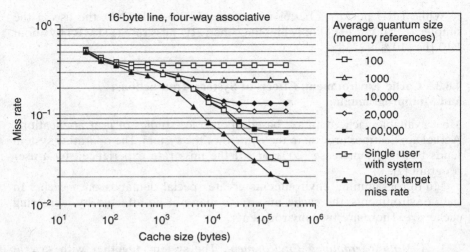

Figure 4.12   Cold cache: cache miss rates for a transaction environment switching processes after Q instructions.

through to completion. Each application consists of Q instructions. This kind of environment is sometimes called a *cold* cache. Figure 4.12 illustrates the situation.

Both of the preceding environments are characterized by passing control from one program to another before completely loading the working set of the program. This can significantly increase the miss rate.

4.9   OTHER TYPES OF CACHE

So far, we have considered only the simple integrated cache (also called a "unified" cache), which contains both data and instructions. In the next few sections, we consider various other types of cache. The list we present (Table 4.5) is hardly exhaustive, but it illustrates some of the variety of cache designs possible for special or even commonplace applications.

Most currently available microprocessors use split I- and D-caches, described in the next section.

4.10   SPLIT I- AND D-CACHES AND THE EFFECT OF CODE DENSITY

Multiple caches can be incorporated into a single processor design, each cache serving a designated process or use. Over the years, special caches for systems

TABLE 4.5   Common Types of Cache

Type	Where It Is Usually Used
Integrated (or unified)	The basic cache that accommodates all references (I and D). This is commonly used as the second- and higher-level cache.
Split caches I and D	Provides additional cache access bandwidth with some increase in the miss rate (MR). Commonly used as a first-level processor cache.
Sectored cache	Improves area effectiveness (MR for given area) for on-chip cache.
Multilevel cache	The first level has fast access; the second level is usually much larger than the first to reduce time delay in a first-level miss.
Write assembly cache	Specialized, reduces write traffic, usually used with a WT on-chip first-level cache.

code and user code or even special input/output (I/O) caches have been considered. The most popular configuration of partitioned caches is the use of separate caches for instructions and data.

Separate instruction and data caches provide significantly increased cache bandwidth, doubling the access capability of the cache ensemble. I- and D-caches come at some expense, however; a unified cache with the same size as the sum of a data and instruction cache has a lower miss rate. In the unified cache, the ratio of instruction to data working set elements changes during the execution of the program and is adapted to by the replacement strategy.

Split caches have implementation advantages. Since the caches need not be split equally, a 75–25% or other split may prove more effective. Also, the I-cache is simpler as it is not required to handle stores.

4.11   MULTILEVEL CACHES

4.11.1   Limits on Cache Array Size

The cache consists of a static RAM (SRAM) array of storage cells. As the array increases in size, so does the length of the wires required to access its most remote cell. This translates into the cache access delay, which is a function of the cache size, organization, and the process technology (feature size, f). McFarland [166] has modeled the delay and found that an approximation can be represented as

$$\text{Access time (ns)} = (0.35 + 3.8f + (0.006 + 0.025f)C) \times (1 + 0.3(1 - 1/A)),$$

where f is the feature size in microns, C is the cache array capacity in kilobyte, and A is the degree of associativity (where direct map = 1).

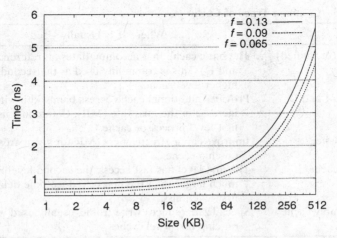

Figure 4.13   Cache access time (for a single array) as a function of cache array size.

The effect of this equation (for $A = 1$) can be seen in Figure 4.13. If we limit the level 1 access time to under 1 ns, we are probably limited to a cache array of about 32 KB. While it is possible to interleave multiple arrays, the interleaving itself has an overhead. So usually, L1 caches are less than 64 KB; L2 caches are usually less than 512 KB (probably interleaved using smaller arrays); and L3 caches use multiple arrays of 256 KB or more to create large caches, often limited by die size.

4.11.2   Evaluating Multilevel Caches

In the case of a multilevel cache, we can evaluate the performance of both levels using L1 cache data. A two-level cache system is termed *inclusive* if all the contents of the lower-level cache (L1) are also contained in the higher-level cache (L2).

Second-level cache analysis is achieved using the principle of inclusion; that is, a large, second-level cache includes the same lines as in the first-level cache. Thus, for the purpose of evaluating performance, we can assume that the first-level cache does not exist. The total number of misses that occur in a second-level cache can be determined by assuming that the processor made all of its requests to the second-level cache without the intermediary first-level cache.

There are design considerations in accommodating a second-level cache to an existing first-level cache. The line size of the second-level cache should be the same as or larger than the first-level cache. Otherwise, if the line size in the second-level cache were smaller, loading the line in the first-level cache would simply cause two misses in the second-level cache. Further, the second-level cache should be significantly larger than the first-level; otherwise, it would have no benefit.

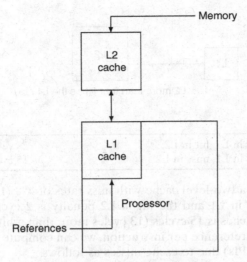

Figure 4.14   A two-level cache.

In a two-level system, as shown in Figure 4.14, with first-level cache, L1, and second-level cache, L2, we define the following miss rates [202]:

1. A local miss rate is simply the number of misses experienced by the cache divided by the number of references to it. This is the usual understanding of *miss rate*.
2. The global miss rate is the number of L2 misses divided by the number of references made by the processor. This is our primary measure of the L2 cache.
3. The solo miss rate is the miss rate the L2 cache would have if it were the only cache in the system. This is the miss rate defined by the principle of inclusion. *If* L2 contains *all* of L1, then we can find the number of L2 misses and the processor reference rate, ignoring the presence of the L1 cache. The principle of inclusion specifies that the global miss rate is the same as the solo miss rate, allowing us to use the solo miss rate to evaluate a design.

The preceding data (read misses only) illustrate some salient points in multi-level cache analysis and design:

1. So long as the L1 cache is the same as or larger than the L2 cache, analysis by the principle of inclusion provides a good estimate of the behavior of the L2 cache.
2. When the L2 cache is significantly larger than the L1 cache, it can be considered independent of the L1 parameters. Its miss rate corresponds to a solo miss rate.

EXAMPLE 4.1

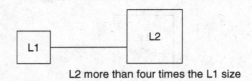

L2 more than four times the L1 size

Miss penalties:

Miss in L1, hit in L2:	2 cycles
Miss in L1, miss in L2:	15 cycles

Suppose we have a two-level cache with miss rates of 4% (L1) and 1% (L2). Suppose the miss in L1 and the hit in L2 penalty is 2 cycles, and the miss penalty in both caches is 15 cycles (13 cycles more than a hit in L2). If a processor makes one reference per instruction, we can compute the excess cycles per instruction (CPIs) due to cache misses as follows:

$$\text{Excess CPI due to L1 misses}$$
$$= 1.0 \text{ refr/inst} \times 0.04 \text{ misses/refr} \times 2 \text{ cycles/miss}$$
$$= 0.08 \text{ CPI}$$

$$\text{Excess CPI due to L2 misses}$$
$$= 1.0 \text{ refr/inst} \times 0.01 \text{ misses/refr} \times 13 \text{ cycles/miss}$$
$$= 0.13 \text{ CPI}.$$

Note: the L2 miss penalty is 13 cycles, not 15 cycles, since the 1% L2 misses have already been "charged" 2 cycles in the excess L1 CPI:

$$\text{Total effect} = \text{excess L1 CPI} + \text{excess L2 CPI}$$
$$= 0.08 + 0.13$$
$$= 0.21 \text{ CPI}.$$

The cache configurations for some recent SOCs are shown in Table 4.6.

TABLE 4.6   SOC Cache Organization

SOC	L1 Cache	L2 Cache
NetSilicon NS9775 [185]	8-KB I-cache, 4-KB D-cache	—
NXP LH7A404 [186]	8-KB I-cache, 8-KB D-cache	—
Freescale e600 [101]	32-KB I-cache, 32-KB D-cache	1 MB with ECC
Freescale PowerQUICC III [102]	32-KB I-cache, 32-KB D-cache	256 KB with ECC
ARM1136J(F)-S [24]	64-KB I-cache, 64-KB D-cache	Max 512 KB

4.11.3 Logical Inclusion

True or logical inclusion, where *all* the contents of L1 reside also in L2, should not be confused with statistical inclusion, where *usually*, L2 contains the L1 data. There are a number of requirements for logical inclusion. Clearly, the L1 cache must be write-through; the L2 cache need not be. If L1 were copy-back, then a write to a line in L1 would not go immediately to L2, so L1 and L2 would differ in contents.

When logical inclusion is required, it is probably necessary to actively force the contents to be the same and to use consistent cache policies.

Logical inclusion is a primary concern in shared memory multiprocessor systems that require a consistent memory image.

4.12 VIRTUAL-TO-REAL TRANSLATION

The TLB provides the real addresses used by the cache by translating the virtual addresses into real addresses.

Figure 4.15 shows a two-way set associative TLB. The page address (the upper bits of the virtual address) is composed of the bits that require translation. Selected virtual address bits address the TLB entries. These are selected

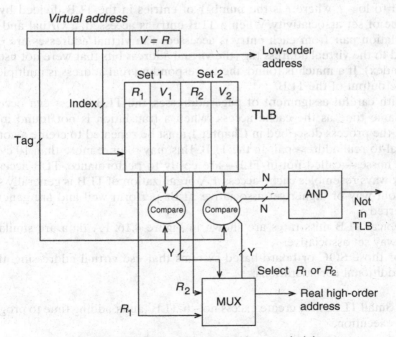

Figure 4.15   TLB with two-way set associativity.

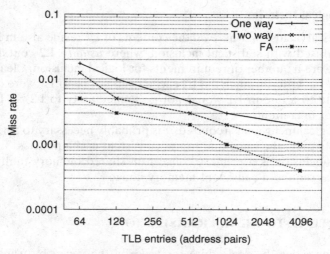

Figure 4.16   Not-in-TLB rate.

(or *hashed*) from the bits of the virtual address. This avoids too many address collisions, as might occur when both address and data pages have the same, say, "000," low-order page addresses. The size of the virtual address index is equal to $\log_2 t$, where t is the number of entries in the TLB divided by the degree of set associativity. When a TLB entry is accessed, a virtual and real translation pair from each entry is accessed. The virtual addresses are compared to the virtual address tag (the virtual address bits that were not used in the index). If a match is found, the corresponding real address is multiplexed to the output of the TLB.

With careful assignment of page addresses, the TLB access can occur at the same time as the cache access. When a translation is not found in the TLB, the process described in Chapter 1 must be repeated to create a correct virtual-to-real address pair in the TLB. This may require more than 10 cycles; TLB misses—called not-in-TLB—are costly to performance. TLB access in many ways resembles cache access. FA organization of TLB is generally slow, but four-way or higher set associative TLBs perform well and are generally preferred.

Typical TLB miss rates are shown in Figure 4.16. FA data are similar to four-way set associative.

For those SOC or board-based systems that use virtual addressing, there are additional considerations:

1. Small TLBs may create excess not-in-TLB faults, adding time to program execution.
2. If the cache uses real addresses, the TLB access must occur before the cache access, increasing the cache access time.

TABLE 4.7 SOC TLB Organization

SOC	Organization	Number of Entries
Freescale e600 [101]	Separate I-TLB, D-TLB	128-entry, two-way set associative, LRU
NXP LH7A404 [186]	Separate I-TLB, D-TLB	64-entry each
NetSilicon NS9775 (ARM926EJ-S) [185]	Mixed	32-entry two-way set associative

Excess not-in-TLB translations can generally be controlled through the use of a well-designed TLB. The size and organization of the TLB depends on performance targets.

Typically, separate instruction and data TLBs are used. Both TLBs might use 128-entry, two-way set associative, and might use LRU replacement algorithm. The TLB conflagrations of some recent SOCs are shown in Table 4.7.

4.13 SOC (ON-DIE) MEMORY SYSTEMS

On-die memory design is a special case of the general memory system design problem, considered in the next section. The designer has much greater flexibility in the selection of the memory itself and the overall cache-memory organization. Since the application is known, the general size of both the program and data store can be estimated. Frequently, part of the program store is designed as a fixed ROM. The remainder of memory is realized with either SRAM or DRAM. While the SRAM is realized in the same process technology as the processor, usually DRAM is not. An SRAM bit consists of a six-transistor cell, while the DRAM uses only one transistor plus a deep trench capacitor. The DRAM cell is designed for density; it uses few wiring layers. DRAM design targets low refresh rates and hence low leakage currents. A DRAM cell uses a nonminimum length transistor with a higher threshold voltage, (V_T), to provide a lower-leakage current. This leads to lower gate overdrive and slower switching. For a stand-alone die, the result is that the SRAM is 10–20 times faster and 10 or more times less dense than DRAM.

eDRAM [33, 125] has been introduced as a compromise for use as an on-die memory. Since there are additional process steps in realizing an SOC with eDRAM, the macro to generate the eDRAM is fabrication specific and is regarded as a hard (or at least firm) IP. The eDRAM has an overhead (Figure 4.17) resulting in less density than DRAM. Process complexity for the eDRAM can include generating three additional mask layers resulting in 20% additional cost than that for the DRAM.

An SOC, using the eDRAM approach, integrates high-speed, high-leakage logic transistors with lower-speed, lower-leakage memory transistors on the same die. The advantage for eDRAM lies in its density as shown in Figure 4.18. Therefore, one key factor for selecting eDRAM over SRAM is the size of the memory required.

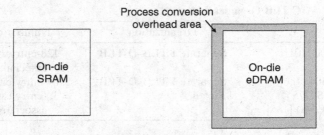

Figure 4.17 On-die SRAM and DRAM. The eDRAM must accommodate the process requirements of the logic, representing an overhead. SRAM is unaffected.

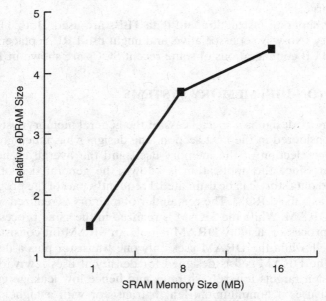

Figure 4.18 The relative density advantage eDRAM improves with memory size.

Having paid the process costs for eDRAM, the timing parameters for eDRAM are much better than conventional DRAM. The cycle time (and access time) is much closer to SRAM, as shown in Figure 4.19. All types of on-die memory enjoy the advantage of bandwidth as a whole memory column can be accessed at each cycle.

A final consideration in memory selection is the projected error rate due to radiation (called the *soft error rate* or *SER*). Each DRAM cell stores significantly larger amounts of charge than in the SRAM cell. The SRAM cells are faster and easier to flip, with correspondingly higher SER. Additionally, for an SRAM cell, as technology scales, the critical amount of charge for determining an error decreases due to scaling of supply voltages and cell capacitances. The differences are shown in Figure 4.20. At even 130-nm

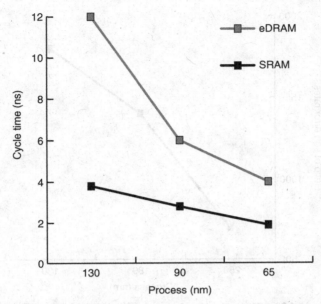

Figure 4.19   Cycle time for random memory accesses.

feature size, the SER for SRAM is about 1800 times higher than for eDRAM. Of course, more error-prone SRAM implementation can compensate by a more extensive use of error-correcting codes (ECCs), but this comes with its own cost.

Ultimately, the selection of on-die memory technology depends on fabrication process access and memory size required.

4.14   BOARD-BASED (OFF-DIE) MEMORY SYSTEMS

In many processor design situations (probably all but the SOC case), the main memory system is the principal design challenge.

As processor ensembles can be quite complex, the memory system that serves these processors is correspondingly complex.

The memory module consists of all the memory chips needed to forward a cache line to the processor via the bus. The cache line is transmitted as a burst of bus word transfers. Each memory module has two important parameters: module access time and module cycle time. The module access time is simply the amount of time required to retrieve a word into the output memory buffer register of a particular memory module, given a valid address in its address register. Memory service (or cycle) time is the minimum time between requests directed at the same module. Various technologies present a significant range of relationships between the access time and the service time. The access time is the total time for the processor to access a line in memory. In a small, simple

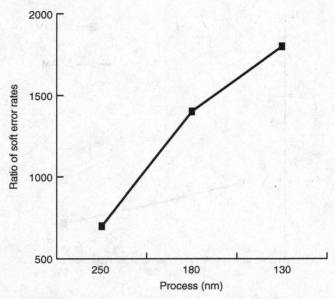

Figure 4.20   The ratio of soft error rates of SRAM to eDRAM.

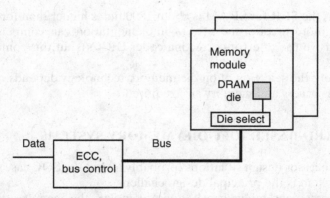

Figure 4.21   Accessing delay in a complex memory system. Access time includes chip accessing, module overhead, and bus transit.

memory system, this may be little more than chip access time plus some multiplexing and transit delays. The service time is approximately the same as the chip cycle time. In a large, multimodule memory system (Figure 4.21), the access time may be greatly increased, as it now includes the module access time plus transit time, bus accessing overhead, error detection, and correction delay.

After years of rather static evolution of DRAM memory chips, recent years have brought about significant new emphasis on the performance (rather than simply the size) of memory chips.

The first major improvement to DRAM technology is synchronous DRAM (SDRAM). This approach synchronizes the DRAM access and cycle time to the bus cycle. Additional enhancements accelerate the data transfer and improves the electrical characteristics of the bus and module. There are now multiple types of SDRAM. The basic DRAM types are the following:

1. *DRAM.* Asynchronous DRAM.
2. *SDRAM.* The memory module timing is synchronized to the memory bus clock.
3. *Double data rate (DDR) SDRAM.* The memory module fetches a double-sized transfer unit for each bus cycle and transmits at twice the bus clock rate.

In the next section, we present the basics of the (asynchronous) DRAM, following that of the more advanced SDRAMs.

4.15 SIMPLE DRAM AND THE MEMORY ARRAY

The simplest asynchronous DRAM consists of a single memory array with 1 (and sometimes 4 or 16) output bits. Internal to the chip is a two-dimensional array of memory cells consisting of rows and columns. Thus, half of the memory address is used to specify a row address, one of $2^{n/2}$ row lines, and the other half of the address is similarly used to specify one of $2^{n/2}$ column lines (Figure 4.22). The cell itself that holds the data is quite simple, consisting merely of a

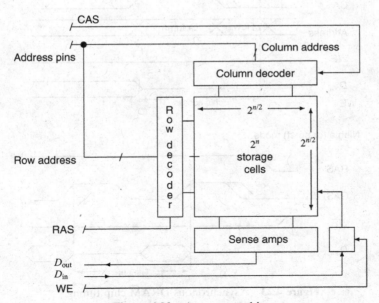

Figure 4.22 A memory chip.

MOS transistor holding a charge (a capacitance). As this discharges over time, it must continually be refreshed, once every several milliseconds.

With large-sized memories, the number of address lines dominates the pinout of the chip. In order to conserve these pins and to provide a smaller package for better overall density, the row and column addresses are multiplexed onto the same lines (input pins) for entry onto the chip. Two additional lines are important here: row address strobe (RAS) and column address strobe (CAS). These gate first the row address, then the column address into the chip. The row and column addresses are then decoded to select one out of the $2^{n/2}$ possible lines. The intersection of the active row and column lines is the desired bit of information. The column line's signals are then amplified by a sense amplifier and are transmitted to the output pin (data out, or D_{out}) during a read cycle. During a write cycle, the write-enable (WE) signal stores the data-in (D_{in}) signal to specify the contents of the selected bit address.

All of these actions happen in a sequence approximated in the timing diagram in Figure 4.23. At the beginning of a read from memory, the RAS line is activated. With the RAS active and the CAS inactive, the information on the address lines is interpreted as the row address and is stored into the row address register. This activates the row decoder and the selected row line in

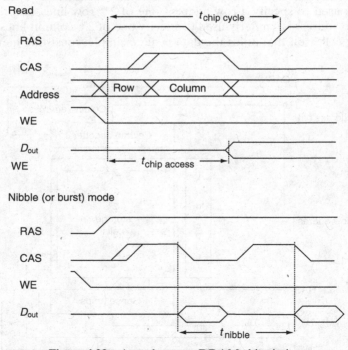

Figure 4.23   Asynchronous DRAM chip timing.

the memory array. The CAS is then activated, which gates the column address lines into a column address register. Note that

1. the two rise times on CAS represent the earliest and latest that this signal may rise with respect to the column address signals and
2. WE is inactive during read operations.

The column address decoder then selects a column line; at the intersection of the row and column line is the desired data bit. During a read cycle, the WE is inactive (low) and the output line (D_{out}) is at a high-impedance state until it is activated either high or low depending on the contents of the selected memory cell.

The time from the beginning of RAS until the data output line is activated is a very important parameter in the memory module design. This is called the chip access time or $t_{chip\ access}$. The other important chip timing parameter is the cycle time of the memory chip ($t_{chip\ cycle}$). This is not the same as the access time, as the selected row and column lines must recover before the next address can be entered and the read process repeated.

The asynchronous DRAM module does not simply consist of memory chips (Figure 4.24). In a memory system with p bits per physical word, and 2^n words in a module, the n address bits enter the module and are usually directed at a dynamic memory controller chip. This chip, in conjunction with a memory timing controller, provides the following functions:

1. multiplexing the n address bits into a row and a column address for use by the memory chips,

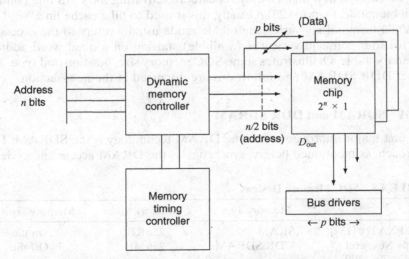

Figure 4.24 An asynchronous DRAM memory module.

2. the creation of the correct RAS and CAS signal lines at the appropriate time, and

3. providing a timely refresh of the memory system.

Since the dynamic memory controller output drives all p bits, and hence p chips, of the physical word, the controller output may also require buffering. As the memory read operation is completed, the data-out signals are directed at bus drivers, which then interface to the memory bus, which is the interface for all of the memory modules.

Two features found on DRAM chips affect the design of the memory system. These "burst" mode-type features are called

1. nibble mode and
2. page mode.

Both of these are techniques for improving the transfer rate of memory words. In nibble mode, a single address (row and column) is presented to the memory chip and the CAS line is toggled repeatedly. Internally, the chip interprets this CAS toggling as a *mod* 2^w progression of low-order column addresses. Thus, sequential words can be accessed at a higher rate from the memory chip. For example, for $w = 2$, we could access four consecutive low-order bit addresses, for example:

$$[00] \rightarrow [01] \rightarrow [10] \rightarrow [11]$$

and then return to the original bit address.

In page mode, a single row is selected and nonsequential column addresses may be entered at a high rate by repeatedly activating the CAS line (similar to nibble mode, Figure 4.23). Usually, this is used to fill a cache line.

While terminology varies, the nibble mode usually refers to the access of (up to) four consecutive words (a nibble) starting on a quad word address boundary. Table 4.8 illustrates some SOC memory size, position and type. The newer DDR SDRAM and follow ons are discussed in the next section.

4.15.1 SDRAM and DDR SDRAM

The first major improvement to the DRAM technology is the SDRAM. This approach, as mentioned before, synchronizes the DRAM access and cycle to

TABLE 4.8 SOC Memory Designs

SOC	Memory Type	Memory Size	Memory Position
Intel PXA27x [132]	SRAM	256 KB	On-die
Philips Nexperia PNX1700 [199]	DDR SDRAM	256 MB	Off-die
Intel IOP333 [131]	DDR SDRAM	2 GB	Off-die

the bus cycle. This has a number of significant advantages. It eliminates the need for separate memory clocking chips to produce the RAS and CAS signals. The rising edge of the bus clock provides the synchronization. Also, by extending the package to accommodate multiple output pins, versions that have 4, 8, and 16 pins allow more modularity in memory sizing.

With the focus on the bus and memory bus interface, we further improve bus bandwidth by using differential data and address lines. Now when the clock line rises, the complement clock falls, but midway through the cycle, the clock line falls and the complement clock rises. This affords the possibility to transmit synchronous data twice during each cycle: once on the rising edge of the clock signal and once on the rising edge of the complement clock. By using this, we are able to double the data rate transmitted on the bus. The resulting memory chips are called **DDR SDRAMs** (Figure 4.25). Also, instead of selecting a row and a column for each memory reference, it is possible to select a row and leave it selected (active) while multiple column references are made to the same row (Figure 4.26).

In cases where spatial locality permits, the read and write times are improved by eliminating the row select delay. Of course, when a new row is referenced,

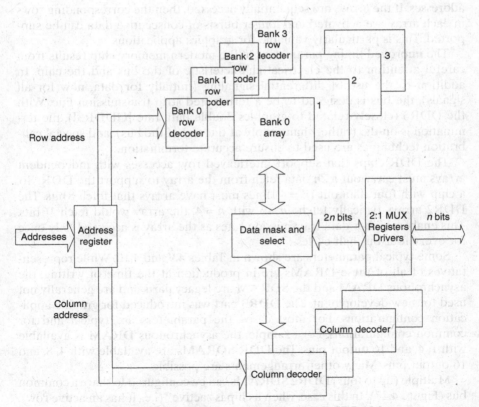

Figure 4.25   Internal configuration of DDR SDRAM.

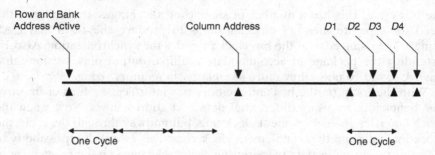

Figure 4.26 A line fetch in DDR SDRAM.

then the row activation time must be added to the access time. Another improvement introduced in SDRAMs is the use of multiple DRAM arrays, usually either four or eight. Depending on the chip implementation, these multiple arrays can be independently accessed or sequentially accessed, as programmed by the user. In the former case, each array can have an independently activated row providing an interleaved access to multiple column addresses. If the arrays are sequentially accessed, then the corresponding rows in each array are activated and longer bursts of consecutive data can be supported. This is particularly valuable for graphics applications.

The improved timing parameters of the modern memory chip results from careful attention to the electrical characteristic of the bus and the chip. In addition to the use of differential signaling (initially for data, now for all signals), the bus is designed to be a terminated strip transmission line. With the DDR3 (closely related to graphics double data rate [GDDR3]), the termination is on-die (rather than simply at the end of the bus), and special calibration techniques are used to ensure accurate termination.

The DDR chips that support interleaved row accesses with independent arrays must carry out a *2n* data fetch from the array to support the DDR. So, a chip with four data out ($n = 4$) lines must have arrays that fetch 8 bits. The DDR2 arrays typically fetch *4n*, so with $n = 4$, the array would fetch 16 bits. This enables higher data transmission rates as the array is accessed only once for every four-bus half-cycles.

Some typical parameters are shown in Tables 4.9 and 4.10. While representatives of all of these DRAMs are in production at the time of writing, the asynchronous DRAM and the SDRAM are legacy parts and are generally not used for new development. The DDR3 part was introduced for graphic application configurations. For most cases, the parameters are typical and for common configurations. For example, the asynchronous DRAM is available with 1, 4, and 16 output pins. The DDR SDRAMs are available with 4, 8, and 16 output pins. Many other arrangements are possible.

. Multiple (up to four) DDR2 SDRAMs can be configured to share a common bus (Figure 4.27). In this case, when a chip is "active" (i.e., it has an active row),

TABLE 4.9 Configuration Parameters for Some Typical DRAM Chips Used in a 64-bit Module

	DRAM	SDRAM	DDR1	DDR2	GDDR3 (DDR3)
Typical chip capacity		1 Gb	1 Gb	1 Gb	256 Mb
Output data pins/chip	1	4	4	4	32
Array data bits fetched	1	4	8	16	32
Number of arrays	1	4	4	8	4
Number of chips/module	64+	16	16	16	4
Burst word transfers	1–4	1, 2, 4	2, 4, 8	4, 8	4, 8, 16
Rows			16 K	16 K	
Columns			2048 × 8	512 × 16	512 × 32
32-byte lines/row/array			2048	1024	2048 × 4

TABLE 4.10 Timing Parameters for Some Typical DRAM Modules (64 bits)

	DRAM	SDRAM	DDR1	DDR2	DDR3
Bus clock rate (MHz)	Asynchronous	100	133	266	600
Active to CAS (ns)	30	30	20	15	12
Column address to data out 1 (read time) (ns)	40	30	20	15	12
Line access (accessing a new row) (ns)	140	90	51	36	28
Line access (within an active row) (ns)	120	60	31	21	16
Rows interleaving	×1	×4	×4	×8	×1

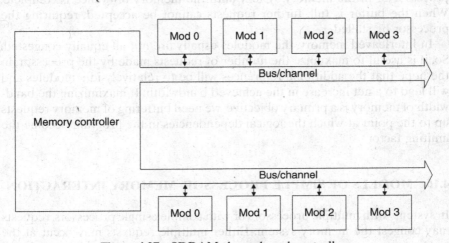

Figure 4.27 SDRAM channels and controller.

the on-die termination is unused. When there are no active rows on the die, the termination is used. Typical server configurations then might have four modules sharing a bus (called a channel) and a memory controller managing up to two buses (see Figure 4.27). The limit of two is caused simply by the large number of tuned strip and microstrip transmission lines that must connect the controller to the buses. More advanced techniques place a channel buffer between the module and a very high-speed channel. This advanced channel has a smaller width (e.g., 1 byte) but a much higher data rate (e.g., 8×). The net effect leaves the bandwidth per module the same, but now the number of wires entering the controller has decreased, enabling the controller to manage more channels (e.g., 8).

4.15.2   Memory Buffers

The processor can sustain only a limited number of outstanding memory references before it suspends processing and the generation of further memory references. This can happen either as a result of logical dependencies in the program or because of an insufficient buffering capability for outstanding requests. The significance of this is that the achievable memory bandwidth is decreased as a consequence of the pause in the processing, for the memory can service only as many requests as are made by the processor.

Examples of logical dependencies include branches and address interlocks. The program must suspend computation until an item has been retrieved from memory.

Associated with each outstanding memory request is certain information that specifies the nature of the request (e.g., a read or a write operation), the address of the memory location, and sufficient information to route requested data back to the requestor. All this information must be buffered either in the processor or in the memory system until the memory reference is complete. When the buffer is full, further requests cannot be accepted, requiring the processor be stalled.

In interleaved memory, the modules usually are not all equally congested. So, it is useful to maximize the number of requests made by the processor, in the hope that the additional references will be to relatively idle modules and will lead to a net increase in the achieved bandwidth. If maximizing the bandwidth of memory is a primary objective, we need buffering of memory requests up to the point at which the logical dependencies in the program become the limiting factor.

4.16   MODELS OF SIMPLE PROCESSOR–MEMORY INTERACTION

In systems with multiple processors or with complex single processors, requests may congest the memory system. Either multiple requests may occur at the same time, providing bus or network congestion, or requests arising from different sources may request access to the memory system. Requests that cannot be immediately honored by the memory system result in memory systems contention. This contention degrades the bandwidth and is possible to achieve from the memory system.

In the simplest possible arrangement, a single simple processor makes a request to a single memory module. The processor ceases activity (as with a blocking cache) and waits for service from the module. When the module responds, the processor resumes activity. Under such an arrangement, the results are completely predictable. There can be no contention of the memory system since only one request is made at a time to the memory module. Now suppose we arrange to have n simple processors access m independent modules. Contention develops when multiple processors access the same module. Contention results in a reduced average bandwidth available to each of the processors. Asymptotically, a processor with a nonblocking cache making n requests to the memory system during a memory cycle resembles the n processor m module memory system, at least from a modeling point of view. But in modern systems, processors are usually buffered from the memory system. Whether or not a processor is slowed down by memory or bus contention during cache access depends on the cache design and the service rate of processors that share the same memory system.

Given a collection of m modules each with service time T_c, access time T_a, and a certain processor request rate, how do we model the bandwidth available from these memory modules, and how do we compute the overall effective access time? Clearly, the modules in low-order interleave are the only ones that can contribute to the bandwidth, and hence they determine m. From the memory system's point of view, it really does not matter whether the processor system consists of n processors, each making one request every memory cycle (i.e., one per T_c), or one processor with n requests per T_c, so long as the statistical distribution of the requests remains the same. Thus, to a first approximation, the analysis of the memory system is equally applicable to the multiprocessor system or the superscalar processor. The request rate, defined as n requests per T_c, is called the offered request rate, and it represents the peak demand that the noncached processor system has on the main memory system.

4.16.1   Models of Multiple Simple Processors and Memory

In order to develop a useful memory model, we need a model of the processor. For our analysis, we model a single processor as an ensemble of multiple simple processors. Each simple processor issues a request as soon as its previous request has been satisfied. Under this model, we can vary the number of processors and the number of memory modules and maintain the address request/data supply equilibrium. To convert the single processor model into

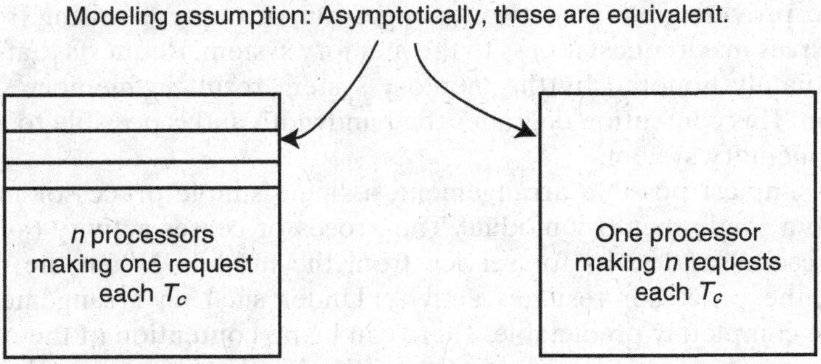

Modeling assumption: Asymptotically, these are equivalent.

n processors
making one request
each T_c

One processor
making n requests
each T_c

Figure 4.28   Finding simple processor equivalence.

an equivalent multiple processor, the designer must determine the number of requests to the memory module per module service time, $T_s = T_c$.

A simple processor makes a single request and waits for a response from memory. A *pipelined processor* makes multiple requests for various buffers before waiting for a memory response. There is an approximate equivalence between n simple processors, each requesting once every T_s, and one pipelined processor making n requests every T_s (Figure 4.28).

In the following discussion, we use two symbols to represent the bandwidth available from the memory system (the achieved bandwidth):

1. *B.* The number of requests that are serviced each T_s. Occasionally, we also specify the arguments that B takes on, for example, B (m, n) or B (m).
2. *Bw.* The number of requests that are serviced per second: $Bw = B/T_s$.

To translate this into cache-based systems, the service time, T_s, is the time that the memory system is busy managing a cache miss. The number of memory modules, m, is the maximum number of cache misses that the memory system can handle at one time, and n is the total number of request per T_s. This is the total number of expected misses per processor per T_s multiplied by the number of processors making requests.

4.16.2   The Strecker-Ravi Model

This is a simple yet useful model for estimating contention. The original model was developed by Strecker [229] and independently by Ravi [204]. It assumes that there are n simple processor requests made per memory cycle and there are m memory modules. Further, we assume that there is no bus contention. The Strecker model assumes that the memory request pattern for the processors is uniform and the probability of any one request to a particular memory module is simply $1/m$. The key modeling assumption is that the state of the memory system at the beginning of the cycle is not dependent upon any previous action on the part of the memory—hence, not dependent upon contention in the past (i.e., Markovian). Unserved requests are discarded at the end of the memory cycle.

The following modeling approximations are made:

1. A processor issues a request as soon as its previous request has been satisfied.
2. The memory request pattern from each processor is assumed to be uniformly distributed; that is, the probability of any one request being made to a particular memory module is $1/m$.
3. The state of the memory system at the beginning of each memory cycle (i.e., which processors are awaiting service at which modules) is ignored by assuming that all unserviced requests are discarded at the end of each memory cycle and that the processors randomly issue new requests.

Analysis:

Let the average number of memory requests serviced per memory cycle be represented by $B(m, n)$. This is also equal to the average number of memory modules busy during each memory cycle. Looking at events from any given module's point of view during each memory cycle, we have

Prob (a given processor does not reference the module) $= (1 - 1/m)$

Prob (no processor references the module) = Prob (the module is idle)

$$= (1 - 1/m)$$

Prob (the module is busy) $= 1 - (1 - 1/m)^n$

$B(m, n) =$ average number of busy modules $= m\left(1 - (1 - 1/m)^n\right)$.

The achieved memory bandwidth is less than the theoretical maximum due to contention. By neglecting congestion in previous cycles, this analysis results in an optimistic value for the bandwidth. Still, it is a simple estimate that should be used conservatively.

It has been shown by Bhandarkar [41] that $B(m, n)$ is almost perfectly symmetrical in m and n. He exploited this fact to develop a more accurate expression for $B(m, n)$, which is

$$B(m, n) = K\left[1 - (1 - 1/K)^l\right],$$

where $K = \max(m, n)$ and $l = \min(m, n)$.

We can use this to model a typical processor ensemble.

EXAMPLE 4.2

Suppose we have a two-processor die system sharing a common memory. Each processor die is dual core with the two processors (four processors total) sharing a 4-MB level 2 cache. Each processor makes three memory references per cycle and the clock rate is 4 GHz. The L2 cache has a miss rate of 0.001 misses per reference. The memory system has an average T_s of 24 ns including bus delay.

We can ignore the details of the level 1 caches by inclusion. So each processor die creates 6×0.001 memory references per cycle or 0.012 references for both cycles. Since there are 4×24 cycles in a T_s, we have $n = 1.152$ processor requests per T_s. If we design the memory system to manage $m = 4$ requests per T_s, we compute the performance as

$$B(m, n) = B(4, 1.152) = 0.81.$$

The relative performance is

$$P_{\text{rel}} = \frac{B}{n} = \frac{0.81}{1.152} = 0.7.$$

Thus, the processor can only achieve 70% of its potential due to the memory system. To do better, we need either a larger level 2 cache (or a level 3 cache) or a much more elaborate memory system ($m = 8$).

4.16.3 Interleaved Caches

Interleaved caches can be handled in a manner analogous to interleaved memory.

EXAMPLE 4.3

An early Intel Pentium™ processor had an eight-way interleaved data cache. It makes two references per processor cycle. The cache has the same cycle time as the processor.

For the Intel instruction set,

$$\text{Prob (data references per instruction)} = 0.6.$$

Since the Pentium tries to execute two instructions each cycle, we have

$$n = 1, 2,$$

$$m = 8.$$

Using Strecker's model, we get

$$B(m, n) = B(8, 1.2) = 1.18.$$

The relative performance is

$$P_{rel} = \frac{B}{n} = \frac{1.18}{1.2} = 0.98;$$

that is, the processor slows down by about 2% due to contention.

4.17 CONCLUSIONS

Cache provides the processor with a memory access time significantly faster than the memory access time. As such, the cache is an important constituent in the modern processor. The cache miss rate is largely determined by the size of the cache, but any estimate of miss rate must consider the cache organization, the operating system, the system's environment, and I/O effects. As cache access time is limited by size, multilevel caches are a common feature of on-die processor designs.

On-die memory design seems to be relatively manageable especially with the advent of eDRAM, but off-die memory design is an especially difficult problem. The primary objective of such designs is capacity (or size); however, large memory capacity and pin limitations necessarily imply slow access times. Even if die access is fast, the system's overhead, including bus signal transmission, error checking, and address distribution, adds significant delay. Indeed, these overhead delays have increased relative to decreasing machine cycle times. Faced with a hundred-cycle memory access time, the designer can provide adequate memory bandwidth to match the request rate of the processor only by a very large multilevel cache.

4.18 PROBLEM SET

1. A 128^{KB} cache has 64^{bits} lines, 8^{bits} physical word, 4^{KB} pages, and is four-way set associative. It uses copy-back (allocate on write) and LRU replacement. The processor creates 30-bit (byte-addressed) virtual addresses that are translated into 24-bit (byte-addressed) real byte addresses (labeled A_0–A_{23}, from least to most significant).

   (a) Which address bits are unaffected by translation $(V = R)$?

   (b) Which address bits are used to address the cache directories?

   (c) Which address bits are compared to entries in the cache directory?

   (d) Which address bits are appended to address bits in (b) to address the cache array?

2. Show a layout of the cache in Problem 1. Present the details as in Figures 4.5–4.7.

3. Plot traffic (in bytes) as a function of line size for a DTMR cache (CBWA, LRU) for
   (a) 4^{KB} cache,
   (b) 32^{KB} cache, and
   (c) 256^{KB} cache.

4. Suppose we define the miss rate at which a copy-back cache (CBWA) and a write-through cache (WTNWA) have equal traffic as the crossover point.
   (a) For the DTMR cache, find the crossover point (miss rate) for $16^B, 32^B$, and 64^B lines. To what cache sizes do these correspond?
   (b) Plot line size against cache size for crossover.

5. The cache in Problem 1 is now used with a 16-byte line in a transaction environment ($Q = 20,000$).
   (a) Compute the effective miss rate.
   (b) Approximately, what is the optimal cache size (the smallest cache size that produces the lowest achievable miss rate)?

6. In a two-level cache system, we have
   • L1 size 8KB with four-way set associative, 16-byte lines, and write-through (no allocate on writes); and
   • L2 size 64-KB direct mapping, 64-byte lines, and copy-back (with allocate on writes).

   Suppose the miss in L1, hit in L2 delay is 3 cycles and the miss in L1, miss in L2 delay is 10 cycles. The processor makes 1.5 refr/I.
   (a) What are the L1 and L2 miss rates?
   (b) What is the expected CPI loss due to cache misses?
   (c) Will *all* lines in L1 always reside in L2? Why?

7. A certain processor has a two-level cache. L1 is 4-KB direct-mapped, WTNWA. The L2 is 8-KB direct-mapped, CBWA. Both have 16-byte lines with LRU replacement.
   (a) Is it always true that L2 includes all lines at L1?
   (b) If the L2 is now 8KB four-way set associative (CBWA), does L2 include all lines at L1?
   (c) If L1 is four-way set associative (CBWA) and L2 is direct-mapped, does L2 include all lines of L1?

8. Suppose we have the following parameters for an L1 cache with 4KB and an L2 cache with 64KB.

The cache miss rate is

4 KB	0.10 misses per reference
64 KB	0.02 misses per reference
1 refr/Instruction	
3 cycles	$L1$ miss, $L2$ hit
10 cycles	Total time $L1$ miss, $L2$ miss

What is the excess CPI due to cache misses?

9. A certain processor produces a 32-bit virtual address. Its address space is segmented (each segment is 1-MB maximum) and paged (512-byte pages). The physical word transferred to/from cache is 4 bytes.

   A TLB is to be used, organized set associative, 128×2. If the address bits are labeled V_0–V_{31} for virtual address and R_0–R_{31} for real address, least to most significant,

   (a) Which bits are unaffected by translation (i.e., $V_i = R_i$)?

   (b) If the TLB is addressed by the low-order bits of the portion of the address to be translated (i.e., no hashing), which bits are used to address the TLB?

   (c) Which virtual bits are compared to virtual entries in the TLB to determine whether a TLB hit has occurred?

   (d) As a minimum, which real address bits does the TLB provide?

10. For a 16-KB integrated level 1 cache (direct mapped, 16-byte lines) and a 128-KB integrated level 2 cache (2 W set associative, 16-byte lines), find the solo and local miss rate for the level 2 cache.

11. A certain chip has an area sufficient for a 16-KB I-cache and a 16-KB D-cache, both direct mapped. The processor has a virtual address of 32 bits, a real address of 26 bits, and uses 4-KB pages. It makes 1.0 I-refr/I and 0.5 D-refr/I. The cache miss delay is 10 cycles plus 1 cycle for each 4-byte word transferred in a line. The processor is stalled until the entire line is brought into the cache. The D-cache is CBWA; use dirty line ratio $w = 0.5$. For both caches, the line size is 64 B. Find

    (a) The CPI lost due to I-misses and the CPI lost due to D-misses.

    (b) For the 64-byte line, find the number of I- and D-directory bits and corresponding rbe (area) for both directories.

12. Find two recent examples of DDR3 devices and for these devices, update the entries of Tables 4.9 and 4.10.

13. List all the operations that must be performed after a "not-in-TLB" signal. How would a designer minimize the not-in-TLB penalty?

14. In Example 4.2, suppose we need a relative performance of 0.8. Would this be achieved by interleaving at $m = 8$?

15. Update the timing parameters for the NAND-based flash memory described in Table 4.3.

16. Compare recent commercially available flash (NAND and NOR) with recent eDRAM offerings.

5 Interconnect

5.1 INTRODUCTION

SOC designs usually involve the integration of intellectual property (IP) cores, each separately designed and verified. System integrators can maximize the reuse of design to reduce costs and to lower risks. Frequently the most important issue confronting an SOC integrator is the method by which the IP cores are connected together.

SOC interconnect alternatives extend well beyond conventional computer buses. We first provide an overview of SOC interconnect architectures: bus and network-on-chip (NOC). Bus architectures developed specifically for SOC designs are described and compared. There are many switch-based alternatives to bus-based interconnects. We will not consider ad hoc or fully customized switching interconnects that are not intended for use with a variety of IP cores. Switch-based interconnects as used in SOC interconnects are referred to as NOC technology.

An NOC usually includes an interface level of abstraction, hiding the underlying physical interconnects from the designer. We follow current SOC usage and refer to interconnect as a bus or as an NOC implemented by a switch. In the NOC the switch can be a crossbar, a directly linked interconnect, or a multistage switching network.

There is a great deal of bus and computer interconnect literature. The units being connected are sometimes referred to as agents (in buses) or nodes (in the general interconnect literature); we simply use the term *units*. Since current SOC interconnects usually involve a modest number of units, the chapter provides a simplified view of the interconnect alternatives. A comprehensive treatment of on-chip communication architectures is available elsewhere [193]. For a general discussion of computer interconnection networks, see any of several standard texts [72, 78].

Computer System Design: System-on-Chip, First Edition. Michael J. Flynn and Wayne Luk.
© 2011 John Wiley & Sons, Inc. Published 2011 by John Wiley & Sons, Inc.

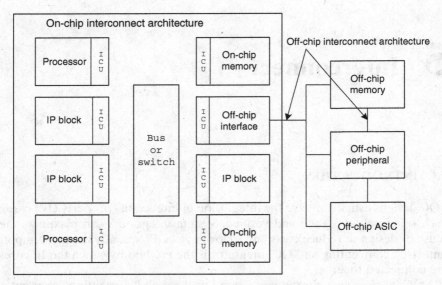

Figure 5.1 A simplified block diagram of an SOC module in a system context.

5.2 OVERVIEW: INTERCONNECT ARCHITECTURES

Figure 5.1 depicts a system that includes an SOC module. The SOC module typically contains a number of IP blocks, one or more of which are processors. In addition, there are various types of on-chip memory serving as cache, data, or instruction storage. Other IP blocks serving application-specific functions, such as graphics processors, video codecs, and network control units, are integrated in the SOC.

The IP blocks in the SOC module need to communicate with each other. They do this through the interconnect, which is accessed through an interconnect interface unit (ICU). The ICU enables a common interface protocol for all SOC modules.

External to the SOC module are off-chip memories, off-chip peripheral devices, and mass storage devices. The cost and performance of the system, therefore, depends on both on-chip and off-chip interconnect structures.

Choosing a suitable interconnect architecture requires the understanding of a number of system level issues and specifications. These are:

1. *Communication Bandwidth.* The rate of information transfer between a module and the surrounding environment in which it operates. Usually measured in bytes per second, the bandwidth requirement of a module dictates to a large extent the type of interconnection required in order to achieve the overall system throughput specification.

WHAT IS AN NOC?

As SOC terminology has evolved there seems to be only two interconnect strategies: the bus or the NOC. So what exactly is the NOC? Professor Nurmi (in a presentation reported by Leibson [156]) summarized the NOC characteristics:

1. The NOC is more than a single, shared bus.
2. The NOC provides point-to-point connections between any two hosts attached to the network either by crossbar switches or through node-based switches.
3. The NOC provides high aggregate bandwidth through parallel links.
4. In the NOC, communication is separate from computation.
5. The NOC uses a layered approach to communications, although with few network layers due to complexity and expense.
6. NOCs support pipelining and provide intermediate data buffering between sender and receiver.

In the context of the SOC when the designer finds that bus technology provides insufficient bandwidth or connectivity, the obvious alternative is some sort of switch. Any well-designed switched interconnect will clearly satisfy points 2, 3, 4, and 6. Point 5 is not satisfied by ad hoc switching interconnects, where the processor nodes and switching interconnect are interfaced by common, specialized design. But in the SOC, incorporating various vendor IPs ad hoc interconnects is almost never the case. The designer selects a common communications interface (layer) separate from the processor node.

2. *Communication Latency.* The time delay between a module requesting data and receiving a response to the request. Latency may or may not be important in terms of overall system performance. For example, long latency in a video streaming application usually has little or no effect on the user's experience. Watching a movie that is a couple of seconds later than when it is actually broadcast is of no consequence. In contrast, even small, unanticipated latencies in a two-way mobile communication protocol can make it almost impossible to carry out a conversation.

3. *Master and Slave.* These terms concern whether a unit can initiate or react to communication requests. A master, such as a processor, controls transactions between itself and other modules. A slave, such as memory, responds to requests from the master. An SOC design typically has several masters and numerous slaves.

4. *Concurrency Requirement.* The number of independent simultaneous communication channels operating in parallel. Usually, additional channels improve system bandwidth.

5. *Packet or Bus Transaction.* The size and definition of the information transmitted in a single transaction. For a bus, this consists of an address with control bits (read/write, etc.) and data. The same information in an NOC is referred to as a *packet*. The packet consists of a header (address and control) and data (sometimes called the payload).

6. *ICU.* In an interconnect, this unit manages the interconnect protocol and the physical transaction. It can be simple or complex, including out-of-order transaction buffering and management. If the IP core requires a protocol translation to access the bus, the unit is called a *bus wrapper*. In an NOC, this unit manages the protocol for transport of a packet from the IP core to the switching network. It provides packet buffering and out-of-order transaction transmission.

7. *Multiple Clock Domains.* Different IP modules may operate at different clock and data rates. For example, a video camera captures pixel data at a rate governed by the video standard used, while a processor's clock rate is usually determined by the technology and architectural design. As a result, IP blocks inside an SOC often need to operate at different clock frequencies, creating separate timing regions known as clock domains. Crossing between clock domains can cause deadlock and synchronization problems without careful design.

Given a set of communication specifications, a designer can explore the different bandwidth, latency, concurrency, and clock domain requirements of different interconnect architectures, such as bus and NOC. Some examples of these are given in Table 5.1. Other examples include the Avalon Bus for Altera field-programmable gate arrays (FPGAs) [10], the Wishbone Interconnect for use in open-source cores and platforms [189], and the AXI4-Stream interface protocol for FPGA implementation [74].

Designing the interconnect architecture for an SOC requires careful consideration of many requirements, such as those listed above. The rest of this chapter provides an introduction to two interconnect architectures: the bus and the NOC.

5.3 BUS: BASIC ARCHITECTURE

The performance of a computer system is heavily dependent on the characteristics of its interconnect architecture. A poorly designed system bus can throttle the transfer of instructions and data between memory and processor, or between peripheral devices and memory. This communication bottleneck is the focus of attention among many microprocessor and system

TABLE 5.1 Examples of Interconnect Architectures [167]

Technology	AMBA	AXI (AMBA 3)	CoreConnect	Smart Interconnect IP	Nexus
Company	ARM	ARM	IBM	Sonics	Fulcrum
Core type	Soft/hard	Soft/hard	Soft	Soft	Hard
Architecture	Bus	Unidirectional channels	Bus	Bus	NOC using direct switch
Bus width	8–1024	8–1024	32/64/128	16	8–128
Frequency	200 MHz	400 MHz*	100–400 MHz	300 MHz	1 GHz
Maximum BW (GB/s)	3	6.4*	2.5–24	4.8	72
Minimum latency (ns)	5	2.5*	15	n/a	2

*As implemented in the ARM PL330 high-speed controller.
BW, bandwidth.

TABLE 5.2   Comparison of Bus Interconnect Architectures [198]

Standard	Speed (MHz)	Area (rbe*)
AMBA(implementation dependent)	166–400	175,000
CoreConnect	66/133/183	160,000

*rbe = register bit equivalent; estimates are approximate and vary by implementation.

manufacturers who, over the last three decades, have adopted a number of bus standards. These include the popular VME bus and the Intel Multibus-II. For systems on a board and personal computers, the evolution includes the instruction set architecture (ISA) bus, the EISA bus, and the now prevalent PCI and PCI Express buses. All these bus standards are designed to connect together integrated circuits (ICs) on a printed circuit board (PCB) or PCBs in a system-on-board implementation.

While these bus standards have served the computing community well, they are not particularly suited for SOC technology. For example, all such system-level buses are designed to drive a backplane, either in a rack-mounted system or on a computer motherboard. This imposes numerous constraints on the bus architecture. For a start, the number of signals available is generally restricted by the limited pin count on an IC package or the number of pins on the PCB connector. Adding an extra pin on a package or a connector is expensive. Furthermore, the speed at which the bus can operate is often limited by the high capacitive load on each bus signal, the resistance of the contacts on the connector, and the electromagnetic noise produced by such fast-switching signals traveling down a PCB track. Finally, drivers for on-chip buses can be much smaller, saving area and power.

Before describing bus operations and bus structures in detail, we provide, in Table 5.2, a comparison of two different bus interconnect architectures, showing size and speed estimates for a typical bus slave.

5.3.1   Arbitration and Protocols

Conceptually, the bus is just wires shared by multiple units. In practice, some logic must be present to provide an orderly use of the bus; otherwise, two units may send signals at the same time, causing conflicts. When a unit has exclusive use of the bus, the unit is said to own the bus. Units can be either potentially master units that can request ownership or slave units that are passive and only respond to requests. A bus master is the unit that initiates communication on a computer bus or input/output (I/O) paths. In an SOC, a bus master is a component within the chip, such as a processor. Other units connected to an on-chip bus, such as I/O devices and memory components, are the "slaves." The bus master controls the bus paths using specific slave addresses and control signals. Moreover, the bus master also controls the flow of data signals directly between the master and the slaves.

A process called arbitration determines ownership. A simple implementation has a centralized arbitration unit with an input from each potential requesting unit. The arbitration unit then grants bus ownership to one requesting unit, as determined by the bus protocol.

A bus protocol is an agreed set of rules for transmitting information between two or more devices over a bus. The protocol determines the following:

- the type and order of data being sent;
- how the sending device indicates that it has finished sending the information;
- the data compression method used, if any;
- how the receiving device acknowledges successful reception of the information; and
- how arbitration is performed to resolve contention on the bus and in what priority, and the type of error checking to be used.

5.3.2 Bus Bridge

A bus bridge is a module that connects together two buses, which are not necessarily of the same type. A typical bridge can serve three functions:

1. If the two buses use different protocols, a bus bridge provides the necessary format and standard conversion.
2. A bridge is inserted between two buses to segment them and keep traffic contained within the segments. This improves concurrency: both buses can operate at the same time.
3. A bridge often contains memory buffers and the associated control circuits that allow write posting. When a master on one bus initiates a data transfer to a slave module on another bus through the bridge, the data is temporarily stored in the buffer, allowing the master to proceed to the next transaction before the data are actually written to the slave. By allowing transactions to complete quickly, a bus bridge can significantly improve system performance.

5.3.3 Physical Bus Structure

The nature of the bus transaction depends on the physical bus structure (number of wire paths, cycle time, etc.) and the protocol (especially the arbitration support). Multiple bus users must be arbitrated for access to the bus in any given cycle. Thus, arbitration is part of the bus transaction. Simple arbiters have a request cycle wherein signals from the users are prioritized, followed by the acknowledge cycle selecting the user. More complex arbiters add bus control lines and associated logic so that each user is aware of pending bus status and priority. In such designs no cycles are added to the bus transaction for arbitration.

5.3.4 Bus Varieties

Buses may be *unified* or *split* (address and data). In the unified bus the address is initially transmitted in a bus cycle followed by one or more data cycles; the split bus has separate buses for each of these functions.

Also, the buses may be single transaction or *tenured*. Tenured buses are occupied by a transaction only during associated addresses or data cycles. Such buses have unit receivers that buffer the messages and create separate address and data transactions.

EXAMPLE 5.1 BUS EXAMPLES

There are many possible bus designs with varying combinations of physical bus widths and arbitration protocols. The examples below consider some obvious possibilities. Suppose the bus has a transmission delay of one processor cycle, and the memory (or shared cache) has a four-cycle access delay after an initial address and requires an additional cycle for each sequential data access. The memory is accessed 4 bytes at a time. The data to be transmitted consist of a 16-byte cache line. Address requests are 4 bytes.

In these examples, T_{access} is the time required to access the first word from memory after the address is issued, and line access is the time required to access the remaining words. Also, the last byte of data arrives at the end of the timing template and can be used only after that point.

(a) *Simple Bus.* This is a single transaction bus with simple request/acknowledge (ack) arbitration. It has a physical width of 4 bytes. The request and ack signals are separate signals but assumed to be part of the bus transaction, so the bus transaction latency is 11 cycles. The first word is sent from memory at the last cycle of T_{access}, while the fourth (and last) word is sent from memory at the last cycle of line access. The final bus cycle is to reset the arbiter.

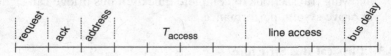

(b) *Bus with Arbitration Support.* This bus has a more sophisticated arbiter but still has a 4-byte physical width and integrates address and data. There is an additional access cycle (five cycles instead of four) to represent the time to move the address from the bus receiver to the memory. This is not shown in case (a), as simple buses are usually slower with immediate coupling to memory. Now the initial cycles for request and ack are overlapped with bus processing, and the final cycle for resetting the arbiter is not shown in the figure for case (b), so the bus transaction now takes 10 cycles.

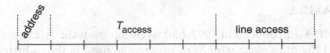

(c) *Tenured Split Bus, 4 Bytes Wide.* The assumption is that the requested line is fetched into a buffer for five cycles and then transmitted in four cycles. While the transaction latency, including the cycle for the address, is no different from that in case (b) at 10 cycles, the transaction occupies the bus for less than half (four cycles) of that time. The address bus is used for only one cycle out of 10. The remaining time is available for other unrelated transactions to improve communication performance.

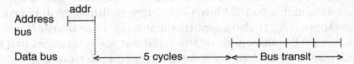

(d) *Tenured Split Bus, 16 Bytes Wide, with a One-Cycle Bus Transaction Time.* As with case (c), the transaction latency is unaffected at 10 cycles. Since the memory clearly limits the system, in this case the memory fetches the entire 16-byte cache line before transmitting it in a single cycle. Both address and data buses are used for only one cycle per transaction. Note that the figure for case (d) allows an additional cycle to reaccess the bus, although this might not be needed and is not accounted for in case (c).

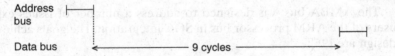

Cases (c) and (d) are interesting, since the bus bandwidth exceeds the memory bandwidth; for instance, in case (d), the memory is busy for seven cycles (four cycles to access the first word and three cycles to assess the remaining words) but the bus is busy for only one cycle. In both of these cases, the "bus"–memory situation is memory limited since that is where the contention will develop.

5.4 SOC STANDARD BUSES

Two commonly used SOC bus standards are the Advanced Microcontroller Bus Architecture (AMBA) bus developed by ARM and the CoreConnect bus developed by IBM. The latter has been adopted in Xilinx's Virtex platform FPGA families.

5.4.1 AMBA

The AMBA, introduced in 1997, had its origin from the ARM processor, which is one of the most successful SOC processors used in the industry. The AMBA bus is based on traditional bus architecture employing two levels of hierarchy. Two buses are defined in the AMBA specification [22]:

- The Advanced High-Performance Bus (AHB) is designed to connect embedded processors, such as an ARM processor core, to high-performance peripherals, direct memory access (DMA) controllers, on-chip memory, and interfaces. It is a high-speed, high-bandwidth bus architecture that uses separate address, read, and write buses. A minimum of 32-bit data operation is recommended in the standard and data widths are extendable to 1024 bits. Concurrent multiple master/slave operations are supported. It also supports burst mode data transfers and split transactions. All transactions on the AHB bus are referenced to a single clock edge, making system-level design easy to understand.
- The Advanced Peripheral Bus (APB) has a lower performance than the AHB bus, but is optimized for minimal power consumption and has reduced interface complexity. It is designed for interfacing to slower peripheral modules.

A third bus, the Advanced System Bus (ASB), is an earlier incarnation of the AHB, designed for lower performance systems using 16/32-bit microcontrollers. It is used where cost, performance, and complexity of the AHB is not justified.

The AMBA bus was designed to address a number of issues exposed by users of the ARM processor bus in SOC integration. The goals achieved by its design are [95]:

1. *Modular Design and Design Reuse.* Since the ARM processor bus interface is extremely flexible, inexperienced designers could inadvertently create inefficient or even unworkable designs by using ad hoc bus and control logic. The AMBA specification encourages a modular design methodology that supports better design partitioning and design reuse.
2. *Well-Defined Interface Protocol, Clocking, and Reset.* AMBA specifies a low-overhead bus interface and clocking structure that is simple yet flexible. The performance of the AMBA bus is enhanced by its multimaster, split transaction, and burst mode operations.
3. *Low-Power Support.* One of the attractions of the ARM processor when compared with other embedded processor cores is its power efficiency. The two-level partitioning of the AMBA buses ensures energy-efficient designs in the peripheral modules, which fits well with the low-power CPU core.

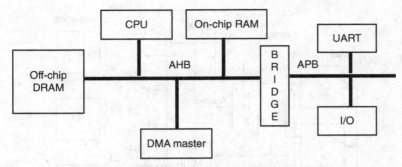

Figure 5.2   A typical AMBA bus-based system [95].

4. *On-Chip Test Access.* AMBA has an optional on-chip test access methodology that reuses the basic bus infrastructure for testing modules that
are connected to the bus.

The AHB   Figure 5.2 depicts a typical system using the AMBA bus architecture. The AHB forms the system backbone bus on which the ARM processor,
the high-bandwidth memory interface and random-access memory (RAM),
and the DMA devices reside. The interface between the AHB bus and the
slower APB bus is through a bus bridge module.

The AMBA AHB bus protocol is designed to implement a multimaster
system. Unlike most bus architectures designed for PCB-based systems, the
AMBA AHB bus avoids tristate implementation by employing a central multiplexer interconnect scheme. This method of interconnect provides higher
performance and lower power than using tristate buffers. All bus masters
assert the address and control signals, indicating the type of transfer each
master requires. A central arbiter determines which master has its address and
control signal routed to all the slaves. A central decoder circuit selects the
appropriate read data and response acknowledge signal from the slave that is
involved in the transaction. Figure 5.3 depicts such a multiplexer interconnect
scheme for a system with three masters and four slaves.

Transactions on the AHB bus involve the following steps:

- *Bus Master Obtains Access to the Bus.* This process begins with the
master asserting a request signal to the arbiter. If more than one master
simultaneously requests the control of the bus, the arbiter determines
which of the requesting masters will be granted the use of the bus.
- *Bus Master Initiates Transfer.* A granted bus master drives the address
and control signals with the address, direction, and width of the transfer.
It also indicates whether the transaction is part of a burst in the case of
burst mode operation. A write data bus operation moves data from the
master to a slave, while a read data bus operation moves data from a
slave to the master.

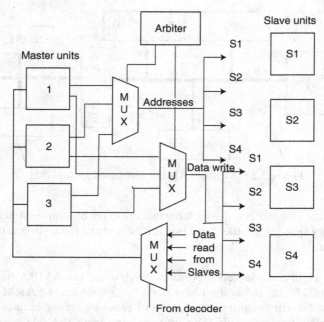

Figure 5.3 Multiplexor (MUX) interconnection for a three masters/four slaves system [22].

- *Bus Slave Provides a Response.* A slave signals to the master the status of the transfer such as whether it was successful, if it needs to be delayed, or that an error occurred.

Figure 5.4a depicts a basic AHB transfer cycle. An AHB transfer consists of two distinct phases: the address phase and the data phase. The master asserts the address (ADDR) and control signals on the rising edge of the clock (CLK) during the address phase, which always lasts for a single cycle. The slave then samples the address and control signals and responds accordingly during the data phase to a data read (RDATA) or write (WDATA) operation, and indicates its completion with the READY signal. A slave may insert wait states into any transfer by delaying the assertion of READY as shown in Figure 5.4b. For a write operation, the bus master holds the data stable throughout the extended data cycles. For a read transfer the slave does not provide valid data until the last cycle of the data phase.

The AHB bus is a pipelined (tenured) bus. Therefore, the address phase of any transfer can occur during the data phase of a previous transfer. This overlapping pipeline feature allows for high-performance operation.

The APB The APB is optimized for minimal power and low complexity instead of performance. It is used to interface to peripherals, which are low bandwidth.

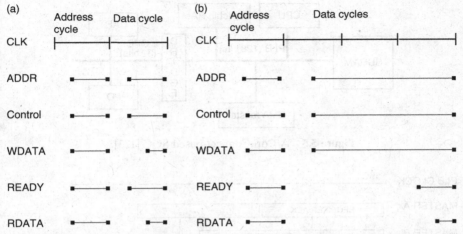

Figure 5.4   A simple AHB transfer [22]. (a) No wait states in transfer; (b) with wait states during transfer.

The operation of the APB is straightforward and can be described by a state diagram with three states. The APB either stays in the Idle state, or loops around the Setup state and the Enable state during data transfer.

5.4.2   CoreConnect

As in the case of AMBA bus, IBM's CoreConnect Bus is an SOC bus standard designed around a specific processor core, the PowerPC, but it is also adaptable to other processors. The CoreConnect Bus and the AMBA bus share many common features. Both have a bus hierarchy to support different levels of bus performance and complexity. Both have advanced bus features such as multiple master, separate read/write ports, pipelining, split transaction, burst mode transfer, and extendable bus width.

The CoreConnect architecture provides three buses for interconnecting cores, library macros, and custom logic:

- processor local bus (PLB),
- on-chip peripheral bus (OPB),
- device control register (DCR) bus.

Figure 5.5 illustrates how the CoreConnect architecture can be used in an SOC system built around a PowerPC. High-performance, high-bandwidth blocks such as the PowerPC 440 CPU core, the PCI-X bus bridge, and the PC133/ DDR133 (DDR1 with a 133 MHz bus) synchronous dynamic RAM (SDRAM) Controller are connected together using the PLB, while the OPB hosts lower data rate on-chip peripherals. The daisy-chained DCR bus provides a

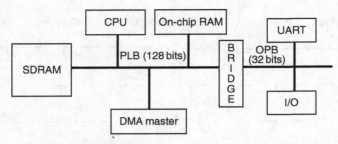

Figure 5.5 A CoreConnect-based SOC [123].

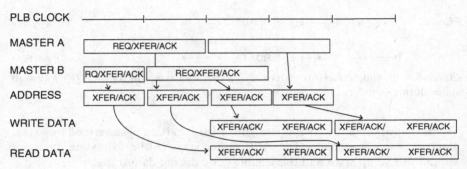

Figure 5.6 PLB transfer protocol [123].

relatively low-speed datapath for passing configuration and status information between the PowerPC 440 CPU core and other on-chip modules.

The PLB The PLB is used for high-bandwidth, high-performance, and low-latency interconnections between the processors, memory, and DMA controllers [123]. It is a fully synchronous, split transaction bus with separate address, read, and write data buses, allowing two simultaneous transfers per clock cycle. All masters have their own Address, Read Data, Write Data, and control signals called transfer qualifier signals. Bus slaves also have Address, Read Data, and Write Data buses, but these buses are shared.

PLB transactions, as in the AMBA AHB, consist of multiple phases that may last for one or more clock cycles, and involve the address and data buses separately. Transactions involving the address bus have three phases: request (RQ), transfer (XFER), and address acknowledge (ACK). A PLB transaction begins when a master drives its address and transfer qualifier signals and requests ownership of the bus during the request phase of the address tenure. Once the PLB arbiter grants bus ownership, the master's address and transfer qualifiers are presented to the slave devices during the transfer phase. The address cycle terminates when a slave latches the master's address and transfer qualifiers during the address acknowledge phase.

Figure 5.6 illustrates two deep read and write address pipelining along with concurrent read and write data tenures. Master A and Master B represent the state of each master's address and transfer qualifiers. The PLB arbitrates between these requests and passes the selected master's request to the PLB slave address bus. The trace labeled Address Phase shows the state of the PLB slave address bus during each PLB clock.

Each data beat in the data tenure has two phases: transfer and acknowledge. During the transfer phase the master drives the write data bus for a write transfer or samples the read data bus for a read transfer. As shown in Figure 5.6, the first (or only) data beat of a write transfer coincides with the address transfer phase.

Split Transaction   The PLB address, read data, and write data buses are decoupled, allowing for address cycles to be overlapped with read or write data cycles, and for read data cycles to be overlapped with write data cycles. The PLB split bus transaction capability allows the address and data buses to have different masters at the same time. Additionally, a second master may request ownership of the PLB, via address pipelining, in parallel with the data cycle of another master's bus transfer. This situation is illustrated in Figure 5.6, with the dependence of various signals indicated by arrows.

The OPB   The OPB is a secondary bus designed to alleviate system performance bottlenecks by reducing capacitive loading on the PLB [126]. Peripherals suitable for attachment to the OPB include serial ports, parallel ports, UARTs, GPIO (general purpose I/O), timers, and other low-bandwidth devices. The OPB is more sophisticated than the AMBA APB. It supports multiple masters and slaves by implementing the address and data buses as a distributed multiplexer. This type of structure is suitable for the less data-intensive OPB bus and allows peripherals to be added to a custom core logic design without changing the I/O on either the OPB arbiter or existing peripherals. Figure 5.7 shows one method of structuring the OPB address and data buses. Both masters and slaves provide enable control signals for their outbound buses. By requiring that each unit provide this signal, the associated bus combining logic can be strategically placed throughout the chip. As shown in the figure, either of the masters is capable of providing an address to the slaves, whereas both masters and slaves are capable of driving and receiving the distributed data bus.

Table 5.3 shows a comparison between the AMBA and CoreConnect bus standards.

5.4.3   Bus Interface Units: Bus Sockets and Bus Wrappers

Using a standard SOC bus for the integration of different reusable IP blocks has one major drawback. Since standard buses specify protocols over wired connections, an IP block that complies with one bus standard cannot be reused with another block using a different bus standard. One approach to alleviate this is to employ a hardware "socket," which is an example of a bus wrapper in Section 5.2, to separate the interconnect logic from the IP

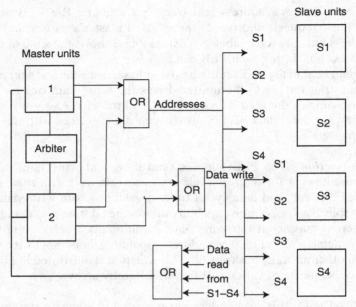

Figure 5.7 The on-chip peripheral bus (OPB) [126].

TABLE 5.3 Comparison between CoreConnect and AMBA Architectures [198]

	IBM CoreConnect PLB	ARM AMBA 2.0 AMBA High-Performance Bus
Bus architecture	32, 64, and 128 bits, extendable to 256 bits	32, 64, and 128 bits
Data buses	Separate read and write	Separate read and write
Key capabilities	Multiple bus masters	Multiple bus masters
	Four-deep read pipelining, two-deep write pipelining	Pipelining
	Split transactions	Split transactions
	Burst transfers	Burst transfers
	Line transfers	Line transfers
	OPB	AMBA APB
Masters supported	Supports multiple masters	Single master: The APB bridge
Bridge function	Master on PLB or OPB	APB master only
Data buses	Separate read and write	Separate or three-state

core using a well-defined IP core protocol that is independent of the physical bus protocol. Core-to-core communication is therefore handled by the interface wrapper. This approach is taken by the Virtual Socket Interface Alliance (VSIA) [44] with their virtual component interface (VCI) [249], and by Sonics Inc. employing the Open Core Protocol (OCP) and Silicon Backplane μNetwork [225].

VSIA proposes a set of standards and interfaces known as virtual socket interface (VSI) that enables system-level interaction on a chip using predesigned blocks (called virtual components [VCs]) [249]. This encourages designs using a component paradigm. The VCs, which are effectively IP blocks that conform to the VSI specifications, can be one of three varieties. *Hard* VCs consist of placed and routed gates with all silicon layers defined. It has predictable performance, area usage, and power consumption, but offers no flexibility. *Soft* VCs are designed in some hardware description language representation, which are mapped to physical design through synthesis, placement, and routing. They can be easily modified but generally take more effort to integrate and verify in the SOC design as well as having less predictable performance. Finally, *firm* VCs offer a compromise between the two. They come in the form of generators or partially placed library blocks that require final routing and/ or placement adjustment. This form of VCs provides more predictable performance than soft VCs, but still offers some degree of flexibility in aspect ratio and configuration.

In order to connect these different VCs together, VSIA has developed a VCI specification to which other proprietary buses can interface. By following the VCI specification, a designer can take a VC and integrate it with any of several buses in order to meet system performance requirements. The VCI standard specifies a family of protocols. Currently three protocols are defined: the peripheral VCI (PVCI), the basic VCI (BVCI), and the advanced VCI (AVCI) [249]. The PVCI is a low-performance protocol where the request and the response data transfer occur during a single control handshake transaction. It is therefore not a split-transaction protocol. The BVCI employs a split-transaction protocol, but responses must arrive in order. In other words, the response data must be supplied in the same order in which the initiator generated the requests. The AVCI is similar to the BVCI, but out-of-order transactions are allowed. Requests are tagged and transactions can be interleaved and reordered.

In addition to the specification of the VCI, VSIA also specifies a number of abstraction layers to define the representation views required to integrate a VC into an SOC design [44]. The idea is that if both the IP block provider (VC provider) and the system integrator (VC integrator) conform to the VSI specifications at all levels of abstraction, SOC designs using an IP component paradigm can proceed with lower risk of errors.

An alternative to VCI is the OCP promoted by the Open Core Protocol International Partnership (OCP-IP) [188]. The OCP defines a point-to-point interface between two communicating entities such as two IP cores using a core-centric protocol. An interface implementing the OCP assumes the attributes of a *socket*, which, as explained earlier, is effectively a bus wrapper that allows interfacing to the target bus. A system consisting of three IP core modules using the OCP and bus wrappers is shown in Figure 5.8. One module is a system initiator, one is a system target, and another is both initiator and target.

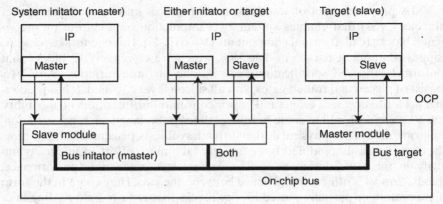

Figure 5.8   A three-core system using OCP and bus wrappers [225].

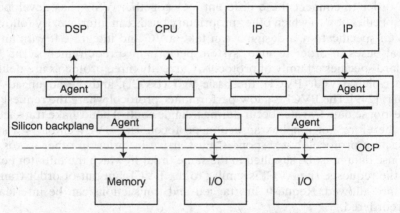

Figure 5.9   Sonics μNetwork configuration [225]. DSP, digital signal processor.

Another layer of interconnection can be made above the OCP in order to help IP integration further. Sonics Inc. proposes their proprietary SiliconBackplane Protocol that seamlessly glues together IP blocks that uses the OCP. The communication between different blocks takes place over the Silicon Backplane μNetwork, which has a scalable bandwidth of 50–4000 MB/s. Figure 5.9 depicts how the Sonics μNetwork components are connected together [225].

Bus interface units using the wrapper-based approach have been demonstrated to reduce the design time of SOC, but at a cost in terms of gates and latency. Attaching simple wrapper hardware increases the access latencies and incurs a hardware overhead of 3–5 K gates [160].

In addition, bus interface units can include first-in–first-out (FIFO) buffers to improve performance. Figure 5.10 shows the amount of hardware overhead

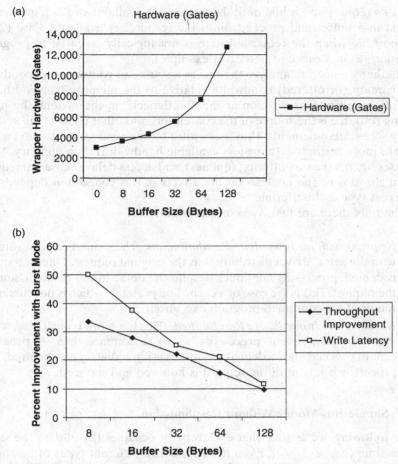

Figure 5.10   (a) Hardware overhead of write buffers; (b) performance impact of buffer for burst mode transfer [9].

incurred and performance improvement achieved by employing write data buffers in a bus interface unit [9].

The write buffer provides several cycles improvement in latency and, depending on the data size, more than 10% improvement in throughput.

5.5   ANALYTIC BUS MODELS

5.5.1   Contention and Shared Bus

Contention occurs wherever two or more units request a shared resource that cannot supply both at the same time. When contention occurs, either (1) it delays its request and is idle until the resource is available or (2) it queues its request in a buffer and proceeds until the resource is available. Case (2) is only possible when the requested item is not logically essential to program execution (as in a cache prefetch, for example).

Whether we need to analyze the bus as a source of contention depends on its maximum (or offered) bandwidth relative to the memory bandwidth. As contention and queues develop at the "bottleneck" in the system, the most limiting resource is the source of the contention, and other parts of the system simply act as delay elements. Thus buses must be analyzed for contention when they are more restrictive (have less available bandwidth) than memory.

Buses often have no buffering (queues), and access delays cause immediate system slowdown. The analysis on the effects of bus congestion depends on the access type and buffering.

Generally there are two types of access patterns:

1. *Requests without Immediate Resubmissions.* The denied request returns with the same arrival distribution as the original request. Once a request is denied, processing continues despite the delay in the resubmission of the request. This is the case of a cache line prefetch, which is not currently required for continued program execution.
2. *Requests Are Immediately Resubmitted.* This is a more typical case, when multiple independent processors access a common bus. A program cannot proceed after a denied request. It is immediately resubmitted. The processor is idle until the request is honored and serviced.

5.5.2 Simple Bus Model: Without Resubmission

In the following, we assume that each request occupies the bus for the same service time (e.g., $T_{line\ access}$). Even if we have two different types of bus users (e.g., word requests and line requests on a single line or [dirty] double line requests), most cases are reasonably approximated by simple computation of the per-processor average (offered) bus occupancy, ρ, given by:

$$\rho = \frac{\text{bus transaction time}}{\text{processor time} + \text{bus transaction time}}.$$

The processor time is the mean time the processor needs to compute before making a bus request. Of course, it is possible for the processor to overlap some of its compute time with the bus time. In this case, the processor time is the net nonoverlapped time between bus requests. In any event, $\rho \leq 1$.

The simplest model for n processors accessing a bus is given by:

$$\text{Prob (processor does not access bus)} = 1 - \rho$$

$$\text{Prob (bus is busy)} = (1-\rho)^n$$
$$= \text{fraction of bus bandwidth realized} = B(\rho, n).$$

The fraction of bandwidth realized times the maximum bus bandwidth gives the realized (or achieved) bus bandwidth, Bw.

The achieved bandwidth fraction (achieved occupancy) per processor (ρ_a) is given by:

$$n\rho_a = B(\rho, n)$$
$$\rho_a = \frac{B(\rho, n) \cdot}{n}$$

A processor slows down by ρ_a/ρ due to bus congestion.

5.5.3   Bus Model with Request Resubmission

A model that supports request resubmission involves a more complex analysis and requires an iterative solution. There are several solutions, each providing similar results. The solution provided by Hwang and Briggs [122] is an iterative pair of equations:

$$a = \frac{\rho}{\rho + (\rho_a/\rho)(1-\rho)}$$

and

$$n\rho_a = 1 - (1-a)^n,$$

where a is the actual offered request rate. To find a final ρ_a, initially set $a = \rho$ to begin the iteration. Convergence usually occurs within four iterations.

5.5.4   Using the Bus Model: Computing the Offered Occupancy

The model in the preceding section does not distinguish among types of transactions. It just requires the mean bus transaction time, which is the average number of cycles that the bus is busy managing a transaction. Then the issue is finding the offered occupancy, ρ.

The offered occupancy is the fraction of the time that the bus would be busy if there were no contention among transactions (bounded by 0.0 and 1.0). In order to find this, we need to determine the mean time for a bus transaction and the compute time between transactions.

The nature of the processor initiating the transaction is another factor. Simple processors make *blocking* transactions. In this case the processor is idle after the bus request is made and resumes computation only after the bus transaction is complete. The alternative for more complex processors is a *buffered* (or nonblocking) transaction. In this case the processor continues processing after making a request, and may indeed make several requests before completion of an initial request. Depending on the system configuration, there are two common cases:

1. *A Single Bus Master with Blocking Transactions.* In this case there is no bus contention as the processor waits for the transaction to complete. Here the achieved occupancy, ρ_a, is the same as the offered occupancy, and $\rho = \rho_a = $ (bus transaction time)/(compute time + bus transaction time).

2. *Multiple (n) Bus Masters with Blocking Transactions.* In this case the offered occupancy is simply $n\rho$ where ρ is as in case (1). Now contention can develop so we use our bus model to determine the achieved occupancy, ρ_a.

Example. Suppose a processor has bus transactions that consist of cache line transfers. Assume that 80% of the transactions move a single line and occupy the bus for 20 cycles and 20% of the transactions move a double line (as in dirty line replacement), which takes 36 cycles. The mean bus transaction time is 23.2 cycles. Now assume that a cache miss (transaction) occurs every 200 cycles.

In case (1), the bus is occupied: $\rho = \rho_a = 23.2/223.2 = 0.10$; there is no contention, but the bus causes a system slow down, as discussed below.

In case (2), suppose we have four processors. Now the offered occupancy is $\rho = 0.104$ and we use our model to find the contention time. Initially we set $a = \rho = 0.104$, $n\rho_a = 1 - (1 - a)^n = 1 - (1 - 0.104)^4$; now we find ρ_a and substitute the value of ρ_a for a and continue.

So initially, $\rho_a = 0.089$; after the next iteration, $\rho_a = 0.010$; and after several iterations, $\rho_a = 0.095$. We always achieve less than what is offered and the difference is delay due to contention. So:

$$\rho_a = 0.095 = \frac{\text{bus transaction time}}{\text{compute time} + \text{bus transaction time} + \text{contention time}}.$$

Solving for the contention time, we get about 21 cycles.

5.5.5   Effect of Bus Transactions and Contention Time

There are two separate effects of bus delays on overall system performance. The first is the obvious case of blocking, which simply inserts a transaction delay into the program execution. The second effect is due to contention. Contention reduces the rate of transaction flow into the bus and memory. This reduces performance proportionally.

In the case of blocking the processor simply slows down by the amount of the bus transaction. So the relative performance compared to an ideal processor with no bus transactions is:

$$\text{Relative performance} = \frac{\text{compute time}}{\text{compute time} + \text{bus transaction time}}.$$

In the case (1) example the processor slows down by $200/223.3 = 0.896$.

Contention, when present, adds additional delay. In case (2) the individual processor slows down by $200/(223.2 + 21) = 0.819$. The result of contention is that it simply slows down the system (without contention) by the ratio of ρ_a/ρ. The supply of transactions is reduced by this ratio.

5.6   BEYOND THE BUS: NOC WITH SWITCH INTERCONNECTS

While bus interconnect has been the predominant architecture for SOC interconnections, it suffers from a number of drawbacks. Even a well-designed bus-based system may suffer from data transfer bottlenecks, limiting the performance of the entire system. It is also not inherently scalable. As more modules are added to a bus, not only does data congestion increase, but power consumption also rises due to the increased load presented to the bus driver circuits. Switch-based NOC interconnections avoid some of these limitations. However, switches are inherently more complex than buses and are most useful in larger SOC configurations. There are broad trade-offs possible in switch design. Large numbers of nodes can be interconnected with relatively low latency but at exponentially increasing cost (as with crossbar switches) or they can be implemented with relatively longer latency and with more modest cost (as in a distributed interconnection).

This section presents some basic concepts and alternatives in the design of the physical interconnect network. This network consists of a configuration of switches to enable the interconnection of N units. The design efficiency or cost–performance of the interconnection network is determined by:

1. The delay in connecting a requesting unit to its destination.
2. The bandwidth between units and the number of connections that can be carried on concurrently.
3. The cost of the network.

In a network, units communicate with one another via a link or a channel, which can be either unidirectional or bidirectional. Links have bandwidth or the number of bits per unit time that can be transmitted concurrently between units (or nodes). The fanout of a node is the number of bidirectional channels connecting it to its neighboring nodes (Figure 5.11).

Networks can be static or dynamic. In a *static network*, the topology or the relationship between nodes in the network is fixed (Figure 5.12). The path between two nodes does not change. In a *dynamic network*, the paths between

SOC INTERCONNECT SWITCHES.

This section is an abstract of some of the basic concepts and results from the computer interconnect literature. In SOC switching, currently the number of nodes (units) is typically limited by die size to 16–64. Since the units are on chip, the link bandwidth, w, is relatively large: 16–128 wires. In SOC, dynamic networks are dominant so far (either crossbar or multistage); static networks, when used, tend to be a grid (torus). As the number of SOC units increases, a greater variety of network implementations are expected.

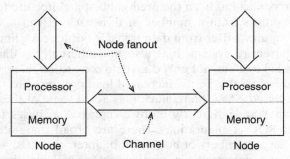

Figure 5.11 Node and channels; the node fanout is the number of channels connecting a node to its neighbors.

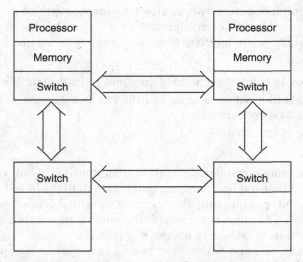

Figure 5.12 Static network (links between units is fixed).

nodes can be altered both to establish connectivity and also to improve network bandwidth (Figure 5.13).

A static network could consist of a 2-D grid of switches [64] to connect together SOC modules. A dynamic network could consist of a centralized crossbar switch. Apart from the advantage of avoiding traffic congestion, a switch-based scheme may allow modules to operate at different clock frequencies as well as alleviating the bus loading problem.

Figure 5.14 shows a crossbar-based interconnect that connects some locally synchronous blocks on the same chip [66]. The crossbar switch is fully

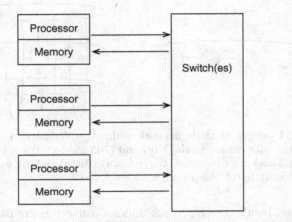

Figure 5.13   Dynamic network (links between units vary to establish connection).

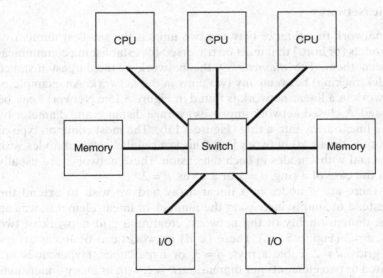

Figure 5.14   A switch-based interconnect scheme [66].

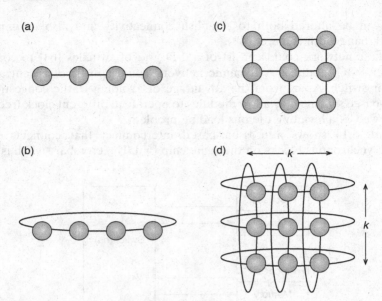

Figure 5.15 Example of static network without preferred sites. (a) Linear array; (b) linear array with closure (a ring); (c) grid (2-D mesh); (d) $k \times k$ grid with closure (a 2-D torus). These are also called (k, d) networks. In (a) and (b), we have $k = 4, d = 1$ (one dimensional). In (c) and (d), we have $k = 3, d = 2$.

asynchronous. Inside the chip, clock domain converters are used to bridge the asynchronous interconnect to the synchronous blocks.

5.6.1 Static Networks

In a static network the *distance* between two units is the smallest number of links or channels (or hops) that must be traversed for establishing communications between them. The *diameter* of the network is the largest distance (without backtracking) between any two units in the network. An example of a static network in a linear network is found in Figure 5.15a. Networks can be open or closed. A closed network improves average distance and diameter by converting a linear array into a ring (Figure 5.15b). The most common type of static network is the (k, d) network [70]. This is a regular array of nodes with dimension d and with k nodes in each dimension. These networks are usually closed as in the case of a ring, $d = 1$ or a torus, $d = 2$.

Assume there are k nodes in a linear array and we wish to extend the network. Instead of simply increasing the number of linear elements, we can increase the dimensionality of the network, creating a grid network of two dimensions, $d = 2$ (Figure 5.15c). These (k, d) networks can be linear arrays, $d = 1$, 2-D grids, $d = 2$, cubic arrays, $d = 3$, or hypercubes. Hypercubes are usually limited to two elements per dimension, $k = 2$, with as many dimensions as needed to contain the network. Higher dimensional networks improve the connectivity but at the expense of connection switches. There must be a switch for each nearest neighbor and generally there are $2d$ neighbors in a (k, d) network. Figure 5.15d represents a torus, commonly referred to as a nearest-neighbor mesh.

In the special case of the binary cube, or hypercube, $k = 2$. The number of hypercube nodes (N) and the diameter can be determined as follows: for $(2, n)$, the binary n-cube with bidirectional channels has:

$$N = 2^n,$$

and for the $(2, n)$ case:

$$\text{Diameter} = n.$$

For general (k, n) with n dimensions and with closure and bidirectional channels, we have

$$N = k^n$$

or

$$n = \log_k N$$

and

$$\text{Diameter} = \left[\frac{k-1}{2}\right] n.$$

Example. Suppose we have a 4×4 grid (torus as in Figure 5.15d). In (k, d) terms it is a $(4, 2)$ network, $N = 16$ and $n = 2$, and the diameter is 4.

In general, it is the dimension of the network and its maximum distance that are important to cost and performance. Some cost and performance comparisons for various (k, d) static networks are shown in Table 5.4.

Links are characterized in three ways:

1. *The Cycle Time of the Link, T_{ch}.* This corresponds to the time it requires to transmit between neighboring nodes. $1/T_{ch}$ is the bandwidth of a wire in the link or channel.
2. *The Width of the Link, w.* This determines the number of bits that may be concurrently transmitted between two nodes.
3. Whether the link is unidirectional or bidirectional.

Associated with the link characterization is the length of the message in bits (l) plus H header bits. The header is simply the address of the destination node. Thus, $T_{ch} \times (l + H)/w$ will be the time required to transmit a message between two adjacent units.

Suppose unit A has a message for unit C, which must be transmitted via unit B. If node B is available, the message is transmitted first from A to B and stored at B. After the message has been completely transmitted, node B accesses node C and transmits the message to C if C is available. Rather than

**TABLE 5.4   Some Cost and Performance Comparisons for Various (k, d) Static
Networks with 64 Nodes ($N = 64$)**

	Ring (64,1)	Torus (16,2)	Cube (4,3)	Hypercube (2,4)
Performance				
Number of hops (average, $dk/4$)	16	8	3	2
Diameter (hops) (maximum internode distance, $dk/2$)	32	16	6	4
Cost				
Node fanout (ports), $2d$	2	4	6	8
Bisection BW, $2wN/k$	32	128	512	1024

Links (and ports) are bidirectional with 16 wires ($w = 16$). Bisection bandwidth (BW) refers to
the number of wires intersected when a network is split into two equal halves.

storing the message at B, we can use *wormhole routing* [70]. As the message
is received at B, it is buffered only long enough to decode its header and
determine its destination. As soon as this minimal amount of information can
be determined, the message is retransmitted to C, assuming that C is available.
The amount of buffering then required at B is significantly reduced and the
overall time of transmission is:

$$T_{\text{wormhole}} = T_{ch}(d \cdot h + l/w),$$

where $h = [H/w]$.

   Example. In a 4×4 grid, $(k, d) = (4, 2)$ and, assuming $T_{ch} = 1$, let $h = 1$, $l =$
256 and $w = 64$. Then $T_{wormhole} = 2 + 4 = 6$ cycles.

   Once the header is decoded at an intermediate node, that node can determine whether the message is for it or for another node. The intermediate node
selects a minimum distance path to the destination node. If multiple paths have
the same distance, then this intermediate node will select the path that is currently unblocked or available to it.

5.6.2   Dynamic Networks

The dynamic indirect network is shown in Figure 5.16a and b.

   Typically, the basic element in the dynamic network is a crossbar switch
(Figure 5.17).

   The crossbar simply connects one of k points to any of another k points.
Multiple messages can be concurrently executed across the crossbar switch, so
long as two messages do not have the same destination. The cost of the crossbar switch increases as n^2, so that for larger networks, use of a crossbar switch
only becomes prohibitively expensive. In order to contain the cost of the
switch, we can use a small crossbar switch as the basis of a multistage network,
frequently referred to as a MIN—*multistage interconnection network* [256].

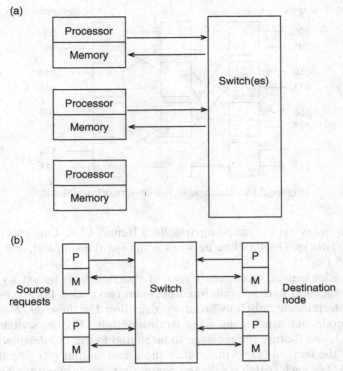

Figure 5.16 A basic dynamic, indirect switching network. P, processor; M, memory. Figure 5.16a represents a centralized switching network, separate from the processors. Figures 5.16b shows a more distributed network.

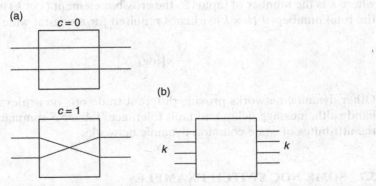

Figure 5.17 (a) A 2×2 crossbar with control c; (b) this can be generalized to a $k \times k$ crossbar switch.

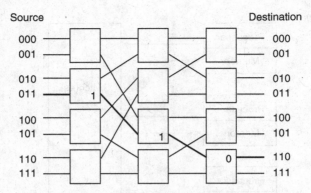

Figure 5.18 Baseline dynamic network topology.

There are many types, including baseline, Benes, Clos, Omega [150], and Banyan networks. The baseline network is among the simplest, and is shown in Figure 5.18.

The header causes successive stages of the switch to be set so that the proper connection path is established between two nodes. For example, consider a deterministic "obvious" routing algorithm for these M, N networks. Suppose node 011 sends a message to destination 110. The switch outputs labeled 1, 1, and 0 cause the message to be routed to the 110 destination node by setting the control (c) so that either the upper output ("0") or the lower output ("1") of each switch is selected. Similarly, the return path is simply 011. The number of stages between two nodes is:

$$\text{Stages} = \lceil \log_k N \rceil,$$

where k is the number of inputs to the crossbar element ($k \times k$) and therefore the total number of ($k \times k$) switches required for a one-bit wide path is:

$$\frac{N}{k} \times \lceil \log_k N \rceil.$$

Other dynamic networks provide different trade-offs on achievable message bandwidth, message delay, and fault tolerance. Table 5.5 summarizes some of the attributes of some common dynamic networks.

5.7 SOME NOC SWITCH EXAMPLES

5.7.1 A 2-D Grid Example of Direct Networks

Data traffic can be distributed over the entire NOC by connecting the user IP cores through a direct interconnect network. Data transfer bottlenecks are

TABLE 5.5   Dynamic Networks, Switching N Inputs $\times$ N Outputs Using $k \times k$ Switches

Network	Other Equivalent Networks	Stages of Delay (in Units of $k \times k$ Switch Delay)	Blocking	Approximate Cost ($k \times k$ Switches)
Baseline	Delta, Omega, SW Banyan	$[\log_k N]$	Yes	$\frac{N}{k}[\log_k N]$
Benes	—	$2[\log_k N] - 1$	Nonblocking if reconfigured	$\frac{2N}{k}[\log_k N]$
Clos	—	$2[\log_k N] - 1$	Strictly nonblocking	$\frac{4N}{k}[\log_k N]$

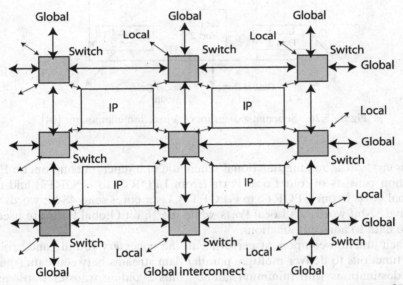

Figure 5.19   Xfabric connecting data processing core via junction components [64]. It is a direct switching network using a 2-D grid topology.

avoided because there are multiple paths between nodes and data transfers can be performed simultaneously. Xfabric uses a 2-D grid direct network approach to connect user cores on a Xilinx FPGA as shown in Figure 5.19 [64]. Data processing cores with one to four communication ports are interconnected via a network of junction components (shown in gray). These data routing junctions manage system data flow autonomously between multiple user cores. Multiple instances of junctions form a direct two-dimensional grid network that can interconnect up to 1024 single-port cores. Horizontal and vertical data transport links between junction components enable efficient data communications between cores.

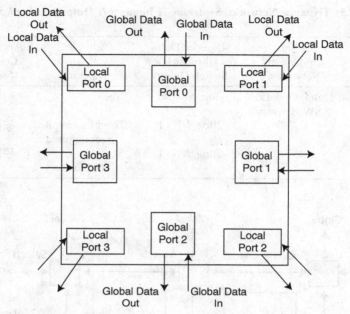

Figure 5.20   Schematic diagram of a junction component [64].

Figure 5.20 shows the functional schematic of a junction component. Each junction consists of four Local Ports (from LPORT0 to LPORT3) and four Global Ports (from GPORT0 to GPORT3). User cores send 48-bit words and receive 32-bit words via Local Ports, while the 16-bit Global Ports are used to route data to adjacent junctions.

Each junction component performs all the necessary routing and arbitration functions to deliver multiple parallel data streams between data sources and destinations with minimum latency, thus avoiding transfer bottlenecks found in bus-based systems.

5.7.2   Asynchronous Crossbar Interconnect for Synchronous SOC (Dynamic Network)

Another NOC for SOC applications is the PivotPoint architecture by Fulcrum [66]. The center of the system is the Nexus crossbar switch (see Figure 5.14), which has a data throughput rate of 1.6Tbps. Nexus uses clockless asynchronous circuits and has the advantages normally associated with this design style, including adaptivity to process technology, environmental variations, and lower system power consumption. The choice of asynchronous design style is partly driven by the need for interconnecting multiple clock domain cores. The synchronous cores can run at different frequencies with independent phase relationships to each other. Clock-domain converters are required to interface between the synchronous cores and the asynchronous crossbar. Since the

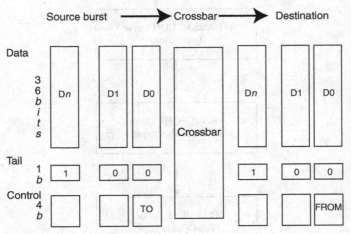

Figure 5.21   Format of burst used on Nexus [66].

crossbar switch does not use any clock signals, integrating different clock domains require no extra effort. In this way, the system is globally asynchronous, but locally synchronous, which is also known as a GALS system.

Data transfer on Nexus is done through bursts. Each burst contains a variable number of data words (36-bit) and is terminated by a tail signal. A 4-bit control is used to indicate a destination channel (TO), which becomes the source channel (FROM) when the burst leaves the crossbar. The format of the burst is shown in Figure 5.21. Bursts are automatically routed by the crossbar and cannot be dropped, fragmented, or duplicated.

The crossbar provides the routing through a physical link that is created when the first word of the burst enters the crossbar and is closed when the last word leaves the crossbar.

5.7.3   Blocking versus Nonblocking

Nexus and PivotPoint are designed to avoid head-of-the-line (HOL) blocking. HOL blocking occurs when one packet failing to progress results in other unrelated packets behind it to be blocked. PivotPoint uses virtual channels (also called ports) to transport separated traffic streams simultaneously. Blocked packets in one channel only blocks packets behind it on the same channel. Packets on other channels are free to progress. In this way communication stalls are minimized.

5.8   LAYERED ARCHITECTURE AND NETWORK INTERFACE UNIT

The network interface unit is a key component in the NOC, since it can overcome a number of limitations found in the conventional bus-based approach

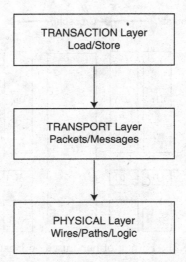

Figure 5.22 The layered architecture of NOC [26].

[40]. Although the bus standards discussed earlier provide some degree of portability and reusability of IP cores, they are difficult to adapt to advances in both process and bus interface technologies. The fundamental weakness of buses is that they do not take a layered approach to interconnection: There is no explicit separation between the transaction level communication in the application layer and the interconnect signals in the physical layer. In contrast, activities in NOC systems are generally separated into transaction, transport, and physical layers as depicted in Figure 5.22. As a result, NOC systems can be adapted more easily to the rapid advances in process technology or in system architecture.

Figure 5.23 shows a general-purpose on-chip interconnect network comprising of a number of modules such as processors, memories, and IP blocks organized as tiles. These module tiles are connected to the network that routes packets of data between them. All communications between tiles are via the network, and the area overhead of the network logic can be as low as 6.6% [71]. The key characteristics of such NOC architectures are that they have: (1) a layered architecture that is easily scalable; (2) a flexible switching topology that can be configured by the user to optimize performance for different applications; and (3) point-to-point communication that effectively decouples the IP blocks from each other.

5.8.1 NOC Layered Architecture

Most NOC architectures adopt a three-layered communication scheme, as shown in Figure 5.22. The *physical layer* specifies how packets are transmitted over the physical interfaces. Any changes in process technology, interconnect-

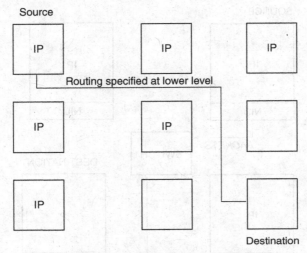

Figure 5.23 A typical NOC architecture [26].

ing switch structure, and clock frequency affect only this layer. Upper layers are not compromised in any way.

The *transport layer* defines how packets are routed through the switch network. A small header cell in the packet is typically used to specify how routing is to be done. The *transaction layer* defines the communication primitives used to connect the IP blocks to the network. The NOC interface unit (NIU) provides the transaction level services to the IP block, governing how information is exchanged between NIUs to implement a particular transaction (Figure 5.24).

The layered architecture of NOC offers a number of benefits [26]:

1. *Physical and Transport Layers can be Independently Optimized.* The physical layer is governed mostly by process technology while the transaction layer is dependent on the particular application. The layered approach allows them to be separately optimized without affecting each other.

2. *Inherently Scalable.* A properly designed switch fabric in an NOC can be scaled to handle any amount of simultaneous transactions. The distributed nature of the architecture allows the switches to be optimized to match the requirements. At the same time, the NIU responsible for the transaction layer can be designed to satisfy the performance requirement of the IP block that it services with no effect on the configuration and performance of the switch fabric.

3. *Better Control of Quality-of-Service.* Rules defined in the transport layer can be used to distinguish between time-critical and best-effort traffic.

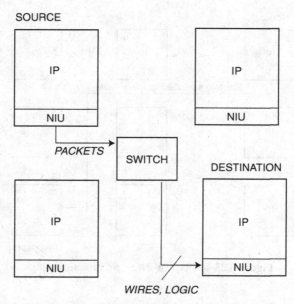

Figure 5.24   The transaction, transport, and physical layers of an NOC [26].

Prioritizing packets helps to achieve quality-of-service requirements enabling real-time performance on critical modules.

4. *Flexible Throughput.* By allocating multiple physical transport links, throughput can be increased to meet the demand of a system statically or dynamically.

5. *Multiple Clock Domain Operation.* Since the notion of a clock only applies to the physical layer and not to the transport and transaction layers, an NOC is particularly suited to an SOC system containing IP blocks that operate at different clock frequencies. Using suitable clock synchronization circuits at the physical layer, modules with independent clock domains can be combined with reduced timing convergence problems.

5.8.2 NOC and NIU Example

For the Nexus crossbar switch in Section 5.7.2, the NIU implements the PivotPoint system architecture connecting nodes using the Nexus crossbar switch. Figure 5.25 shows a simplified PivotPoint architecture. In addition to the Nexus crossbar switch, the FIFO buffer provides data-buffering function for the transmit (TX) and the receive (RX) channels. The System Packet Interface (SPI-4.2, represented simply as SPI-4 in the figure) implements a standard protocol for chip-to-chip communication at data rates of 9.9–16 Gbps.

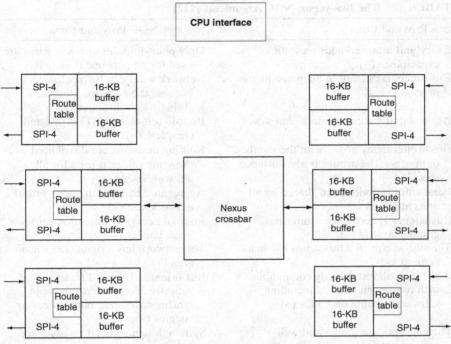

Figure 5.25 PivotPoint architecture [66].

5.8.3   Bus versus NOC

When compared with buses, NOC is not without drawbacks. Perhaps the most significant weakness of NOC is the extra latency that it introduces. Unlike data communication networks, where quality of service is governed mainly by bandwidth and throughput, SOC applications usually also have very strict latency constraints. Furthermore, the NIU and the switch fabric add to the area overhead of the system. Therefore, direct implementation of a conventional network architecture in SOC generally results in unacceptable area and latency overheads. Table 5.6 presents the pros and cons between buses and NOC approaches to SOC interconnect qualitatively.

5.9   EVALUATING INTERCONNECT NETWORKS

There have been a number of important analyses about the comparative merits of various network configurations [137, 145, 194]. The examples below illustrate the use of simple analytic models in evaluating interconnect networks.

TABLE 5.6   The Bus-versus-NOC Arguments [112]

Bus Pros and Cons	NOC Pros and Cons
Every unit attached adds parasitic capacitance (−)	Only point-to-point one-way wires are used for all network sizes (+)
Bus timing is difficult in deep submicron process (−)	Network wires can be pipelined because the network protocol is globally asynchronous (+)
Bus testability is problematic and slow (−)	Built-in self-test (BIST) is fast and complete (+)
Bus arbiter delay grows with the number of masters. The arbiter is also instance specific (−)	Routing decisions are distributed and the same router is used for all network sizes (+)
Bandwidth is limited and shared by all units attached (−)	Aggregated bandwidth scales with the network size (+)
Bus latency is zero once arbiter has granted control (+)	Internal network contention causes a small latency (−)
The silicon cost of a bus is low for small systems (+)	The network has a significant silicon area (−)
Any bus is almost directly compatible with most available IPs, including software running on CPUs (+)	Bus-oriented IPs need smart wrappers. Software needs clean synchronization in multiprocessor systems (−)
The concepts are simple and well understood (+)	System designers need re-education for new concepts (−)

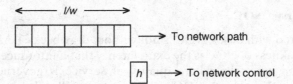

Figure 5.26   Message transmission from node to switch.

5.9.1   Static versus Dynamic Networks

In this section, we present the results and largely follow the analyses performed by Agarwal [8] in his work on network performance.

Dynamic Networks   Assume we have a dynamic indirect network made up of $k \times k$ switches with wormhole routing. Let us assume this network has n stages and channel width w with message length l. In the indirect network, we assume that the header network path address is transmitted in one cycle just before the message leaves the node, so that there is only one cycle of header overhead to set up the interconnect; see Figure 5.26.

Assuming the switches have unit delay (T_{ch} = one cycle), the total time for a message to transit the network without contention is:

$$T_c = n + \frac{l}{w} + 1 \text{ cycles.}$$

For all our subsequent analysis we assume that $n + l/w \gg 1$, so

$$T_c \approx n + \frac{l}{w} \text{ cycles.}$$

In a blocking dynamic network, each network switch has a buffer. If a block is detected, a queue develops at the node; so each of N units with occupancy ρ requests service from the network. Since the number of connection lines at each network level is the same (N), then the expected occupancy for each is ρ. At each switch, the message transmits experiences a waiting time. Kruskal and Snir [145] have shown that this waiting time is (assume that $T_{ch} = 1$ cycle and express time in cycles):

$$T_w = \frac{\rho(l/w)(1 - 1/k)}{2(1 - \rho)}.$$

The channel occupancy is

$$\rho = m \frac{l}{w},$$

where m is the probability that a node makes a request in a channel cycle. The total message transit time, $T_{dynamic}$, is:

$$T_{dynamic} = T_c + n T_w$$
$$= \left(n + \frac{l}{w} + \frac{np}{2(1 - \rho)} \left(\frac{l}{w} \right) (1 - 1/k) \right) T_{ch}.$$

Static Networks A similar analysis may be performed on a static (k, n) network. Let k_d be the average number of hops required for a message to transit a single dimension. For a unidirectional network with closure $k_d = \frac{(k-1)}{2}$ and for a bidirectional network $k_d = \frac{k}{4}$ (k even), the total time for a message to pass from source to destination is:

$$T_c = \left(h \times n \times k_d + \frac{l}{w} \right) T_{ch}.$$

Again, we assume that $T_{ch} = 1$ cycle and perform the remaining computations on a cycle basis. Agarwal [8] computes the waiting time ($M/G/1$) as:

$$T_w = \frac{\rho}{1-\rho} \frac{l}{w} \frac{k_d-1}{k_d^2}(1+1/n).$$

The total transit time for a message to a destination ($h = 1$) is:

$$T_{static} = T_c + nk_dT_w$$
$$= nk_d + l/w + \frac{nk_d\rho}{1-\rho}\left(\frac{l}{wk_d}\right)(1+1/n).$$

The preceding cannot be used for low k (i.e., $k = 2, 3, 4$). In this case [1],

$$T_w = \frac{\rho}{2(1-\rho)} \frac{l}{w}$$

and $\rho = \frac{mk_dl}{2w}$ or, for hypercube, $\frac{mk_dl}{w}$.

5.9.2 Comparing Networks: Example

In the following example assume that m, the probability that a unit requests service in any channel cycle, is 0.1; $h = 1, l = 256$, and $w = 64$. Compare a 4×4 grid (torus) static network with $N = 16, k = 4, n = 2$, and a MIN dynamic network with $N = 16, k = 2$.

For the dynamic network, the number of stages is:

$$n = \log_2 16 = 4,$$

while the channel occupancy is:

$$\rho = m\frac{l}{w} = 0.1\frac{256}{64} = 0.4.$$

The message transit time without contention is:

$$T_c = n + \frac{l}{w} + 1 = 4 + \frac{256}{64} + 1 = 9 \text{ cycles,}$$

while the waiting time is:

$$T_w = \frac{\rho(l/w)(1-1/k)}{2(1-\rho)} = \frac{0.4(256/64)(1-1/2)}{2(1-0.4)} = \frac{0.8}{1.2} = 0.67 \text{ cycle.}$$

Hence the total message transit time is:

$$T_{dynamic} = T_c + nT_w = 9 + 4(0.67) = 11.68 \text{ cycles.}$$

For the static network, the average number of hops $k_d = k/4 = 1$, and the total message time is:

$$T_c = \left(h \times n \times k_d + \frac{l}{w} \right) T_{ch} = (1 \times 2 \times 1 + (256/64)) = 6.$$

Since

$$\rho = \frac{m k_d l}{2w} = \frac{0.1 \times 1 \times 256}{2 \times 64} = 0.2$$

and T_w for low k is given by:

$$T_w = \frac{\rho}{2(1-\rho)} \frac{l}{w} = \frac{0.2}{2(1-0.2)} \frac{256}{64} = 0.5,$$

the waiting time is given by

$$
\begin{aligned}
T_{\text{static}} &= T_c + n k_d T_w \\
&= 6 + 2(1)(0.5). \\
&= 7 \text{ cycles}
\end{aligned}
$$

5.10 CONCLUSIONS

The interconnect subsystem is the backbone of the SOC. The system's performance can be throttled by limitations in the interconnect. Because of its importance, a great deal of attention has been afforded to optimize cost–performance interconnect strategies.

Excluding fully custom designs, there are two distinct approaches to SOC interconnect: bus based and network based (NOC). However, even here these can be complementary approaches. An NOC can connect nodes that can themselves be a bus-based cluster of processors or other IPs.

In the past most SOCs were predominantly bus based. The number of nodes to be connected were small (perhaps four or eight IPs) and each node consisted solely of a single IP. This remains a tried and tested method of interconnect that is both familiar and easy to use. The use of standard protocols and bus wrappers make the task of IP core integration less error prone. Also, the large number of bus options available allows users to trade-off between complexity, ease of use, performance, and universality.

As the number of interconnected nodes increases, the bandwidth limitations of bus-based approaches become more apparent. Switches overcome the bandwidth limitations but with additional cost and, depending on the configuration, additional latency. As switches (whether static or dynamic) are translated into IP and supported with experience and the emergence of tools, they will become the standard SOC interconnect especially for high-performance systems.

Modeling the performance of either bus- or switch-based interconnects is an important part of the SOC design. If initial analysis of bus-based interconnection demonstrates insufficient bandwidth and system performance, switch-based design is the alternative. Initial analysis and design selection is usually based on analytic models, but once the selection has been narrowed to a few alternatives, a more thorough simulation should be used to validate the final selection. The performance of the SOC will depend on the configuration and capability of the interconnection scheme.

In NOC implementations, the network interface unit has a key role. For a relatively small overhead, it enables a layering of the interconnect implementation. This allows designs to be re-engineered and extended to include new switches without affecting the upper level SOC implementation. Growth in NOC adoption facilitates easier SOC development.

There are various topics in SOC interconnect that are beyond the scope of this chapter. Examples include combination of design and verification of on-chip communication protocols [46], self-timed packet switching [105], functional modeling and validation of NOC systems [210], and the AMBA 4 technology optimized for reconfigurable logic [74]. The material in this chapter, and other relevant texts such as that by Pasricha and Dutt [193], provide the foundation on which the reader can follow and contribute to the advanced development of SOC interconnect.

5.11 PROBLEM SET

1. A tenured split (address plus bidirectional data bus) bus is 32 + 64 bits wide. A typical bus transaction (read or write) uses a 32-bit memory address and subsequently has a 128-bit data transfer. If the memory access time is 12 cycles,

   (a) show a timing diagram for a read and a write (assuming no contention).

   (b) what is the (data) bus occupancy for a single transaction?

2. If four processors use the bus described above and ideally (without contention) each processor generates a transaction every 20 cycles,

   (a) what is the offered bus occupancy?

   (b) using the bus model without resubmissions, what is the achieved occupancy?

   (c) using the bus model with resubmissions, what is the achieved occupancy?

   (d) what is the effect on system performance for the (b) and (c) results?

3. Search for current products that use the AMBA bus; find at least three distinct systems and tabularize their respective parameters (AHB and APB): bus width, bandwidth, and maximum number of IP users per bus. Provide additional details as available.

4. Search for current products that use the CoreConnect bus; find at least three distinct systems and tabularize their respective parameters (PLB and OPB): bus width, bandwidth, and maximum number of IP users per bus. Provide additional details as available.

5. Discuss some of the problems that you would expect to encounter in creating a bus wrapper to convert from an AMBA bus to a CoreConnect bus.

6. A static switching interconnect is implemented as a 4×4 torus (2-D) with wormhole routing. Each path is bidirectional with 32 wires; each wire can be clocked at 400 Mbps. For a message consisting of an 8-bit header and 128-bit "payload,"
   (a) what is the expected latency (in cycles) for a message to transit from one node to an adjacent node?
   (b) what is the average distance between nodes and the average message latency (in cycles)?
   (c) if the network has an occupancy of 0.4, what is the delay due to congestion (waiting time) for the message?
   (d) what is the total message transit time?

7. A dynamic switching interconnect is to connect 16 nodes using a baseline switching network implemented with 2×2 crossbars. It takes one cycle to transit a 2×2. Each path is bidirectional with 32 wires; each wire can be clocked at 400 Mbps. For a message consisting of an 8 bit header and 128 bit "payload,"
   (a) what is the expected latency (in cycles) for a message to transit from one node to any other?
   (b) draw the network.
   (c) what is the message waiting time, if the network has an occupancy of 0.4?
   (d) what is the total message transit time?

8. The bisection bandwidth of a switching interconnect is defined as the maximum available bandwidth across a line dividing the network into two equal parts (number of nodes). What is the bisection bandwidth for the static and dynamic networks outlined above?

9. Search for at least three distinct NOC systems; compare their underlying switches (find at least one dynamic and one static example). Provide details in table form.

6 Customization and Configurability

6.1 INTRODUCTION

To broaden SOC applicability while reducing cost, one can adopt a common hardware platform that can be customized to improve efficiency for specific applications. This chapter looks at different *customization* technologies, particularly those based on *configurability*. Here configurability covers both *one-time configurability*, when application-oriented customization takes place once either before or after chip fabrication, and *reconfigurability*, when customization takes place multiple times after chip fabrication.

Customization opportunities at design time, particularly those exploited in device fabrication, often result in high performance but at the expense of flexibility when the design is deployed. Such postfabrication flexibility is achieved by devices with various degrees of programmability, including coarse-grained reconfigurable architectures (CGRAs), application-specific instruction processors (ASIPs), fine-grained field-programmable gate arrays (FPGAs), digital signal processors (DSPs), and general-purpose processors (GPPs). The trade-off between programmability and performance is shown in Figure 6.1, which is introduced in Chapter 1.

Structured ASIC (application-specific integrated circuit) technology supports limited customization before fabrication compared with custom ASIC technology. In Figure 6.1, the ASIPs are assumed to be customized at fabrication in ASIC technology. ASIPs can also be customized at compile time if implemented in FPGA technology as a soft processor; a customizable ASIP processor will be presented in Section 6.8.

There are many ways of customizing SOC designs, and this chapter focuses on three of them:

1. customization of instruction processors (Sections 6.4 and 6.8), illustrating how (a) availability of processor families and (b) generation of application-specific processors can offer architectural optimizations such as very long instruction word (VLIW), vectorization, fused operation,

Computer System Design: System-on-Chip, First Edition. Michael J. Flynn and Wayne Luk.
© 2011 John Wiley & Sons, Inc. Published 2011 by John Wiley & Sons, Inc.

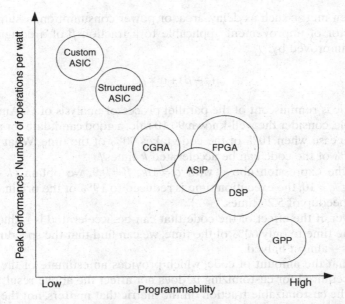

Figure 6.1 A simplified comparison of different technologies: programmability versus performance. GPP stands for general-purpose processor, while CGRA stands for coarse-grained reconfigurable architecture.

and multithreading to meet requirements in performance, area, energy efficiency, and costs;

2. customization of reconfigurable fabrics (Sections 6.5 and 6.6), showing that fine-grained reconfigurable functional units (FUs) and the related interconnect resources are versatile but incur large overheads—hence coarse-grained blocks are increasingly adopted to reduce such overheads;

3. customization techniques for optimizing implementations, such as instance-specific design (Section 6.7) and run-time reconfiguration strategies (Section 6.9), together with methods for assessing related trade-offs in performance, size, power, and energy efficiency.

Other customization methods, such as those based on multiprocessors, would not be treated in detail. Pointers to references on various related topics are included in Section 6.10.

6.2   ESTIMATING EFFECTIVENESS OF CUSTOMIZATION

It is important to be able to estimate and compare the effectiveness of different ways of customization applied to part of a design. The method is simple.

For a given metric such as delay, area, or power consumption, assume that α is the factor of improvement applicable to a fraction β of a design. So the metric is improved by:

$$(1 - \beta) + \alpha \times \beta.$$

This metric is reminiscent of the parallel processor analysis of G. Amdahl. As an example, consider the well-known 90:10 rule: a good candidate for acceleration is the case when 10% of the code takes 90% of the time. What happens if that 10% of the code can be accelerated k times?

From the expression above with $\alpha = 1/k$, $\beta = 0.9$, we obtain $(k + 9)/10k$. Assuming $k = 10$, the execution time is reduced to 19% of the original, resulting in a speedup of 5.26 times.

However, if the effect of the code that can be accelerated is reduced from 90% of the time to only 60% of the time, we can find that the speedup is only 2.17 times—almost halved.

Note that the amount of code, which provides an estimate of the amount of effort required for customizing it, does not affect the above result; it is the effect of the customizable fraction on the metric that matters, not the fraction itself.

This method can be applied in various ways. As another example, consider the use of embedded coarse-grained blocks to customize a fine-grained reconfigurable fabric, as we shall explain in a later section. Assume that 50% of the fine-grained fabric can be replaced by coarse-grained blocks, which are three times more efficient in speed and 35 times more efficient in area. One can find that the design could be improved up to 50% faster with its area reduced by half.

There are, however, several reasons against customizability. Tools for customizable processors such as performance profilers and optimizers are often not as mature as those for noncustomizable processors; backwards compatibility and verification can also become an issue. One approach is to develop customizable processors that are compatible with existing noncustomizable building blocks, such that there is interoperability between customizable and noncustomizable technologies [94].

6.3   SOC CUSTOMIZATION: AN OVERVIEW

Customization is the process of optimizing a design to meet application requirements and implementation constraints. It can take place at design time and at run time. Design time has two components: fabrication time and compile time. During fabrication time, a physical device is constructed. If this device is configurable, then after fabrication it can be customized by a program produced at compile time and executed at run time.

There are three common means of implementing computations: standard instruction processors, ASICs, and reconfigurable devices.

1. For standard instruction processors such as those from ARM, AMD, and Intel, fabrication-time customization produces a device supporting a fixed instruction set architecture, and compile-time customization produces instructions for that architecture; run-time customization corresponds to locating or generating appropriate code for execution at run time.

2. For ASICs, much of the customization to perform application functions takes place at fabrication time. Hence the high efficiency but low flexibility, since new functions not planned before fabrication cannot easily be added. Structured ASICs, such as gate array or standard-cell technologies, reduce design effort by limiting the options of customization to the user to, for instance, the metal layers. One-time customization of antifuse technology can be performed in the field.

3. Reconfigurable devices generally include FPGA and complex programmable logic device (CPLD) technology, as well as instruction processors coupled with a reconfigurable fabric to support custom instructions [25]. In this case, fabrication-time customization produces a device with a reconfigurable fabric, typically containing reconfigurable elements joined together by reconfigurable interconnections. At compile time, configuration information is produced from a design description for customizing the device at appropriate instants at run time.

The standard instruction processors are general purpose. There are, however, opportunities to customize the instruction set and the architecture for a specific application. For instance, the standard instruction set can be customized to remove unused instructions or to include new instructions that would result in improved performance. Custom instruction processors can be customized during fabrication in ASIC technology or during configuration in reconfigurable hardware technology.

- Processors that are customized during fabrication include those from ARC and Tensilica. Typically some of the building blocks are hardwired at fabrication to support, for instance, domain-specific optimizations, including instructions that are customized for specific applications. To reduce risk, there are often reconfigurable prototypes before designs are implemented in ASIC technology.

- For soft processors such as MicroBlaze [259] from Xilinx or Nios [11] from Altera, the challenge is to support instruction processors efficiently using resources in a reconfigurable fabric such as an FPGA. Efficiency can be improved by exploiting device-specific features or run-time reconfigurability [213].

- Another alternative is to implement the instruction processor in ASIC technology, and a suitable interface is developed to enable the processor to benefit from custom instructions implemented in a reconfigurable fabric. An example is the software configurable processor from Stretch [25], which consists of the Xtensa instruction processor from Tensilica and a coarse-grained reconfigurable fabric. These devices can offer higher efficiency than FPGAs when an application requires resources that match their architecture.

A key consideration for deciding which technology to use is volume. Recall from Chapter 1 that the product cost usually has a fixed or nonrecurring component that is independent of volume and has a variable or recurrent component that varies with volume. Reconfigurable technologies like FPGAs have little fixed cost, but have a higher unit cost than ASIC technologies. Hence, below a certain volume threshold, reconfigurable technologies offer the lowest cost—and this threshold moves in favor of reconfigurable technologies with time, since the cost of mask sets and other fixed fabrication costs increase rapidly with each new generation of technology.

There are various ways of classifying a customizable SOC. A customizable SOC typically consists of one or more processors, reconfigurable fabrics, and memories. One way is to classify such SOCs according to the coupling between the reconfigurable fabric and the processor [61].

Figure 6.2a shows the reconfigurable fabric attached to the system bus. Figure 6.2b illustrates the situation when the reconfigurable fabric is a coprocessor of the CPU, with a closer coupling between them than the ones in Figure 6.2a.

Next, Figure 6.2c shows an architecture in which the processor and the fabric are tightly coupled. In this case, the reconfigurable fabric is part of the processor itself, perhaps forming a reconfigurable subunit that supports custom instructions. An example of this organization is the software configurable processor from Stretch.

Figure 6.2d shows another organization. In this case, the processor is embedded in the programmable fabric. The processor can either be a "hard" core [261] or can be a "soft" core, which is implemented using the resources of the reconfigurable fabric itself; examples include the MicroBlaze and the Nios processors mentioned earlier.

It is also possible to integrate configurable analog and digital functionality on the same chip. For instance, the PSoC (programmable system on a chip) device [68] from Cypress has an array of analog blocks that can be configured as various combinations of comparators, filters, and analog-to-digital converters, with programmable interconnects. The inputs and outputs of these and the reconfigurable digital blocks can be flexibly routed to the input/output (I/O) pins. Moreover, these blocks can be reconfigured to perform different functions when the system is operating.

6.4 CUSTOMIZING INSTRUCTION PROCESSORS

Microprocessors in desktop machines are designed for general-purpose computation. Instruction processors in an SOC are often specialized for particular

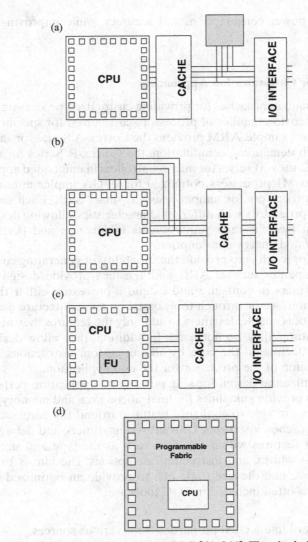

Figure 6.2   Four classes of customizable SOC [61; 244]. The shaded box denotes the reconfigurable fabric. (a) Attached processing unit; (b) coprocessor; (c) reconfigurable FU; (d) processor embedded in a reconfigurable fabric.

types of computations such as media processing or data encryption. Hence they can benefit from customization that is highly specific to their intended function, eliminating hardware elements that would not be needed. Such customization usually takes place before fabrication, although many techniques can also be applied to the design of soft processors. Customization allows designers to optimize their designs to meet requirements such as those in speed, area, power consumption, and accuracy, while improving product differentiation.

6.4.1   Processor Customization Approaches

There are two main approaches for providing customized processors. The first approach is to provide families of processors customized for specific application domains. For example, ARM provides the Cortex-A Series for supporting applications with demanding computation, the Cortex-R Series for real-time processing, the Cortex-M series for microcontrollers in embedded applications (with the Cortex-M1 processors optimized for FPGA implementation), and the SecurCore processors for tamper-resistant smart cards. Each series contains a range of processors with different characteristics, allowing designers to choose one that best fits their requirements in function and performance, including power and energy consumption.

The second approach is to provide the capability of generating customized processors. Companies such as ARC and Tensilica provide design tools to allow SOC designers to configure and extend a processor, either through a graphical user interface or through tools based on an architecture description language. Such tools enable designers to add only the features they need while deleting the features they do not need. In addition, they allow designers to extend the architecture of the core by adding custom instructions, allowing further optimization of the processor for the end application.

To help optimize the design for size, power, and application performance, some SOC tools provide guidelines for final silicon area and memory requirements. Designers are able to configure features around the core, such as the type and size of caches, interrupts, DSP subsystem, timers, and debug components, as well as features within the core, such as the type and size of core registers, address widths, and instruction set options. The aim is to support rapid performance and die-size trade-offs to provide an optimized solution. Specific functions often included in SOC tools are:

- Integration of intellectual properties from various sources.
- Generation of simulation scripts and test benches for system verification.
- Enhancement of software development tools to support, for instance, custom instructions for the customizable processor.
- Automated generation of FPGA designs for an emulation platform.
- Documentation of selected configuration for inclusion in licensees' chip specifications and customer-level documentation.

Such tools can usually configure and deliver a custom processor within minutes. Also, by generating all configuration-specific information required for testing, downstream development tools, and documentation, the configurator reduces time to silicon and reduces project risk.

Further information about tools and applications of customizable embedded processors can be found in various publications [127, 207].

6.4.2 Architecture Description

As processors become increasingly complex, it is useful to provide a significant degree of automation in implementing both the processor and the software tools associated with that processor. Without automation, much design and verification effort is needed to build a processor and its tools from scratch for every application.

To automate development of processors and tools, architecture description languages or processor description languages can help [179]. Such languages should be sufficiently concise and high level for designers to adopt them for different applications; they should also be comprehensive enough to produce realistic, efficient implementations. Many languages have been proposed for describing instruction processors. The goal of these languages is to capture the design of a processor so that supporting tools and the processor itself can be automatically generated.

Architecture description languages can be classified by the description style and by the level and type of automation provided. For example, one can classify architecture description languages as either behavioral, structural, or a combination of the two.

Behavioral descriptions are instruction-set centric: The designer specifies the instruction set and then uses tools to generate a compiler, assembler, linker, and simulator. The nML [87] and TIE [240] languages fall into the behavioral category. Automating generation of a compiler backend from a behavioral description is facilitated when the instructions can be expressed as a tree grammar for a code-generator-generator tool such as BURG [100]. Many behavioral languages support synthesis of processor hardware, and synthesis tools are available for the above examples. In the case of TIE, synthesis is simplified since the base processor is fixed and only extensions to this base processor can be specified by designers. The nML "Go" tool designs the processor architecture automatically [86] from the instruction set, inferring structure from explicitly shared resources such as the register file.

The main advantage of a behavioral description is the high level of abstraction: only an instruction set specification is required to generate a custom processor. The main disadvantage is the lack of flexibility in the hardware implementation. Synthesis tools must fix some aspects of the microarchitecture [87] or even the entire base processor [240]. Efficient synthesis from an instruction set alone is a difficult design automation problem when resource sharing [50] is taken into account.

Structural descriptions capture the FUs, storage resources, and interconnections of a processor. SPREE [269] is a library built onto C++ that generates

TABLE 6.1 Features of Some Architecture Description Languages

Feature	Expression [114]	CUSTARD [77]	LISA [119]	SPREE [269]	nML [239]	TIE [240]
Whole processor	√	√	√	√	√	
Toolchain configuration	√	√	√	√	√	√
Hardware generation		√	√	√	√	√
Memory system	√	√	√			
Behavioral	√	√	√		√	√
Structural	√		√	√		

FPGA soft processors using a structural description. In particular, the designer can remove instructions or change the implementation of FUs, since SPREE provides a method for connecting functional blocks, with built-in support for common functions such as forwarding networks and interlocks.

The main advantage of structural descriptions is that they can be directly converted into a form suitable for synthesis to hardware. Additionally, most structural description styles maintain the generality of a hardware description language (HDL). This generality provides much scope for describing diverse microarchitectures, for example, superscalar or multithreaded ones. The prime disadvantage is the lower level of abstraction: the designer needs to manually specify FUs and control structures.

We present a summary of existing processor description languages in Table 6.1. For each language, we indicate the description style, the scope (whole processor or just instruction set), and the tools available to automate generation of a processor system.

Some systems, such as LISA [119], cover both structural and behavioral information. This combines the advantages of pure behavioral and structural descriptions, but there is a need to ensure that related behavioral and structural elements are consistent.

All languages except TIE are whole processor descriptions, meaning that the entire processor design is specified, as opposed to just the instruction set. However, many processor description languages are specific to a particular basic processor architecture, such as in-order execution in the case of LISA and nML. Customizable threaded architecture (CUSTARD) [77], which would be covered in Section 6.8, is based on the MIPS instruction set while supporting various customization options, such as the type of multithreading and the use of custom instructions.

Possible tools for such languages include [179]:

- *Model Generation.* Tools for producing hardware prototypes and validation models for checking that the architecture specification captures the requirements.

- *Test Generation.* Tools for producing test programs, assertions, and test benches.
- *Toolkit Generation.* Tools for profiling, exploring, compiling, simulating, assembling, and debugging designs.

6.4.3 Identifying Custom Instructions Automatically

Various approaches have been proposed for automatic identification of instruction set extensions from high-level application descriptions. One can cluster related dataflow graph (DFG) nodes heuristically as sequential or parallel templates. Input and output constraints are imposed on the subgraphs to reduce the exponential search space.

Various architectural optimizations—some described in the earlier chapters—can benefit the automatically generated designs, such as [110]:

- VLIW techniques enable a single instruction to support multiple independent operations. A VLIW format partitions an instruction into a number of slots, each of which may contain one of a set of operations. If the instruction set is designed to use VLIW, a source language compiler can use software-pipelining and instruction-scheduling techniques to pack multiple operations into a single VLIW instruction.
- Vector operations increase throughput by creating operations that operate on more than one data element. A vector operation is characterized by the operation it performs on each data element and by the number of data elements that it operates on in parallel, that is, the vector length. For example, a four-wide vector integer addition operation sums two input vectors, each containing four integers, and produces a single result vector of four integers.
- Fused operations involve creating operations composed of several simple operations. A fused operation potentially has one or more of the input operands fixed to a constant value. Using the fused operation in place of the simple operations reduces code size and issue bandwidth, and may reduce register file port requirements. Also, the latency of the fused operation may be lower than the combined latency of the simple operations.

Application of constraint propagation techniques results in an efficient enumerative algorithm. However, the applicability of this approach is limited to DFGs with around 100 nodes. Search space can be further reduced by imposing additional constraints such as single output, or connectivity constraints on the subgraphs.

The identification of instruction set extensions under input and output constraints can be formulated as an integer linear programming problem. Biswas et al. [45] propose an extension to the Kernighan–Lin heuristic based on input and output constraints. Optimality is often limited by either an approximate search algorithm or some artificial constraints—such as I/O constraints—to make subgraph enumeration tractable.

An integer linear programming formulation can replace I/O constraints with the actual data bandwidth constraints and data transfer costs. The instruction set extensions that are generated may have an unlimited number of inputs and outputs. A baseline machine with architecturally visible state registers makes this approach feasible. Promising results are obtained by integrating the data bandwidth information directly into the optimization process, by explicitly accounting for the cost of the data transfers between the core register file and custom state registers [28].

There are many approaches in customizing instruction processors. A technology-aware approach could involve a clustering strategy to estimate the resource utilization of lookup table (LUT)-based FPGAs for specific custom instructions, without going through the entire synthesis process [148]. An application-aware approach could, in the case of video applications, exploit appropriate intermediate representations and loop parallelism [165]. A transformation-aware approach could adopt a method based on combined but phased searching of the source-level transformation design space and the instruction set extension design space [182].

6.5 RECONFIGURABLE TECHNOLOGIES

Among various technologies, FPGAs are well known. Their capacity and capability have improved rapidly in the last few years to support high-performance designs. Their low cost and support for rapid development make them ideal for designs requiring fast time to market, as well as for education and student projects.

The following covers the reconfigurable fabric that underpins FPGAs and other reconfigurable devices. The reconfigurable fabric consists of a set of reconfigurable FUs, a reconfigurable interconnect, and a flexible interface to connect the fabric to the rest of the system. We shall review each of these components and show how they have been used in both commercial and academic reconfigurable systems. The treatment here follows that of Todman et al. [244].

In each component of the fabric, there is a trade-off between flexibility and efficiency. A highly flexible fabric is typically larger and slower than a less flexible fabric. On the other hand, a more flexible fabric can better adapt to application requirements. This kind of trade-off can influence the design of reconfigurable systems. A summary of the main features of various architectures can be found in Table 6.2. There are many related devices, such as those from Elixent [82], that we are unable to include due to limited space.

6.5.1 Reconfigurable Functional Units (FUs)

Reconfigurable FUs can be classified as either coarse grained or fine grained. A fine-grained FU can typically implement a single function on a single bit,

TABLE 6.2 Comparison of Reconfigurable Fabrics and Devices

Fabric or Device	Granularity	Base Logic Component	Routing Architecture	Embedded Memory	Special Features
Actel Axcelerator [2]	Fine	Four-input mux and inverter	Horizontal and vertical tracks	4-Kbit blocks	Antifuse, low-power mode
Actel IGLOO [3], ProASIC [4;5]	Fine	Three-input logic function	Horizontal and vertical tracks	4-Kbit blocks or 1K FlashROM	Flash-based, low-power mode
Altera Stratix III [15], Stratix IV [16]	Fine	Eight-input adaptive logic module	Horizontal and vertical tracks	640-bit, 9-Kbit, 144-Kbit blocks	DSP blocks, 1.6–8.5 Gbps I/Os programmable power
Xilinx Virtex II Pro [262], Virtex 4 [263]	Fine	Four-input LUTs	Horizontal and vertical tracks	18-Kbit blocks	Block multipliers, DSP blocks, PowerPC 405 processor, 3.1–6.5 Gbps I/Os
Xilinx Virtex 5 [264], Virtex 6 [265]	Fine	Six-input LUTs or dual five-input	Horizontal and vertical tracks	36-Kbit blocks	DSPs, 6.5 Gbps I/Os PowerPC 440 processor
Lattice XP2 [149]	Fine	Four-input LUTs	Horizontal and vertical tracks	18-Kbit blocks	DSPs, internal flash memory
SiliconBlue iCE65 [219]	Fine	Four-input LUTs	Horizontal and vertical tracks	4-Kbit blocks	Low power mode, internal flash memory
Silicon Hive Avispa [220]	Coarse	ALUs, shifters, accumulators, and multipliers	Buses	4 × 4K dual port local data memories	75 FUs, 95 register files, OFDM radio applications

OFDM: orthogonal frequency-division multiplexing.

or a small number of bits. The most common kind of fine-grained FUs are the small LUTs that are used to implement the bulk of the logic in a commercial FPGA. A coarse-grained FU, on the other hand, is typically much larger, and may consist of arithmetic and logic units (ALUs) and possibly even a significant amount of storage. In this section, we describe the two types of FUs in more detail.

Many reconfigurable systems use commercial FPGAs as a reconfigurable fabric. These commercial FPGAs contain many three to six input LUTs, each of which can be thought of as a fine-grained FU. Figure 6.3a illustrates a LUT; by shifting in the correct pattern of bits, this FU can implement any single

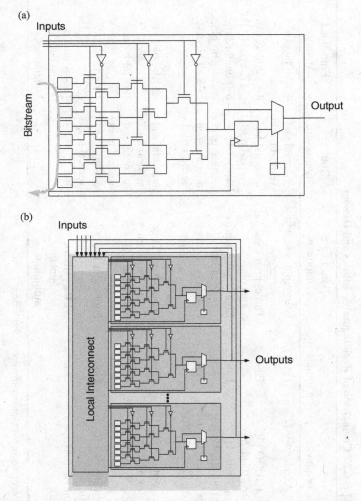

Figure 6.3 Fine-grained reconfigurable FUs [244]. (a) Three-input LUT; (b) cluster of LUTs.

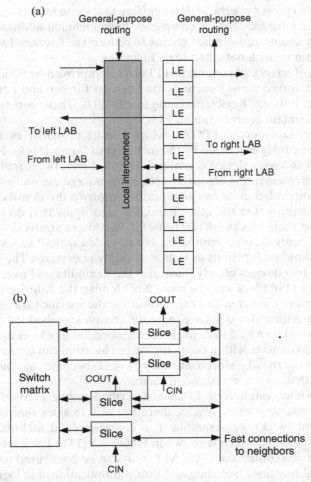

Figure 6.4 Commercial logic block architectures. (a) Altera LAB [14]; (b) Xilinx CLB [262].

function of up to three inputs—the extension to LUTs with larger numbers of inputs is clear. Typically, LUTs are combined into clusters, as shown in Figure 6.3b. Figure 6.4 shows clusters in two popular FPGA families. Figure 6.4a shows a cluster in the Altera Stratix device; Altera calls these clusters "logic array blocks" (LABs) [14]. Figure 6.4b shows a cluster in the Xilinx architecture [262]; Xilinx calls these clusters "configurable logic blocks" (CLBs). In the Altera diagram, each block labeled "LE" is an LUT, while in the Xilinx diagram, each "Slice" contains two LUTs.

Reconfigurable fabrics containing LUTs are flexible and can be used to implement any digital circuit. However, compared to the coarse-grained structures described below, these fine-grained structures have significantly more area, delay, and power overhead. Recognizing that these fabrics are often used for arithmetic purposes, FPGA companies have included additional features such as carry chains and cascade chains to reduce the overhead when implementing common arithmetic and logic functions.

While the efficiency of commercial FPGAs is improved by adding architectural support for common functions, one can go further and embed significantly larger, but less flexible, reconfigurable FUs. There are two kinds of devices that contain coarse-grained FUs.

First, many commercial FPGAs, which consist primarily of fine-grained FUs, are increasingly enhanced by the inclusion of larger blocks. For instance, the early Xilinx Virtex device contains embedded 18×18 bit multiplier units [262]. When implementing algorithms requiring a large amount of multiplication, these embedded units can significantly improve the density, speed, and power consumption. On the other hand, for algorithms that do not perform multiplication, these blocks are rarely useful. The Altera Stratix devices contain a larger, but more flexible embedded block, called a DSP block, which can perform accumulate functions as well as multiply operations. The comparison between the two devices clearly illustrates the flexibility and overhead trade-off: the Altera DSP block may be more flexible than the Xilinx multiplier, but it consumes more chip area and runs slower for the specific task of multiplication. Recent Xilinx devices have a more complex embedded unit, called DSP48. It should be noted that, while such embedded blocks eliminate reconfigurable interconnects within them, their fixed location can cause wiring congestion and overhead. Moreover, they would become an overhead for applications that do not make use of them.

Second, while commercial FPGAs described above contain both fine-grained and coarse-grained blocks, there are also devices that contain only coarse-grained blocks. An example of a coarse-grained architecture is the ADRES architecture, which is shown in Figure 6.5 [171]. Each reconfigurable FU in this device contains a 32-bit ALU that can be configured to implement one of several functions including addition, multiplication, and logic functions, with two small register files. Clearly, such an FU is far less flexible than the fine-grained FUs described earlier; however, if the application requires functions that match the capabilities of the ALU, these functions can be efficiently implemented in this architecture.

6.5.2 Reconfigurable Interconnects

Regardless of whether a device contains fine-grained FUs, coarse-grained FUs, or a mixture of the two, the FUs needed to be connected in a flexible way. Again, there is a trade-off between the flexibility of the interconnect (and hence the reconfigurable fabric) and the speed, area, and power efficiency of the architecture.

Reconfigurable interconnect architectures can be classified as fine grained or coarse grained. The distinction is based on the granularity with which wires are switched. This is illustrated in Figure 6.6, which shows a flexible intercon-

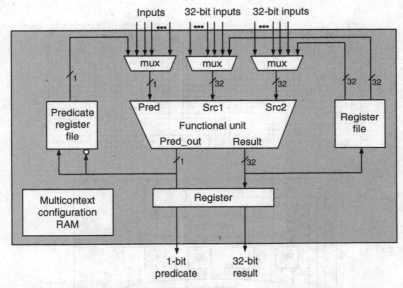

Figure 6.5   ADRES reconfigurable FU [171]. Pred is a one-bit control input selecting either Src1 or Src2 for the functional unit.

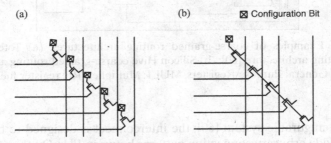

Figure 6.6   Routing architectures. (a) Fine grained; (b) coarse grained.

nect between two buses. In the fine-grained architecture in Figure 6.6a, each wire can be switched independently, while in Figure 6.6b, the entire bus is switched as a unit. The fine-grained routing architecture in Figure 6.6a is more flexible, since not every bit needs to be routed in the same way; however, the coarse-grained architecture in Figure 6.6b contains fewer programming bits, and hence has lower overhead.

Fine-grained routing architectures are usually found in commercial FPGAs. In these devices, the FUs are typically arranged in a grid pattern and they are connected using horizontal and vertical channels. Significant research has been performed in the optimization of the topology of this interconnect [157].

Coarse-grained routing architectures are commonly used in devices containing coarse-grained FUs. Figure 6.7 shows two examples of coarse-grained routing architectures. The routing architecture in Figure 6.7a is used in the

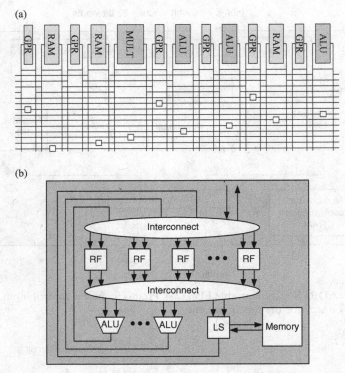

Figure 6.7 Examples of coarse-grained routing architectures. (a) Totem coarse-grained routing architecture [60]; (b) Silicon Hive coarse-grained routing architecture [220]. GPR: General Purpose Registers, MULT: Multiplier. RF: register file, LS: Load/Store Unit.

Totem reconfigurable system [60]; the interconnect is designed to be flexible and to provide arbitrary connection patterns between FUs. On the other hand, the routing architecture in Figure 6.7b, which is used in the Silicon Hive reconfigurable system, is less flexible, but faster and smaller [220]. In the Silicon Hive architecture, only connections between units that are likely to communicate are provided.

6.5.3 Software Configurable Processors

Software configurable processors are devices introduced by Stretch. They have an architecture that couples a conventional instruction processor to a reconfigurable fabric to allow application programs to dynamically customize the instruction set. Such architectures have two benefits. First, they offer significant performance gains by exploiting data parallelism, operator specialization, and deep pipelines. Second, application builders can develop their programs using the Stretch C compiler without having expertise in electronic design.

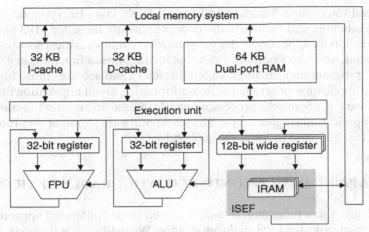

Figure 6.8 The Stretch S6 Software Configurable Processor Engine [230]. IRAM denotes embedded memory for the instruction set extension fabric (ISEF).

A software configurable processor consists of a conventional 32-bit RISC processor coupled with a programmable instruction set extension fabric (ISEF). There are also an ALU for arithmetic and logic operations and a floating-point unit (FPU) for floating-point operations. Figure 6.8 shows the S6 Software Configurable Processor Engine.

The ISEF consists of an array of blocks, each containing an array of 4-bit ALUs and an array of multiplier elements, interconnected by a programmable routing fabric. The 4-bit ALUs can be cascaded through a fast carry circuit to form up to 64-bit ALUs. Each 4-bit ALU may also implement up to four 3-input logic functions, with four register bits for extension instruction state variables or for pipelining.

The ISEF supports multiple application-specific instructions as extension instructions. Arguments to extension instructions are provided from 32 wide registers, which are 128 bits wide. Each extension instruction may read up to three 128-bit operands and write up to two 128-bit results. A rich set of dedicated load and store instructions are provided to move data between the 128-bit wide register and the 128-bit wide cache and memory subsystem. The ISEF supports deep pipelining by allowing extension instructions to be pipelined.

In addition to the load/store model, a group of extension instructions may also define arbitrary state variables to be held in registers within the ISEF. State values may be read and modified by any extension instruction in the group, thereby reducing the Wide Register traffic.

In addition to the Software Configurable Processor Engine, there is also a programmable accelerator, which consists of a list of functions implemented in dedicated hardware. These functions include motion estimation for video encoding, entropy coding for H.264 video, cryptographic operations based on

Advanced Encryption Standard (AES) and Triple Data Encryption Standard (3DES) schemes, and various audio codecs including those for MP3 and AC3.

To develop an application, the programmer identifies critical sections to be accelerated, writes one or more extension instructions as functions in a variant of the C programming language called Stretch C, and accesses those functions from the application program. Further information about application mapping for software configurable processors can be found in the next section, and related application studies for the Stretch S5 Software Configurable Processor Engine can be found in Sections 7.6.2 and 7.7.2.

6.6 MAPPING DESIGNS ONTO RECONFIGURABLE DEVICES

The resources in a reconfigurable device need to be configured appropriately to implement a design for a given application. We shall look at the ways designs are mapped onto an FPGA and onto a software configurable processor.

A typical tool flow for an FPGA is shown in Figure 6.9 [56]. In the conventional tool flow, HDLs such as VHDL and Verilog are widely used to target commercial devices to describe the circuit to be implemented in the FPGA. The description of the circuit is written at the register transfer level (RTL), which specifies the operations at each clock cycle. The description is then synthesized to a netlist of logic blocks before being placed and routed for the FPGA.

In the first stage of the synthesis process, the datapath operations in an RTL design such as control logic, memory blocks, registers, adders, and multipliers are identified and elaborated into a set of basic boolean logic gates such as AND, OR, and XOR.

Next, the netlist of basic gates is optimized independent of the FPGA architecture. The optimization includes: boolean expression minimization, removing the redundant logic, buffering sharing, retiming, and finite-state machine encoding. The optimized netlist of basic gates is then mapped to the specific FPGA architecture such as Xilinx Virtex devices or Altera Stratix devices. There is further optimization based on the specific architecture such as carry chains for adders and dedicated shift functions in logic block for shift registers. The final stage in the synthesis process is packing and clustering groups of several LUTs and registers into logic blocks like Figure 6.4. The packing and clustering minimize the number of connections between different logic blocks. After the synthesis process, the logic blocks in the mapped netlist are placed onto the FPGA based on the different optimization goals, such as circuit speed, routability, and wire length. Once the location of the logic blocks is determined, the connection between I/Os, logic blocks, and other embedded elements are routed onto the programmable routing resources in FPGA. The routing process determines which programmable switches should be used to connect the logic block input and output pins. Finally, a configuration bitstream for all inputs and outputs, logic blocks, and routing resources for the circuit in specific FPGA is generated.

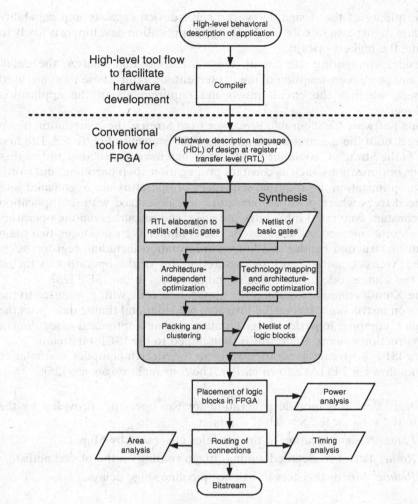

Figure 6.9 Tool flow for FPGA.

The above description covers design mapping for fine-grained FPGA resources. Many reconfigurable devices also have coarse-grained resources for computation and for storage (see Section 6.5.1), so FPGA design tools need to take such resources into account.

To improve productivity, high-level programming languages are included in the tool flow for FPGAs (the upper part of Figure 6.9). These languages and tools, such as AutoPilot [272], Harmonic [159], and ROCC [248], enable application developers to produce designs without detailed knowledge of the implementation technology. Some of these compilers are able to extract parallelism in the computation from the source code, and to optimize for pipelining. Such tools often improve productivity of application developers, at the expense of the quality of the design. However, since device capacity and capability continue to increase rapidly, productivity of application developers is likely to become the highest priority.

Besides configuring the circuit, there are tools that analyze the delay, area, and power consumption of the implemented circuit. These tools are used to check whether the circuit meets the requirements of the application developer.

For a Software Configurable Processor from Stretch, the compilation needs to target both the execution unit and the ISEF shown in Figure 6.8. The first stage of the Stretch C compiler [25] takes an extension instruction and applies various optimizations, such as constant propagation, loop unrolling, and word-length optimization. In addition, sequences of operators are aggregated into balanced trees where possible; operators are specialized with multiplication by a constant converted into shifts and adds; and resources among operators for different instructions are shared. The compiler then produces two main outputs: instruction header and latency information including register usage for the Xtensa compiler, and a structured netlist of the operators extracted from the source code for mapping to the resources in the ISEF [25].

The Xtensa compiler compiles the application code with references to the extension instructions. It uses the instruction header and timing data from the Stretch C compiler to perform register allocation and optimized scheduling of the instruction stream. The result is then linked to the ISEF bitstream.

The ISEF bitstream generation stage in the Stretch compiler is similar to the tool flow for FPGAs shown earlier. The four main stages are [25]:

- *Map.* Performs module generation for the operators provided by the initial stage of the Stretch C compiler.
- *Place.* Assigns location to the modules generated by Map.
- *Route.* Performs detailed, timing-driven routing on the placed netlist.
- *Retime.* Moves registers to balance pipeline stage delays.

The linker packages the components of the application into a single executable file, which contains a directory of the ISEF configurations for the operating system or the run-time system to locate instruction groups for dynamic reconfiguration.

6.7 INSTANCE-SPECIFIC DESIGN

Instance-specific design is often used in customizing both hardware and software. The aim for instance-specific design is to optimize an implementation for a particular computation. The main benefits are improving speed and reducing resource usage, leading to lower power and energy consumption at the expense of flexibility.

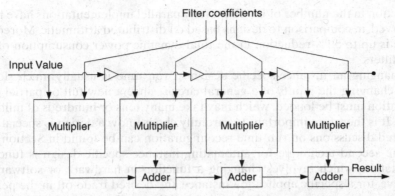

Figure 6.10 An FIR filter containing two-input multipliers that support variable filter coefficients. The triangular blocks denote registers [197].

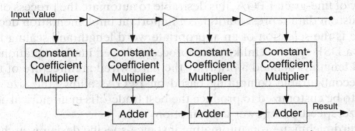

Figure 6.11 An FIR filter containing one-input constant-coefficient multipliers that support instance-specific filter coefficients [197].

We describe three techniques for automating instance-specific design. The first technique is constant folding: propagating static input values through a computation to eliminate unnecessary hardware or software. As an example, an instance-specific version of the hardware design in Figure 6.10 specialized to particular filter coefficients is shown in Figure 6.11. The improvement in efficiency is due to the fact that one-input constant-coefficient multipliers are smaller and faster than two-input multipliers.

The ability to implement specialized designs, while at the same time providing flexibility by allowing different specialized designs to be loaded onto a device, can allow reconfigurable logic to be more effective than ASICs in implementing some applications. For other applications, performance improvements from optimizing designs to a particular problem instance can help to shift the price/performance ratio away from ASICs and toward FPGAs.

Significant benefits for instance-specific design have been reported for a variety of applications. For FIR (Finite Impulse Response) filters, a modified common subexpression elimination algorithm can be used to reduce the number of adders used in implementing constant-coefficient multiplication [180]. Up to 50% reduction in the number of FPGA slices and up to 75%

reduction in the number of LUTs for fully parallel implementations have been observed, in comparison to designs based on distributed arithmetic. Moreover, there is up to 50% reduction in the total dynamic power consumption of the FIR filters.

Changing an instance-specific design at run time is usually much slower than changing the inputs of a general circuit, since a new full or partial configuration must be loaded, which may take many tens or hundreds of milliseconds. It is therefore important to carefully choose how a design is specialized. Related discussions on run-time reconfiguration can be found in Section 6.9.

The second technique for automating instance-specific design is function adaptation, which involves changing a function in hardware or software to achieve, for a specific application instance, the desired trade-off in the performance or resource usage of the function and the quality of the result produced by the function.

An example of function adaptation is word-length optimization. Given the flexibility of fine-grain FPGA, it is desirable to automate the process of finding a good custom data representation. An important implementation decision to automate is the selection of an appropriate word length and scaling for each signal in a DSP system. Unlike microprocessor-based implementations where the word length is defined a priori by the hard-wired architecture of the processor, reconfigurable computing based on FPGAs allows the size of each variable to be customized to produce the best trade-offs in numerical accuracy, design size, speed, and power consumption.

The third technique for automating instance-specific design is architecture adaptation, which involves changing the hardware and software architecture to optimize for a specific application instance, such as supporting relevant custom instructions. We shall discuss this technique in more detail in the next section.

An illustration of the above three techniques is given in Table 6.3. Further information about instance-specific design can be found elsewhere [197].

TABLE 6.3   Some Illustrations of Instance-Specific Design

Technique	Purpose	Example	Benefits in Example
Constant folding	Optimize operation for static input values	FIR filter [180]	Up to 50% reduction in dynamic power consumption
Function adaptation	Optimize function for quality of result	Word-length optimization [62]	87% reduction in power consumption
Architecture adaptation	Optimize architecture for application instance	Instruction processor customization [77]	Speed improved by 72%, area increased by 3%

6.8 CUSTOMIZABLE SOFT PROCESSOR: AN EXAMPLE

This section describes a multithreaded soft processor called CUSTARD with a customizable instruction set [77]. It illustrates the material from the preceding sections: we show how an instruction processor can be customized by adapting the architecture to support different types of multithreading and custom instructions; we then present the associated tool flow targeting reconfigurable technology.

CUSTARD supports multiple contexts within the same processor hardware. A context is the state of a thread of execution, specifically the state of the registers, stack, and program counter. Supporting threads at the hardware level brings two significant benefits. First, a context switch—changing the active thread—can be accomplished within a single cycle, enabling a uniprocessor to interleave execution of independent threads with little or no overhead. Second, a context switch can be used to hide latency where a single thread would otherwise busy-wait.

The major cost of supporting multiple threads stems from the additional register files required for each context. Fortunately, current FPGAs are rich in on-chip block memories that could be used to implement large register files. Additional logic complexity must also be added to the control of the processor and the current thread must be recorded at each pipeline stage. However, the bulk of the pipeline and the FUs are effectively shared between multiple threads, so we would expect a significant area reduction over a multiprocessor configuration.

Instances of CUSTARD processors are generated using a parameterizable model. The key elements of this parameterizable model are shown in Figure 6.12. This model is used both in instantiating a synthesizable hardware description and in configuring a cycle-accurate simulator.

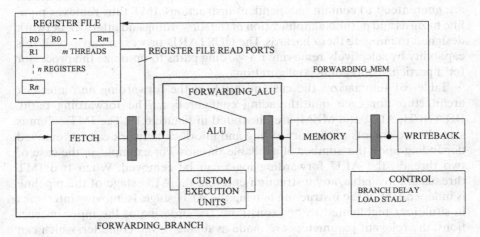

Figure 6.12 CUSTARD microarchitecture showing threading, register file, and forwarding network parameterizations.

The CUSTARD base architecture is typical of a soft processor, with a fully bypassed and interlocked 4-stage pipeline. It is a load/store RISC architecture supporting the MIPS integer instruction set. It is also capable of augmenting the pipeline with custom instructions using spare portions of the MIPS opcode space.

There are four sets of parameters for customizing CUSTARD. The first set covers multithreading support: one can specify the number of threads and the threading type, either block multithreading (BMT) or interleaved multithreading (IMT). The second set covers custom instructions and the associated datapaths at the execution stage of the pipeline as well as custom memory blocks. The third set covers the forwarding and interlock architecture: whether the Branch delay slot, the Load delay slot, and the forwarding paths are necessary. The fourth set covers the register file: the number of registers and the number of register file ports.

Two types of multithreading, BMT and IMT, are supported. Both types simultaneously maintain the context—the state of registers, program counter, and so on—of multiple independent threads. The types of threading differ in the circumstances that context switches are triggered.

BMT triggers a context switch as a result of some run-time event in the currently active thread, for example, a cache miss, an explicit "yield" of control, or the start of some long latency operation such as a custom instruction. When only a single thread is available, the BMT processor behaves exactly as a conventional single-threaded processor. When multiple threads are available, any latency in the active thread is hidden by a context switch. The context switch is triggered at the execution stage of the pipeline, such that the last instruction fetched must be flushed and refilled from the new active thread.

IMT performs a mandatory context switch every single cycle, resulting in interleaved execution of the available threads. IMT permits simplification of the processor pipeline since, given sufficient threads, certain pipeline stages are guaranteed to contain independent instructions. IMT thus removes pipeline hazards and permits simplification of the forwarding and interlock network designed to mitigate these hazards. The CUSTARD processor can exploit this capability by selectively removing forwarding paths to optimize the processor for a particular threading configuration.

Table 6.4 summarizes the customization of the forwarding and interlock architecture for each multithreading configuration. The forwarding paths, BRANCH, ALU, and MEM, are illustrated in Figure 6.12. The IMT columns show how elements of the forwarding and interlock network can be removed depending upon the number of available threads. For example, in the case of two threads, the ALU forwarding logic can be removed. When two IMT threads are available, any instruction entering the ALU stage of the pipeline is independent of the instruction leaving the ALU stage. Removing interlocks in situations highlighted by "*" constrains the ordering of the input instructions; the relevant parameters are made available to the compiler, which can then adapt the scheduling of instructions.

TABLE 6.4 Summary of Forwarding Paths (As Shown in Figure 5.12) and Interlocks That Can Be "Optimized Away" for Single-Threaded, Block Multithreaded (BMT), and Interleaved Multithreaded (IMT) Parameterizations

Disable Configuration Number of Threads	BMT ≥ 1	IMT 2	IMT ≥ 4
FORWARDING BRANCH		√	√
FORWARDING ALU	√	√	
FORWARDING MEM		√	
BRANCH DELAY	√*	√	√
LOAD INTERLOCK	√*	√	√

*Optimizing away this element in this configuration changes the compiler scheduler behavior to prevent hazards.

Multiple contexts are supported by multiple register files that are implemented as dual-port RAM on the FPGA. Each register file access is indexed by the register number and also the ID of the thread that generated the access. Each register file is also parameterizable in terms of the number of ports and the number of registers per thread. Increasing the number of register file ports allows custom instructions to be selected by the compiler that take a greater number of operands.

An approach based on compiling a parallel imperative language into hardware [191] is used to implement the parameterizable processor. This implementation of CUSTARD provides a framework for parameterization of the processor together with a route to hardware. The associated compiler outputs MIPS integer instructions and custom instructions to optimize CUSTARD for a given application; Table 6.5 shows the custom instructions for some benchmarks.

Figure 6.13 shows the flow through the CUSTARD tools. Custom instructions are generated based on a technique known as similar sub-instructions [77]. Prior to finding custom instructions, a preoptimization stage performs standard source-level optimizations together with loop unrolling to expose loop parallelism. After custom instructions have been selected, custom and base instructions are scheduled to minimize pipeline stalls. This scheduling stage is parameterizable to support the microarchitectural changes afforded by the CUSTARD multithreading modes.

The result of compilation comprises hardware datapaths to implement custom instructions and software to execute on the customized processor. Custom instruction datapaths are added to the CUSTARD processor, and the decoding logic is revised to map new instructions to unused portions of the opcode space.

There is a cycle-accurate simulator based upon the SimpleScalar framework [30]. The simulator can be configured directly from the processor hardware description and simulates a parameterizable memory system.

Five benchmarks—Blowfish, Colourspace, AES, discrete cosine transform (DCT), and SUSAN—have been developed for a CUSTARD processor

TABLE 6.5 A Summary of the Custom Instructions Automatically Generated for a Set of Benchmarks

Benchmark	Custom Instruction(s) (Input Registers $r_0 - r_3$, Immediate Value imm_0)	Num. Uses	Latency (Cycles)	BRAM (Bytes)
Blowfish	$LUT(r_0 \gg 24) + LUT(r_1 \gg 16)$	2	1	1024
	$LUT([r_0 \gg 8]\&255)$	2	1	
Color space	$([r_0 \gg 8]\&0xFF)|(r_1\&0xFF00)$ $|([r_2 \ll 8]\&0xFF0000)$	1	1	32
DCT	$LUT(r_1) + r_2 * (r_0 \ll 8)$	65	2	64
	$LUT(r_1) + r_2 * ([r_0\&255] - 128)$	65	2	
Edge detect	$LUT(r_0 + 1 + imm_0)$	3	1	64
Susan	$LUT(r_0)$	31	1	516
AES	$LUT(r_0) \wedge LUT(r_1 \gg 8)$ $\wedge LUT(r_2 \gg 16) \wedge LUT(r_3 \gg 24)$	64	1	1024

Inputs $r_0 - r_3$ are allocated to registers from the general purpose file. $LUT(a) =$ table lookup from dedicated block RAM (BRAM) address a. "Num. Uses" demonstrates the extent of reuse by showing the number of times the instruction is used in the benchmark assembly code. Latency is the number of execution cycles required before the output is available to the forwarding network or in the register file.

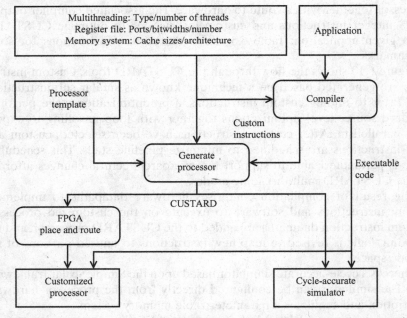

Figure 6.13 Tool flow for the CUSTARD processor customized for a particular application.

implemented on a Xilinx XC2V2000 FPGA. It is found that the IMT4 (IMT with four threads) and BMT4 (BMT with four threads) configurations add only 28% and 40% area, respectively, to the single-threaded processor, while allowing interleaved execution of four threads with no software overhead. Moreover, custom instructions give a significant performance increase, an average of 72% with a small area overhead above the same configuration without custom instructions, an average of only 3%. CUSTARD accelerates AES by 355%.

The IMT processors without custom instructions provide a higher maximum clock rate than both BMT (41% higher) and single-threaded (5% higher) processors. The number of cycles is also reduced by an average of 10%. The IMT processors hide pipeline latencies by tightly interleaving independent threads. We anticipate that the relatively low (10%) improvement is caused by the short latency of the custom instructions generated (Table 6.5), at most two cycles in every case. It is not possible to build longer latency instructions within the register file port constraints, so we expect that deeply pipelined processors or floating point custom instructions are needed to create latencies long enough for significant benefit in this area. However, the IMT processors allow a higher maximum clock rate by removing the forwarding logic around the ALU. The ALU forwarding logic is necessarily on the critical path in the BMT and single-threaded processors, as indicated by the timing analyzer reports.

6.9 RECONFIGURATION

There are many motivations for reconfiguration. One motivation is to share resources that are not required concurrently. Another motivation is to upgrade to support new functions, new standards, or new protocols. A third reason is to adapt the hardware based on run-time conditions.

Run-time reconfiguration has shown promise for many applications, including automotive systems [35], high-performance computing [81], interconnection networks [161], video processing [211], and adaptive Viterbi decoding [241]. The treatment below abstracts from the specific technology, focusing on overhead analysis of designs involving run-time reconfiguration.

6.9.1 Reconfiguration Overhead Analysis

Adapting an architecture to specific applications aims to improve performance by applying application-specific optimizations. However the performance gained by adaptation has to outweigh the cost of reconfiguration. Consider a software function $f()$ that takes t_{si} time to execute on an architecture with a standard, general-purpose instruction set. When adapted to support a custom instruction, it takes t_{ci} time to execute, and can be expressed as a fraction of the original execution time as αt_{si}, where $0 < \alpha < 1$. The device on which $f()$

executes requires t_r time to reconfigure. We define a reconfiguration ratio R that helps us decide if reconfiguration to this new architecture is desirable by analyzing the overhead involved:

$$R = \frac{t_{si}}{t_{ci} + t_r} = \frac{t_{si}}{\alpha t_{si} + t_r}. \tag{6.1}$$

The reconfiguration ratio R gives us a measure of the benefits of reconfiguring to the new adapted architecture; R provides the improvement factor of the new implementation after reconfiguration, over the current implementation. The point where $R = 1$ is the threshold: if $R > 1$, reconfiguration will be beneficial. It is, however, important to note that an R value of 2 does not necessarily translate to an overall twofold system performance increase. The maximum reconfiguration ratio R_{max} is a measure of the absolute performance gain, discounting reconfiguration time. It is the maximum possible R value for a custom instruction. This is determined as follows:

$$R_{max} = \lim_{t_r \to 0} R = \frac{t_{si}}{t_{ci}} = \frac{1}{\alpha}. \tag{6.2}$$

The maximum potential reconfiguration ratio R_{pot} is a measure of the maximum rate at which performance improvement is possible; it gives an idea of how quickly a custom instruction will cross the reconfiguration threshold:

$$R_{pot} = \lim_{\alpha \to 0} R = \frac{t_{si}}{t_r}. \tag{6.3}$$

R_{pot} provides an indication on the granularity of reconfiguration and size of functions that will benefit from adaptation. A function with a higher R_{pot} value can be adapted more easily. It can be shown that:

$$\frac{t_{ci}}{t_{si}} = \frac{R_{pot} - 1}{R_{pot}}. \tag{6.4}$$

Hence an R_{pot} of 5 means that the custom instruction produced need only be four-fifths the speed of the original software version, before it becomes worth implementing. An R_{pot} of 4 requires the custom instruction to be three-fourths the speed of the original, while an R_{pot} of 3, two-thirds the speed of the original, and so on.

If function $f()$ has an R_{pot} value of 1, the adaptation and subsequent reconfiguration of that function will not be beneficial.

The reconfiguration ratio can also be described in terms of the number of clock cycles of an FIP. Consider a software function $f()$, which takes t_{si} units of time to execute. The function takes n_{si} clock cycles to execute, and the cycle time is T_{si}. The function $f()$ is called F times over the period we are investigating, in this case one execution of the application. Similarly with t_{ci}:

$$t_{si} = n_{si}T_{si}F$$
$$t_{ci} = n_{ci}T_{ci}F. \qquad (6.5)$$

The reconfiguration time t_r can be rewritten as the product of the reconfiguration cycle time T_r and the number of configuration cycles n_r. The reconfiguration cycle time, T_r, is platform dependent and is independent of the cycle time of designs implemented on the programmable device. The number of configuration cycles models the time required for either full or partial reconfiguration. In full reconfiguration, n_r is a constant associated with a particular programmable device; in partial reconfiguration, n_r varies with the amount of changes in the configuration. n_r may also be reduced through improvements in technology and architectures that support fast reconfiguration through caches or context switches. There is a factor τ that represents certain reconfiguration overheads, such as stopping of the device prior to reconfiguration and starting of the device after reconfiguration:

$$t_r = n_rT_r + \tau. \qquad (6.6)$$

In modern programmable devices, the time taken to start and stop a device can often be ignored. For instance, in Xilinx Virtex devices, this value can be as small as 10% of the time required to reconfigure a frame, the smallest atomic reconfigurable unit.

Other overheads include the time taken to save and restore the state of the processor. In the most extreme case, the state of the processor includes all storage components in the processor, for instance the register file, pipeline registers, program counter, or cache. By reinstating the state of a processor, a processor can be put back into the condition it was in when the state was saved.

After substituting Equations 6.5 and 6.6 into Equation 6.1, the reconfiguration ratio R becomes:

$$R = \frac{t_{si}}{t_{ci} + t_r} = \frac{n_{si}T_{si}F}{n_{ci}T_{ci}F + n_rT_r + \tau}. \qquad (6.7)$$

This equation can be used to produce a graph showing how R changes with increasing F, the number of times that the function $f()$ is called. When $R > 1$, then reconfiguration is profitable. More information about this approach can be found in a description of the adaptive flexible instruction processor [213].

6.9.2 Trade-Off Analysis: Reconfigurable Parallelism

In the following we describe a simple analytical model [37] for devices that are partially reconfigurable: the larger the configured area, the longer the configuration time. For applications involving repeated independent processing of the same task on units of data that can be supplied sequentially or concurrently, increasing parallelism reduces processing time but increases configuration time. The model below would help identify the optimal trade-off: the amount of parallelism that would result in the fastest overall combination of processing time and configuration time.

The three implementation attributes are performance, area, and storage: processing time t_p for one unit of data, with area A, configuration time t_r, and configuration storage size Ψ. There are s processing steps, and the amount of parallelism is P.

We can also identify parameters of the application: the required data throughput is ϕ_{app}, while there are n units of data n processed between successive configurations. The reconfigurable device has available area A_{max}. The data throughput of the configuration interface is ϕ_{config}.

Designs on volatile FPGAs require external storage for the initial configuration bitstream. Designs using partial run-time reconfiguration also need additional storage for the precompiled configuration bitstreams of the reconfigurable modules. Given A denotes the size of a reconfigurable module in FPGA tiles (e.g., CLBs) and Θ denotes a device-specific parameter that specifies the number of bytes required to configure one tile, the partial bitstream size and storage requirement Ψ (in bytes) of a reconfigurable module is directly related to its area A:

$$\Psi = A \cdot \Theta + h \approx A \cdot \Theta, \tag{6.8}$$

where h denotes the header of configuration bitstreams. In most cases, this can be neglected because the header size is very small.

The time overhead of run-time reconfiguration can consist of multiple components, such as scheduling, context save and restore, as well as the configuration process itself. In our case there is no scheduling overhead as modules are loaded directly as needed. There is also no context that needs to be saved or restored since signal processing components do not contain a meaningful state once a dataset has passed through. The reconfiguration time is proportional to the size of the partial bitstream and can be calculated as follows:

$$t_r = \frac{\Psi}{\phi_{config}} \approx \frac{A \cdot \Theta}{\phi_{config}}. \tag{6.9}$$

ϕ_{config} is the configuration data rate and measured in *bytes per second*. This parameter not only depends on the native speed of the configuration interface but also on the configuration controller and the data rate of the memory where the configuration data are stored.

We can distinguish between run-time reconfigurable scenarios where data do not have to be buffered during reconfiguration and scenarios where data

TABLE 6.6   Buffer Size for Various Functions and Reconfiguration Times

Function	Data Throughput	Buffer Size for a Given Reconfiguration Time		
		100 ms	10 ms	1 ms
Downconversion (16 bits)	800 Mbit/s	80 Mbit	8 Mbit	800 Kbit
Downconversion (14 bits)	700 Mbit/s	70 Mbit	7 Mbit	700 Kbit
Demodulation UMTS	107.52 Mbit/s	10.75 Mbit	1.07 Mbit	107 Kbit
Demodulation GSM	7.58 Mbit/s	758 Kbit	75.8 Kbit	7.58 Kbit
Error correction UMTS	6 Mbit/s	600 Kbit	60 Kbit	6 Kbit
Error correction GSM	22.8 Kbit/s	2.28 Kbit	228 bit	22.8 bit
Decryption UMTS	2 Mbits/s	200 Kbit	20 Kbit	2 Kbit
Encryption GSM	13 Kbit/s	1.3 Kbit	130 bit	13 bit

UMTS: Universal Mobile Telecommunications System, GSM: Global System for Mobile Communications

buffering is needed during reconfiguration. For the latter case we can calculate the buffer size B depending on reconfiguration time t_r and the application data throughput ϕ_{app}:

$$B = \phi_{app} \cdot t_r = \frac{\phi_{app}}{\phi_{config}} \cdot \Psi. \tag{6.10}$$

Table 6.6 outlines the buffer size for several receiver functions and a range of reconfiguration times. We can observe that the data rate is reduced through all stages of the receiver. Hence, a reconfiguration-during-call scenario becomes easier to implement toward the end of the receiver chain. Obviously, the buffer size also increases with the bandwidth of the communication standard and the duration of the reconfiguration time.

A buffer can be implemented with on-chip or off-chip resources. Most modern FPGAs provide fast, embedded RAM blocks that can be used to implement first in–first out buffers. For example, Xilinx Virtex-5 FPGAs contain between 1 and 10 Mbit of RAM blocks. Larger buffers have to be realized with off-chip memories.

The performance of a run-time reconfigurable system is dictated by the reconfiguration downtime. If reconfigurable hardware is used as an accelerator for software functions, overall performance is usually improved despite the configuration overhead. In our case, we use reconfiguration to support multiple hardware functions in order to improve flexibility and reduce area requirements. In this case, the reconfigurable version of a design will have a performance penalty over a design that does not use reconfiguration. The reconfiguration of hardware usually takes much longer than a context switch on a processor. This is due to the relatively large amount of configuration data that need to be loaded into the device. The efficiency I of a reconfigurable design compared to a static design can be expressed as:

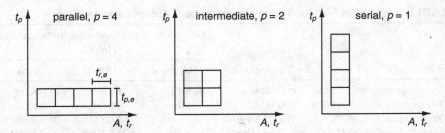

Figure 6.14   Different spatial and temporal mappings of an algorithm with $s = 4$ steps.

$$I = \frac{t_{static}}{t_{reconf}} = \frac{n \cdot t_p}{n \cdot t_p + t_r} = \frac{n}{n + \frac{t_r}{t_p}}. \tag{6.11}$$

The reconfigurable system becomes more efficient by processing more data between configurations and by improving the ratio of configuration time to processing time. We propose a more detailed analysis where we consider the effect of parallelism on processing time and configuration time. Many applications can be scaled between a small and slow serial implementation, and a large and fast parallel or pipelined implementation. FIR filter, AES encryption, or CORDIC (COordinate Rotation DIgital Computer) are examples of such algorithms.

Figure 6.14 illustrates the different spatial and temporal mappings of an algorithm with regard to processing time, area, and reconfiguration time. The processing time per datum t_p is inversely proportional to the degree of parallelism P. It can be calculated based on $t_{p,e}$, the basic processing time of one processing element, s, the number of steps or iterations in the algorithm, and P, the degree of parallelism:

$$t_p = \frac{t_{p,e} \cdot s}{p}. \tag{6.12}$$

Parallelism speeds up the processing of data but slows down reconfiguration. This is because a parallel implementation is larger than a sequential one, and the reconfiguration time is directly proportional to the area as shown in Equation 6.9. The reconfiguration time t_r is directly proportional to the degree of parallelism P, where $t_{r,e}$ is the basic reconfiguration time for one processing element:

$$t_r = t_{r,e} \cdot p. \tag{6.13}$$

We can now calculate the total processing time for a workload of n data items:

$$t_{total} = n \cdot t_p + t_r = \frac{t_{p,e} \cdot s \cdot n}{p} + t_{r,e} \cdot p. \tag{6.14}$$

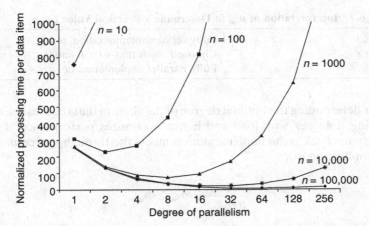

Figure 6.15 Normalized processing times for a range of workload sizes n and different levels of parallelism p. The number of steps s is set to 256 and we assume $t_{r,e} = 5000 t_{p,e}$.

Figure 6.15 illustrates how parallelism can affect the optimality of the processing time. We consider an algorithm with $s = 256$ steps, which is inspired by the observation that filters can have orders of 200 or higher. The plots are normalized to processing time per datum and we assume that the reconfiguration time $t_{r,e}$ of one processing element is 5000 times the processing time $t_{p,e}$ of one processing element. This value can vary depending on the application and target device but we estimate that at least the order of magnitude is realistic for current devices. We can observe that fully sequential implementations are beneficial for small workloads. In this case, the short configuration time outweighs the longer processing time. However, the overall time is still high due to the large influence of the configuration time. Large workloads benefit from a fully parallel implementation since the processing time is more dominant than reconfiguration time. In case of medium workloads, the degree of parallelism can be tuned to optimize the processing time.

In order to find the optimal degree of parallelism, we calculate the partial derivative of the function given in Equation 6.14 with respect to P:

$$\frac{\partial t_{total}}{\partial p} = \frac{t_{p,e} \cdot s \cdot n}{p^2} + t_{r,e}. \tag{6.15}$$

To find the minimum, we set Equation 6.15 to 0 and solve for P:

$$p_{opt} = \sqrt{\frac{s \cdot n \cdot t_{p,e}}{t_{r,e}}}. \tag{6.16}$$

The result p_{opt} is usually a real number, which is not a feasible value to specify parallelism. In order to determine a practical value for P, p_{opt} can be interpreted according to Table 6.7.

TABLE 6.7   Interpretation of p_{opt} to Determine a Practical Value for p

$0 < p_{opt} \leq 1$	Fully serial implementation, $p = 1$
$1 < p_{opt} < s$	Choose P such that $s/P \in \mathbf{Z}$ and $|p_{opt} - p|$ minimal
$S \leq p_{opt}$	Fully parallel implementation, $p = s$

After determining the optimal degree of parallelism that reduces the overall processing time per workload and hence maximizes performance, it is still necessary to check if the implementation meets the throughput requirements of the application Φ_{app}:

$$\frac{n}{t(p)_{total}} = \Phi_{hw} \geq \Phi_{app}. \tag{6.17}$$

The resulting area requirement A also has to be feasible within the total available area A_{max}. In summary, to implement an optimized design according to our model, the following steps have to be carried out:

1. Derive Φ_{app}, s and n from application.
2. Obtain Φ_{config} for target technology.
3. Develop one design and determine t_p and A.
4. Calculate t_r, $t_{p,e}$, and $t_{r,e}$ using Equations 6.9, 6.12, and 6.13.
5. Find p_{opt} from Equation 6.16 and find a feasible value according to Table 6.7.
6. Calculate t_{total} using Equation 6.14 and verify throughput using Equation 6.17.
7. Implement design with P from step 5 and verify if its actual throughput satisfies the requirement.
8. Calculate buffer size B using Equation 6.10 and check $A \leq A_{max}$.

The above methodology can be adopted for a wide variety of applications and target technologies; it will find the highest performing version of the design. In order to find the smallest design that satisfies a given throughput requirement, one can try smaller values for P while checking Equation 6.17.

This approach can also be extended to address energy efficiency for reconfigurable designs [38]; a reconfigurable FIR filter is shown to be up to 49% more energy efficient and up to 87% more area efficient than a nonreconfigurable design.

6.10   CONCLUSIONS

Customization techniques can be applied in various ways to ASIC and to configurable technologies. We provide an overview of such techniques and show how instance-specific designs and custom instruction processors can exploit customizability.

As technology advances, two effects become increasingly prominent:

1. integrated-circuit mask costs grow rapidly, making ASIC less affordable,
2. complexity of SOC design and verification keeps rising.

The technologies discussed in this chapter address these issues directly: various degrees of prefabrication customization reduce both the need for ASIC technology and the design complexity. Reconfigurable technologies such as FPGAs offer significant flexibility in the form of postfabrication customization, at the expense of overheads in speed, area, and power consumption.

Customization and configurability, in addition to their widespread adoption in commercial systems, also constitute exciting research areas, with recent progress in SOC design reuse [215], synthesizable datapath fabric [253], dynamically extensible microprocessors [48], customizable multiprocessors [90], and many others. Moreover, dynamically reconfigurable processors are beginning to be adopted commercially, such as the D-Fabrix from Panasonic, DRP-1 from NEC Electronics, and FE-GA from Hitachi [17]. It is also reported [74] that ARM processor and interconnect technologies, including ARM cell libraries and AMBA interconnect technology, would be adopted and optimized for Xilinx FPGA architectures. There is little doubt that customization and configurability will continue to play an important part in electronic systems for many years to come.

6.11 PROBLEM SET

1. Provide examples for several application domains that would benefit from postfabrication customization.

2. Some reconfigurable devices support pipelined interconnects. What are the pros and cons of pipelined interconnects?

3. Some FPGA companies provide a way of producing a structured ASIC implementation of an FPGA design, effectively removing the reconfigurability. Why do they do that?

4. Early FPGAs contain just a homogeneous array of fine-grained logic cells, while more recent ones are more heterogeneous; in addition to the fine-grained cells, they also contain configurable memory blocks, multiplier arrays, and even processor cores. Explain this evolution of FPGA architectures.

5. A subset of the instructions for a machine M can be accelerated by n times using a coprocessor C.
   (a) A program P is compiled into instructions of M such that a fraction k belongs to this subset. What is the overall speedup that can be achieved using C with M?

(b) The coprocessor C in part (a) above costs j times as much as M. Calculate the minimum fraction of instructions for a program that C has to accelerate, so that the combined system of M and C is j times faster than M.

(c) The performance of M is improving by m times per month. How many months will pass before M alone, without the coprocessor C, can execute the program P in part (a) as fast as the current combined system of M and C?

6. Explain how Equation 6.7 can be generalized to cover m custom instructions.

7. A database search engine makes use of run-time reconfiguration of the hash functions to reduce the amount of processing resources. The search engine contains P processors operating in parallel; each processor can be reconfigured to implement one of h hash functions. The total number of words, w, in the input dataset is divided into ℓ subsets of words; each subset is processed using a particular hash function with one bit per word used to indicate whether a match has occurred. The indicator bit is stored along with the corresponding word in temporary memory, and such temporary data are processed by the next hash function in the processor after reconfiguration. The match indicator bit is updated in each iteration and the process continues until the data have been processed by all h hash functions. Let T_h denote the critical path delay of the hash function processor, and T_r is the time for reconfiguring the processor to support a different hash function. It takes m cycles to access the memory, and the average number of characters per word is c. Consider the worst case that all the hash functions are required all the time—the analysis will become more complex if it is possible to abort the matching process if a match does not occur.

(a) How long does it take to process one subset of data?

(b) How long does it take to process all the data?

(c) Given that each character contains b bits, how many bits are required for the temporary storage?

8. To assess the effect of reconfiguration overheads on energy efficiency, consider developing an analytical model in the same spirit as the one in Section 6.9.2, involving an application with:

- n, the number of packets or data items processed between two successive reconfigurations,
- s, the number of processing steps in the algorithm.

A reconfigurable implementation is characterized by the following parameters:

- A, the area requirement of the implementation,
- P, the amount of parallelism in the implementation,
- t_p, the processing time for one packet or datum,

- t_r, the reconfiguration time,
- P_p, the power consumed during processing,
- P_c, the computation power which is a component of P_p,
- P_o, the power overhead which is a component of P_p,
- Pr, the power consumed during reconfiguration. ·

The reconfigurable device is characterized by:

- ϕ_{config}, the data throughput of the configuration interface,
- Θ, the configuration size per resource or unit of area.

Recall that energy is the product of power consumption and the associated time duration.

Given power consumption for computation, P_c, is directly proportional to P, the degree of parallelism, and there is a constant power consumption overhead, P_o, and a constant power consumption for reconfiguration, P_r:

(a) What is the computation energy E_c for processing n data items?

(b) What is the energy overhead E_o due to P_o?

(c) What is the energy for reconfiguration E_r, given that the reconfiguration time is directly proportional to P?

(d) What is the total energy per data item involved in computation and reconfiguration?

(e) Find the optimal degree of parallelism that minimizes the energy per datum.

7 Application Studies

7.1 INTRODUCTION

This chapter describes various applications to illustrate the opportunities and trade-offs in SOC design. It also shows how some of the techniques described in earlier chapters can be applied.

We first present an approach for developing SOC designs. Then we illustrate the proposed techniques in analyzing simple designs for the Advanced Encryption Standard (AES). Next, we have a look at 3-D computer graphics, showing the use of analysis and prototyping techniques and their application to a simplified PS2 system. After that we describe compression methods for still image and real-time video, as well as a few other applications to illustrate the variety of requirements and architectures of SOCs.

Our discussion separates *requirements* from *designs* that can be shown to meet the requirements. Requirements cover what are needed, while a design includes sufficient implementation detail for it to be evaluated against the requirements.

7.2 SOC DESIGN APPROACH

Figure 7.1 shows a simplified SOC design approach based on the material from the preceding chapters. Chapter 2 introduces five big issues in SOC design: performance, die area, power consumption, reliability, and configurability. These issues provide the basis on which design specification and run-time requirements for SOC designs can be captured. An initial design can then be developed, which would show promise in meeting the key requirements. This initial design can then be systematically optimized by addressing issues related to memory (Chapter 4), interconnect (Chapter 5), processor (Chapter 3) and cache (Chapter 4), and customization and configurability (Chapter 6). This process is repeated until reaching a design that meets the specification and run-time requirements. More details will be given later in this section.

Following this approach, however, can appear to be a formidable task. System design is often more challenging than component or processor design,

Computer System Design: System-on-Chip, First Edition. Michael J. Flynn and Wayne Luk.
© 2011 John Wiley & Sons, Inc. Published 2011 by John Wiley & Sons, Inc.

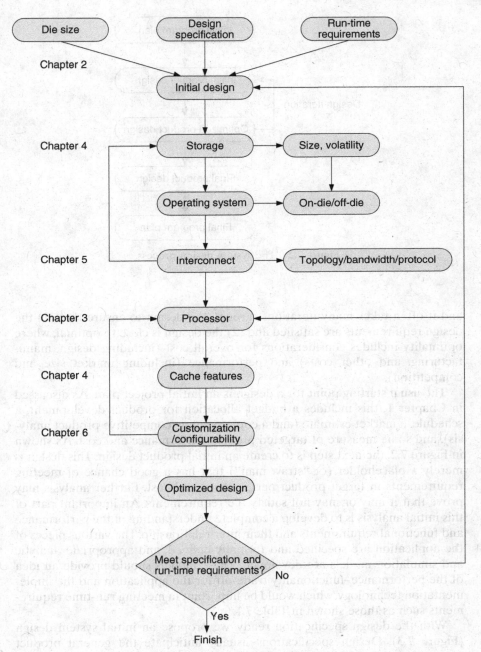

Figure 7.1 An approach for designing SOC devices.

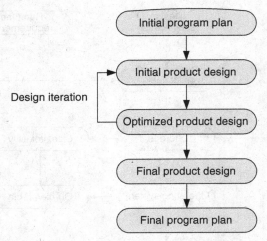

Figure 7.2   The system design process.

and it often takes many iterations through the design to ensure that (1) the design requirements are satisfied and (2) the design is close to optimal, where optimality includes considerations for overall cost (including design, manufacturing, and other costs) and performance (including market size and competition).

The usual starting point for a design is an initial project plan. As discussed in Chapter 1, this includes a budget allocation for product development, a schedule, a market estimate (and a corresponding competitive product analysis), and some measure of targeted product performance and cost. As shown in Figure 7.2, the next step is to create an initial product design. This design is merely a placeholder (or "straw man") that has a good chance of meeting requirements in target product performance and cost. Further analysis may prove that it may or may not satisfy the requirements. An important part of this initial analysis is to develop a complete understanding of the performance and functional requirements and their inter-relationship. The various pieces of the application are specified and formally defined, and appropriate analytic and simulation models are developed. These models should provide an idea of the performance–functionality trade-off for the application and the implementation technology, which would be important in meeting run-time requirements such as those shown in Table 7.1.

With the design specification ready, we propose an initial system design (Figure 7.3). Design specifications usually anticipate the general product layout, addressing issues such as having all on one die or system on a board, operating system selection, total size of memory, and backing store. The development of the initial design then proceeds as follows, to ensure that the critical requirements are met:

REQUIREMENTS AND DESIGN

The input to the requirement understanding task is usually a requirement specification from customers or from a marketing study. The output is often a functional requirement specification for the design. The specification may be detailed and carefully written for review; this is the case in large companies. However, the specification may also be brief, captured, for example, in a spreadsheet; this is often the case in small companies and startups. The specification, whether detailed or brief, is essential for design review, documentation, and verification, and must be clear and consistent. Moreover, mathematical, executable, or diagrammatic descriptions can be used to capture data flow and control flow for the main operations or selected functions of the SOC, during various system design stages. Such descriptions can help designers to understand the functional requirements. Once the functional requirements are understood, these descriptions can be mapped to possible implementations of the main components and their interactions in the SOC.

1. Selection and allocation of memory and backing store. This generally follows the discussions in Chapter 4.
2. Once the memory has been allocated, the processor(s) are selected. Usually a simple base processor is selected to run the operating system and manage the application control functions. Time critical processes can be assigned to special processors (such as VLIW and SIMD processors discussed in Chapter 1 and Chapter 3) depending on the nature of the critical computation.
3. The layout of the memory and the processors generally defines the interconnect architecture covered in Chapter 5. Now the bandwidth requirements must be determined. Again the design specifications and processor target performance largely determine the overall requirement but cache memory can act as an important buffer element in meeting specifications.

TABLE 7.1   Run-Time Requirements Showing Various Constraints to Be Met for Some Video and Graphics Applications

Application	Real-Time Constraint (fps)	Other Constraints
Video conference	16	Frame size, error rate, missed frames
3-D graphics	30	Image size, shading, texture, color

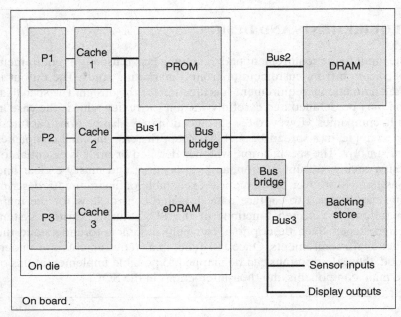

Figure 7.3   An example of an initial design, with three processors P1, P2, and P3.

Usually the initial design assumes that the interconnect bandwidth is sufficient to match the bandwidth of memory.

4. The memory elements are analyzed to assess their effects on latency and bandwidth. The caches or data buffers are sized to meet the memory and interconnect bandwidth requirements. Some details can be covered later, so for instance bus latency is usually determined without considering the effects of bus contention. Processor performance models are developed.

5. Some applications require peripheral selection and design, which must also meet bandwidth requirements. Example peripherals are shown in Section 7.5.1, which covers the JPEG system for a digital still camera, and also in Section 8.7, which covers radio frequency and optical communications for future autonomous SOCs.

6. Rough estimates of overall cost and performance are determined.

Following initial design, the design optimization and verification phase begins. This phase is supported by various tools, including profiling facilities and optimizing compilers. All components and allocations are reassessed with the view toward lowering cost (area) and improving both performance and functionality. For instance, customization and configurability techniques, such as the use of custom instructions or the adoption of run-time reconfiguration as discussed in Chapter 6, can be applied to enhance flexibility or performance. As another example, software optimizations, such as those that improve locality of reference, can often provide large performance improvement for little hardware cost. The optimization would, where applicable, involve repartitioning between hardware and software, which could affect the complexity of embedded software programs [151] and the choice of real-time operating systems [34].

After each optimization, its impact on accuracy, performance, resource usage, power and energy consumption, and so on needs to be analyzed. Also the design needs to be verified to make sure that its correctness would not be affected by the optimizations [53]. Such analysis and verification can often be supported by electronic system-level design tools (see box), as well as by prototyping.

ESL: ELECTRONIC SYSTEM LEVEL DESIGN AND VERIFICATION

There does not seem to be a standard description of what ESL covers. Wikipedia describes ESL design and verification to be "an emerging electronic design methodology that focuses on the higher abstraction level concerns first and foremost." Another definition of ESL is the utilization of appropriate abstractions in order to increase comprehension about a system, and to enhance the probability of a successful implementation of functionality in a cost-effective manner [32]. Various ESL tools have been developed, which are capable of supporting a design flow that can generate systems across hardware and software boundaries from an algorithmic description [108].

When the design appears optimal after several iterations, another complete program plan is developed to understand any changes made to schedule fixed costs and to address issues involved in system integration and testing. Finally, the product market is assessed based on the final design and the overall program profitability can be assessed.

7.3   APPLICATION STUDY: AES

We adopt the AES as a case study to illustrate how techniques discussed in the preceding chapters can be used for exploring designs that meet specified requirements.

7.3.1   AES: Algorithm and Requirements

The AES cipher standard [69] has three block sizes: 128 (AES-128), 192 (AES-192), and 256 (AES-256) bits. The whole process from original data to

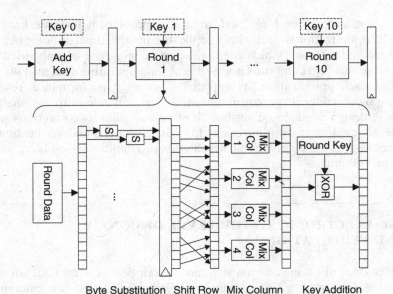

Byte Substitution   Shift Row   Mix Column   Key Addition

Figure 7.4   Fully pipelined AES architecture [107].

encrypted data involves one initial round, $r - 1$ standard rounds, and one final round. The major transformations involve the following steps (Figure 7.4):

- *SubBytes.* An input block is transformed byte by byte by using a special design substitution box (S-Box).
- *ShiftRows.* The bytes of the input are arranged into four rows. Each row is then rotated with a predefined step according to its row value.
- *MixColumns.* The arranged four-row structure is then transformed by using polynomial multiplication over GF (2^8) per column basis.
- *AddRoundKey.* The input block is XOR-ed with the key in that round.

There is one round *AddRoundKey* operation in the initial round; the standard round consists of all four operations above; and the *MixColumns* operation is removed in the final round operation, while the other three operations remain. On the other hand, the inverse transformations are applied for decryption. The round transformation can be parallelized for fast implementation.

Besides the above four main steps, the AES standard includes three block sizes: 128 (AES-128), 192 (AES-192), and 256 (AES-256) bits. The whole block encryption is divided into different rounds. The design supporting AES-128 standard consists of 10 rounds.

Run-time requirements are shown in Table 7.2 for various applications, such as Wi-Fi and VoIP (Voice over Internet Protocol); our task is to find designs that meet one or more of these throughput requirements.

TABLE 7.2   Different Application Throughput Requirements, PAN: Personal Area Network

Application	Throughput requirement
Wi-Fi 802.11b	11 Mbps
Wi-Fi 802.11g	54 Mbps
Wi-Fi 802.11i/802.11n	500 Mbps
Metropolitan area network (MAN) 802.16a	75 Mbps
PAN 802.15 TG4 (low rate)	250 Kbps
PAN 802.15 TG3 (high rate)	55 Mbps
VoIP	64 Kbps
Cisco PIX firewall router	370 Mbps

7.3.2   AES: Design and Evaluation

Our initial design starts with a die size, design specification, and run-time requirement (Figure 7.1). We assume that the requirements specify the use of a PLCC68 (Plastic Leaded Chip carrier) package, with a die size of $24.2 \times 24.2 \, mm^2$.

Our task is to select a processor that meets the area constraint while capable of performing a required function. Let us consider ARM7TDMI, a 32-bit RISC processor. Its die size is $0.59 \, mm^2$ for a 180 nm process, and $0.18 \, mm^2$ for a 90 nm process. Clearly, both processors can fit into the initial area requirement for the PLCC68 package. The cycle count for executing AES from the SimpleScalar tool set is 16,511, so the throughput, given an 115-MHz clock (as advertised by the vendor) with the 180-nm device, is $(115 \times 32)/16,511 = 222.9 \, Kbps$; for a 236-MHz clock with the 90-nm device, the throughput is 457.4 Kbps. Hence the 180-nm ARM7 device is likely to be capable of performing only VoIP in Table 7.2, while the 90 nm ARM7 device should be able to support PAN 802.15 TG4 as well.

Let us explore optimization of this SOC chip such that we can improve the total system throughput without violating the initial area constraint. We would apply the technique used in Chapter 4 for modifying the cache size and evaluate its effect, using facilities such as the SimpleScalar tool set [30] if a software model for the application is available.

Using SimpleScalar with an AES software model, we explore the effects of doubling the block size of a 512-set L1 direct mapped instruction cache from 32 bytes to 64 bytes; the AES cycle count reduces from 16,511 to 16,094, or 2.6%. Assume that the initial area of the processor with the basic configuration without cache is 60K rbe, and the L1 instruction cache has 8K rbe. If we double the size of the cache, we get a total of 76K rbe instead of 68K. The total area increase is over 11%, which does not seem worthwhile for a 2.6% speed improvement.

The ARM7 is already a pipelined instruction processor. Other architectural styles, such as parallel pipelined datapaths, have much potential as shown in Table 7.3; these FPGA designs meet the throughput requirements for all the

TABLE 7.3   Performance and Area Trade-off on a Xilinx Virtex XCV-1000 FPGA [107]

	Basic Iterative	Inner-Round Pipelined	Fully Pipelined
Maximum clock frequency (MHz)	47	80	95
Encrypt/decrypt throughput (128 bits) (Mbps)	521	888	11,300
Area (number of slices)	1228	2398	12,600
Area (number of BRAM)	18	18	80
Slices and BRAM usages	10% and 56%	19% and 56%	103% and 250%

BRAM: block RAM. Note that a fully pipelined design requires more resources than the XCV-1000 device can support.

applications in Table 7.2, at the expense of larger area and power consumption than ASICs [146]. Another alternative, mentioned in Chapter 6, is to extend the instruction set of a processor by custom instructions [28]; in this case they would be specific to AES.

A note of caution: the above discussion is intended to illustrate what conclusions can be drawn given a set of conditions. In practice, various other factors should be taken into account, such as how representative are the numbers derived from, for instance, benchmark results or application scenarios based on the SimpleScalar tool set. In any case, such analysis should only be used for producing evaluations similar to those from back-of-envelope estimates—useful in providing a feel for promising solutions, which should then be confirmed by detailed design using appropriate design tools.

Two further considerations. First, as shown in Figure 7.4, an AES design can be fully pipelined and fitted into an FPGA device. To achieve over 21 Gbit/s throughput, the implementation exploits technology-specific architectures in FPGAs, such as block memories and block multipliers [107].

Second, AES cores are often used as part of a larger system. Figure 7.5 shows one such possibility for implementing the AES core, in the ViaLink FPGA fabric on a QuickMIPS device [116]. This device has a separate 32-bit MIPS 4Kc processor core and various memory and interface elements. Another possibility is to use AES in the implementation of designs involving secure hash methods [88].

7.4   APPLICATION STUDY: 3-D GRAPHICS PROCESSORS

This section considers 3-D graphics accelerators, similar to the Sony PS2 architecture [237]. Our study illustrates two useful techniques in deriving an initial design:

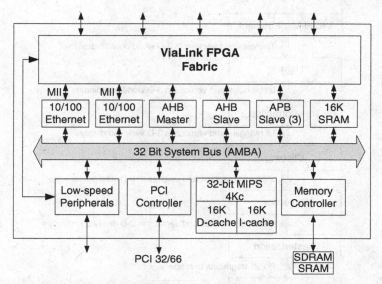

Figure 7.5 QuickMIPS block diagram for the AES SOC system [116].

- *Analysis.* The application is viewed as a high-level algorithm for back-of-envelope-type estimates about, for instance, the amount of computation and communication so that a preliminary choice of design styles and components can be made.
- *Prototyping.* A simplified version of the application is developed using common software tools and off-the-shelf hardware platforms, for example using a standard PC or a general-purpose FPGA platform. The experience gained will suggest areas that are likely to require attention, such as performance bottlenecks. It may also help identify noncritical components that do *not* need to be optimized, saving development time.

The analysis and prototyping activities can often be assisted by ESL techniques and tools [32, 108].

7.4.1 Analysis: Processing

In 3-D graphics, objects are represented by a collection of triangles in 3-D space, and there are lighting and texture effects on each picture element—or pixel—to make objects look realistic. Such 3-D representations are transformed into a 2-D space for viewing. Animation consists of providing successive frames of pixels over time.

There are two main stages in the graphics pipeline (Figure 7.6): transformation and lighting, and rasterization. We cover them in turn.

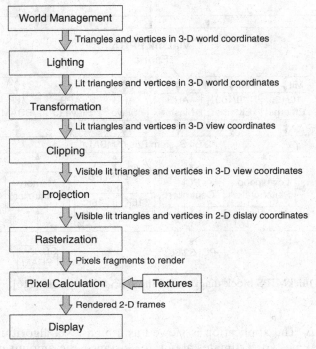

Figure 7.6 3-D graphics pipeline.

Requirements For transformation and lighting, consider v visible triangles per frame, and l light sources; the realism and complexity of the objects improve with larger v and l. To facilitate perspective projection, a system of four coordinates is used: three space dimensions and one homogeneous component capturing the location of the plane to which the 3-D image is projected.

During transformation and lighting, each triangle vertex is transformed from world space to view space, requiring a 4×4 matrix multiplication; then projected into 2-D, requiring a division and a further four multiplies for perspective correction. This can be approximated as about 24 FMACs (floating-point multiply and accumulate) per vertex, where a floating-point division (FDIV) is assumed to take the equivalent of four FMACs. The lighting process requires another 4×4 multiplication to rotate the vertex normal, followed by a dot product and some further calculations. This is approximated as 20 FMACs per light source. This results in $24 + 20l$ FMACs per vertex. In the worst case of three distinct vertices per triangle, $v(72 + 60l)$ FMACs are needed per frame; if vertices between adjacent triangles can be shared, we would only need $v(24 + 20l)$ in the best case.

Let n be the number of triangles processed per second and m be the number of FMAC per second. Given there are f frames per second (fps), $n = fv$ and:

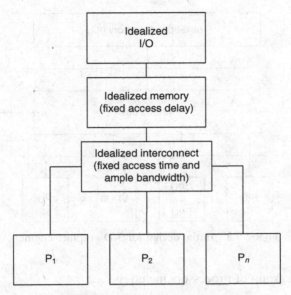

Figure 7.7   Idealized SOC architecture.

$$n \times (24 + 20l) \leq m \leq n \times (72 + 60l). \tag{7.1}$$

If $n = 50M$ $(M = 10^6)$ triangles per second and no lights $(l = 0)$, then $1200M \leq m \leq 3600M$; if $n = 30 \times 10^6$ triangles per second and with one light $(l = 1)$, then $1320\ M \leq m \leq 3960M$.

Design   Let us describe how we come up with a design that meets the requirements. Our initial design is based on the simple structure in Figure 7.7, introduced in Chapter 1.

The proposed design is inspired by the Emotion Engine, which contains two groups of processors as shown in Figure 7.8. The first group of processors includes:

- CPU, a MIPS-III processor with 32 registers, 128 bits, dual issue;
- Floating-point unit (FPU), supporting basic FMAC and floating-point division;
- VPU0, a vector processing unit that can operate as a slave to the MIPS or as an independent SIMD/VLIW processor.
- IPU, an image processing unit for decoding compressed video streams.

These components are connected by a 128-bit bus at 150 MHz.

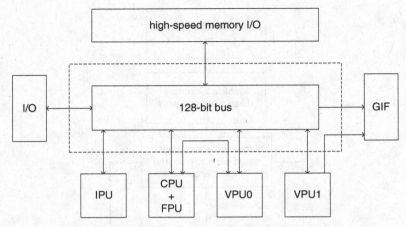

Figure 7.8   Initial design for 3-D graphics engine.

The second group of processors includes:

- VPU1, the same as VPU0, but only operates as a SIMD/VLIW processor.
- GIF, a graphics interface that mainly shunts data onto the graphics synthesizer using a dedicated 128-bit bus.

Since VPU0 and VPU1 each contains four floating-point multipliers at 300 MHz, their performance is given by $300\,\text{MHz} \times 8 = 2400M$ FMAC/s; this value is within the range of $1200M \leq m \leq 3960M$ derived earlier.

There are other components that we do not cover in detail. An example is IPU, an image processing unit for decoding compressed video streams.

Requirements   The rasterization process needs to scan convert each 2-D triangle, calculating the set of output pixels corresponding to each triangle. This is usually performed by stepping vertically along the edges of the triangles using DDA (digital differential analyzer) or another line-drawing method, allowing each horizontal span to be handled at once. Within each span, it is necessary to use more DDAs to interpolate the values of Z (for occlusion testing), color, and texture coordinates where appropriate. We ignore the vertical DDAs and approximate this as requiring $2 + 2t$ DDA steps per pixel.

Design   If each DDA step requires four integer instructions, and the operation at each pixel (such as comparing updating frame and z-buffer) also requires four integer instructions, then the number of instructions for each rendered pixel is:

$$4 + 8(1 + t). \tag{7.2}$$

These steps must be performed each time a pixel is rendered, even if the pixel has already been rendered. Given there are o output pixels in each frame and each output pixel needs to be recalculated p times due to overlapping shapes, the total number of instructions required per frame is

$$(12 + 8t) \times o \times p. \tag{7.3}$$

We would use this result in the prototyping process below. Note that we have ignored the time taken to perform the vertical DDAs, so we would expect there to be some additional computation time that varies with v, but overall computation time is dominated by the per-pixel operation time.

7.4.2 Analysis: Interconnection

In our model of the 3-D graphics pipelines, there are two main intertask logical communications channels: lists of 3-D triangles passed from the creation/management task to the transformation task, and lists of 2-D triangles passed from the transformation task to the rendering task. Both these channels are essentially unidirectional: once a task has passed a set of triangles (2-D or 3-D) onto the next stage, there is no substantial flow of data needed in the other direction apart from obvious data flow signals such as status indicators.

Requirements In the first channel, between world management and transformation, all the 3-D coordinates consist of three single-precision floating point components, requiring $4 \times 3 = 12$ bytes. The minimal triangle size, where each triangle consists only of three coordinates, requires $3 \times 12 = 36$ bytes. However, in most cases there will need to be additional information, such as texture information and lighting information. In order to support lighting, it is sufficient to store the surface normal at each vertex. This applies no matter how many lights are applied, so the size of each vertex then becomes $3 \times (12 + 12 \times \min(l,1))$. Texture information additionally requires the storage of a 2-D texture coordinate for each vertex; assuming floating-point texture coordinates, this adds 8 bytes to each vertex per applied texture. With n visible triangles, the total bandwidth on the channel is:

$$3n \times (12 + 12 \times \min(l, 1) + 8t). \tag{7.4}$$

As an example, given $n = 50 \times 10^6, l = 0, t = 1$, the bandwidth required is 3 GB/s; for $n = 30 \times 10^6, l = 1, t = 1$, the bandwidth required is 2.88 GB/s.

In the second channel, each point is now in screen coordinates, so each point can be represented as two 16-bit integers. In addition the depth of each pixel is needed, but this is stored in greater precision, so the total size is 4 bytes per vertex. Assuming that lights have been applied, the vertices also require a color intensity, requiring 1 byte per channel, or approximately 4 bytes per vertex: $4 + 4 \min(l,1)$. Each texture coordinate must still be applied individually at rasterization, so a 4-byte (2×16 bit integers) coordinate must be retained. This results in a total required bandwidth for the second channel as:

$$3n \times (4 + 4 \times \min(l, 1) + 4t). \tag{7.5}$$

This time, given $n = 50 \times 10^6$, $l = 0$, $t = 1$, the bandwidth required is 1.2 GB/s; for $n = 30 \times 10^6$, $l = 1$, $t = 1$, the bandwidth required is 1.08 GB/s.

Design   As shown in Figure 7.8, the interconnect consists of a 128-bit bus. Since the peak transfer rate of a 128-bit bus at 150 MHz is 2.4 GB/s, which meets the bandwidth required for the second channel but not the first, an additional 64-bit dedicated interface to the rendering engine is included.

7.4.3   Prototyping

A prototype 3-D renderer is written in the C language. This prototype incorporates a world management stage that creates a random pattern of triangles, a transformation stage that projects triangles into 2-D using a single-precision floating point, and a z-buffer-based renderer using integer DDAs. Among the parameters of the renderer that can be varied are:

- number of triangles;
- size of triangles;
- width and height of output.

By adjusting these parameters, it is possible to selectively adjust parameters such as o, v, and p. For example, p can be varied by increasing the size of triangles, as this increases the chance that each triangle is covered by another.

Figure 7.9 shows the changes in execution time on an Athlon 1200 when the number of output pixels are increased. As expected, both the creation and transformation stages show no significant variation as the number of output pixels is increased. In contrast, the rendering stage's execution time is clearly increasing linearly with output pixel count. The fitted line has a correlation coefficient of 0.9895, showing a good linear fit. The fitted linear relationship between rasterization time and pixel count is given by Equation 7.3: $t = o \times 5 \times 10^{-8} + 0.0372$. The large offset of 0.0372 is caused by the per-triangle setup time mentioned (and ignored) in the analysis section. Based on this prototype we might now feel it appropriate to include the effects, as they are clearly more significant than expected.

According to Equation 7.2, the instructions per output pixel is $p \times 12$ in the case that no textures are applied ($t = 0$). In this experiment $P = 1.3$, so the instructions per frame should be 15.6. The reported performance in million instructions per second (MIPS) of the Athlon 1200 is 1400, so according to the model each extra pixel should require $15.6/1.4 \times 10^{-9} = 1.1 \times 10^{-8}$. Comparing the predicted growth of 1.1×10^{-8} with the observed growth of 5×10^{-8}, we see that they differ by a factor of 5. The majority of this error can probably be

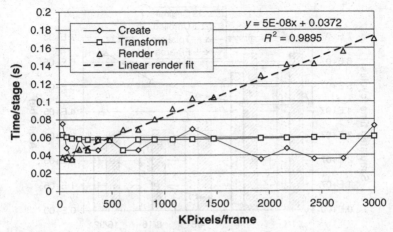

Figure 7.9   Increase in execution times of stages as pixel count increases.

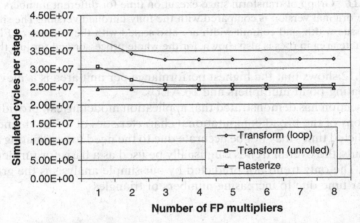

Figure 7.10   Graph of transform stage execution time for different numbers of FPUs when original version is compared to fully unrolled version. The size of the queues, issue width, and commit width are held at a constant (fairly large) value.

attributed to the unoptimized nature of the prototype and to the approximations in our models.

In Figure 7.10 and Figure 7.11 the performance of the transformation stage for different numbers of FPUs is tested using the PISA simulator [30]. When four multipliers are used the performance increases significantly, although there is little benefit when more than four are used. This suggests that a VLIW or SIMD processor that can perform four floating-point operations at once would be efficient. Also shown in the graph is the performance when the matrix multiply loop is unrolled, rather than being implemented as a doubly nested loop. The unrolling allows the processor to use the FPUs to better advantage, but the cost is still significant compared to the speedup. Finally,

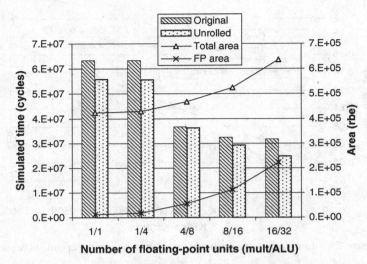

Figure 7.11   Graph of transform stage execution time for different numbers of FPUs when the original version is compared with the fully unrolled version. The size of the queues, issue width, and commit width are also scaled with the number of FPUs. The approximate area in rbes is also shown, for the whole processor and for just the FPUs.

Figure 7.12 shows that the highest performance per unit area is achieved with eight floating-point multipliers and 16 ALUs.

This section has demonstrated that application modeling can provide useful predictions of the broad computational characteristics of a 3-D engine. While the predicted times may not be accurate due to the need for estimating instruction counts, the overall trends can usually be used as a basis for further development. The only trend not predicted by our simple analysis is the growth in rasterizer time due to increasing numbers of triangles.

7.5   APPLICATION STUDY: IMAGE COMPRESSION

A number of intraframe operations are common to both still image compression methods such as JPEG, and video compression methods such as MPEG and H.264. These include color space transformation and entropy coding (EC). Video compression methods usually also include interframe operations, such as motion compensation (MC), to take advantage of the fact that successive video frames are often similar; these will be described in Section 7.6.

7.5.1   JPEG Compression

The JPEG method involves 24 bits per pixel, eight each of red, green, and blue (RGB). It can deal with both lossy and lossless compression. There are three main steps [42].

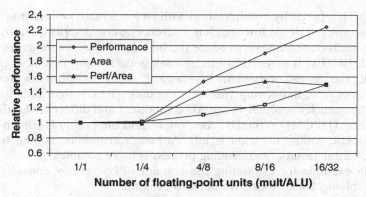

Figure 7.12   Comparison of increases in area and performance for unrolled transform stage. The maximum performance per area is achieved with eight floating-point multipliers (mult) and 16 ALUs.

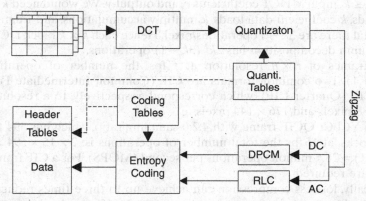

Figure 7.13   Block diagram for JPEG compression. Color space transformation is not shown.

First, color space transformation. The image is converted from RGB into a different color space such as YCbCr. The Y component represents the brightness of a pixel, while the Cb and Cr components together represent the chrominance or color. The human eye can see more detail in the Y component than in Cb and Cr, so the latter two are reduced by downsampling. The ratios at which the downsampling can be done on JPEG are 4:4:4 (no downsampling), 4:2:2 (reduce by factor of 2 in horizontal direction), and most commonly 4:2:0 (reduce by factor of 2 in horizontal and vertical directions). For the rest of the compression process, Y, Cb, and Cr are processed separately in a similar manner. These three components form the input in Figure 7.13.

Second, discrete cosine transform (the DCT block in Figure 7.13). Each component (Y, Cb, Cr) of the image is arranged into tiles of 8×8 pixels each, then each tile is converted to frequency space using a two-dimensional forward

DCT (DCT, type II) by multiplication with an 8×8 matrix. Since much information is covered by the low-frequency pixels, one could apply quantization—another matrix operation—to reduce the high-frequency components.

Third, EC. EC is a special form of lossless data compression. It involves arranging the image components in a "zigzag" order accessing low-frequency components first, employing run-length coding (RLC) algorithm to group similar frequencies together in the AC component and differential pulse code modulation (DPCM) on the DC component, and then using Huffman coding or arithmetic coding on what is left. Although arithmetic coding tends to produce better results, the decoding process is more complex.

As an example for estimating the amount of operations, consider a 2-D DCT involving $k \times k$ blocks. We need to compute:

$$y_i = \sum_{0 < j \le k} c_{i,j} \times j$$

for $0 < i \le k$, input x, DCT coefficients c, and output y. We would need k image data loads, k coefficient data loads, k multiply accumulations, and 1 data store. So in total there are $3k + 1$ operations/pixel. Hence each $k \times k$ block DCT with row–column decomposition has $2k^2 (3k + 1)$ operations.

For frames of $n \times n$ resolution at f fps, the number of operations is $2fn(3k + 1)$. Two common formats are CIF (Common Intermediate Format) and QCIF (Quarter CIF), which correspond, respectively, to a resolution of 352×288 pixels and 176×144 pixels.

For a YCbCr QCIF frame with 4:2:0 sampling ratio, which has 594 tiles of 8×8 blocks, at 15 fps the total number of operations is: $2 \times 15 \times 594 \times 8 \times 8 \times (24 + 1) = 28.5$ million operations per second (MOPS). For a CIF frame, 114 MOPS are required.

Typically, lossless compression can achieve up to three times reduction in size, while lossy compression can achieve up to 25 times reduction.

7.5.2 Example JPEG System for Digital Still Camera

A typical imaging pipeline for a still image camera is shown in Figure 7.14 [128]. The TMS320C549 processor, receiving 16×16 blocks of pixels from SDRAM, implements this imaging pipeline.

Since the TMS320C549 has 32K of 16-bit RAM and 16K of 16-bit ROM, all imaging pipeline operations can be executed on chip since only a small 16×16 block of the image is used. In this way, the processing time is kept short, because there is no need for slow external memory.

This device offers performance up to 100 MIPS, with low power consumption in the region of 0.45 mA/MIPS. Table 7.4 illustrates a detailed cycle count for the different stages of the imaging pipeline software. The entire imaging pipeline, including JPEG, takes about 150 cycles/pixel, or about 150 instructions/pixel given a device of 100 MIPS at 100 MHz.

A TMS320C54x processor at 100 MHz can process 1 megapixel CCD (charge coupled devices) image in 1.5 second. This processor supports a

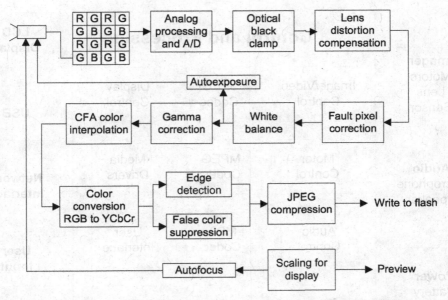

Figure 7.14 Block diagram for a still image camera [128]. A/D: analog to digital conversion; CFA: color filter array.

TABLE 7.4   TMS320C54X Performance [128]

Task	Cycles/Pixel
Preprocessing: for example, gain, white balancing	22
Color space conversion	10
Interpolation	41
Edge enhancement, false color suppression	27
4:1:1 decimation, JPEG encoding	62
Total	152

2 second shot-to-shot delay, including data movement from external memory to on-chip memory. Digital cameras should also allow users to display the captured images on the LCD screen on the camera, or on an external TV monitor. Since the captured images are stored on a flash memory card, playback-mode software is also needed on this SOC.

If the images are stored as JPEG bitstreams, the playback-mode software would decode them, scale the decoded images to appropriate spatial resolutions, and display them on the LCD screen and/or the external TV monitor. The TMS320C54x playback-mode software can execute 100 cycles/pixel to support a 1 second playback of a megapixel image.

This processor requires 1.7 KB for program memory and 4.6 KB for data memory to support the imaging pipeline and compress the image according to the JPEG standard. The complete imaging pipeline software is stored on-chip, which reduces external memory accesses and allows the use of slower

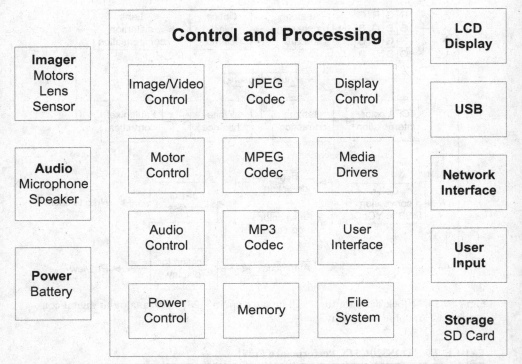

Figure 7.15 Block diagram for a camera chip with video, audio, and networking capabilities.

external memory. This organization not just improves performance, but it also lowers the system cost and enhances power efficiency.

More recent chips for use in digital cameras would need to support, in addition to image compression, also video compression, audio processing, and wireless communication [217]. Figure 7.15 shows some of the key elements in such a chip.

7.6   APPLICATION STUDY: VIDEO COMPRESSION

Table 7.5 summarizes the common video formats used in various applications, together with the associated compression methods such as MPEG1, MPEG2, and MPEG4. Video quality depends on the bitrate and the video resolution—higher bitrate and higher resolution generally mean better video quality, but requiring higher bandwidth.

There is another set of compression methods known as H.261, H.262, H.363, and H.264; some of these are related to the MPEG methods, for instance MPEG2 and H.262 are the same and H.264 corresponds to MPEG4/Part 10. Generally the more recent methods such as H.264 offer higher quality and

TABLE 7.5 Some Common Video Formats

Format	VCD	SVCD	DVD	HDDVD HDTV (WMVHD)	AVI DivX XviD WMV	MOV Quick-Time
Resolution	352×240	480×480	$720 \times 480*$	$1920 \times 1080*$	$640 \times 480*$	$640 \times 480*$
NTSC/PAL	352×288	480×576	$720 \times 576*$	$1280 \times 720*$		
Video compression	MPEG1	MPEG2	MPEG2, MPEG1	MPEG2 (WMV-MPEG4)	MPEG4	MPEG4 (from Sorenson Media)
Video bitrate	1150 Kbps	2000 Kbps†	5000 Kbps†	20 Mbps† (8 Mbps†)	1000 Kbps†	1000 Kbps†
Size/min	10 MB/min	10–20 MB/min	30–70 MB/min	150 MB/min† (60 MB/min†)	4–10 MB/min	4–20 MB/min

From http://www.videohelp.com/svcd.
*Approximate resolution, can be higher or lower.
†Approximate bitrate, can be higher or lower.
Kbps, thousand bits per second; Mbps, million bits per second; min, minutes.

higher compression ratio. In the following we shall provide an overview of some of these video compression methods [42, 270], without going into the details.

7.6.1 MPEG and H.26X Video Compression: Requirements

In addition to intraframe compression methods for still images described earlier, video compression methods also deploy interframe compression methods such as motion estimation. Motion estimation is one of the most demanding operations in standard-based video coding, as shown in the requirement below for H.261 involving CIF images with 352×288 pixels at 30 fps:

968 MOPS for compression:

RGB to YCbCr	27
Motion estimation	608 (25 searches in 16×16 region)
Inter/intraframe coding	40
Loop filtering	55
Pixel prediction	18
2-D DCT	60
Quant., zigzag scanning	44
EC	17
Frame reconstruct	99

Most compression standards involve asymmetric computations, such that decompression is usually much less demanding than compression. For instance, for H.261, the amount of operations for decompression (around 200 MOPS) is around 20% of that for compression (about 1000 MOPS):

198 MOPS for decompression:

Entropy decode	17
Inverse quantization	9
Inverse DCT (IDCT)	60
Loop filter	55
Prediction	30
YCbCr to RGB	27

The motion estimation method involves three kinds of frames (Figure 7.16). First, the intrapicture I, which does not include motion information, so it is like lossy JPEG. Second, the picture P, which covers motion prediction based on earlier I frames; it contains motion vectors (MVs) and error terms. Since error terms are small, quantizing gives good compression. Third, the bidirectional picture B, which supports motion prediction based on past and future I or P frames.

The goal of the motion estimator is to describe the information in the current frame based on information in its reference frame. The reference frame is typically the reconstructed version of the immediately preceding frame in the sequence, which is known to both the encoder and decoder.

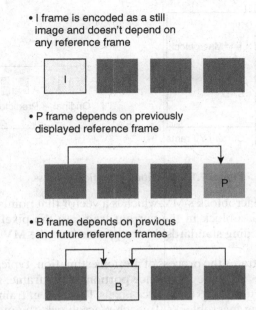

Figure 7.16   Three kinds of frames in MPEG motion estimation.

In the motion estimator for video compression methods such as H.264, pixel values are examined between these pairs of frames. Based on the operations of the motion estimator, the pixel values in the current frame can be alternately represented by a combination of two quantities: pixel values from a predictor based on the reference frame plus a prediction error that represents the difference between the predictor values and the actual pixel values in the current frame.

The function of the motion estimator can be interpreted in the following way. Suppose that the image of a moving object is represented by a group of pixels in the current frame of the original video sequence, as well as by a group of pixels in the previous frame of the reconstructed sequence. The reconstructed sequence is the designated reference frame. To achieve compression, the pixel representation of the object in the current frame is deduced from the pixel values in the reference frame. The pixel values representing the object in the reference frame is called the predictor, because it predicts the object's pixel values in the current frame. Some changes are usually needed in the predictor to attain the true pixel values of the object in the current frame; these differences are known as the prediction error.

In block-based motion estimation, the boundaries of objects represented in the current frame are assumed to approximately align along the boundaries of macroblocks. Based on this assumption, objects depicted in the frame can be represented well by one or more macroblocks. All pixels within a macroblock share the same motion characteristics. These motion characteristics are

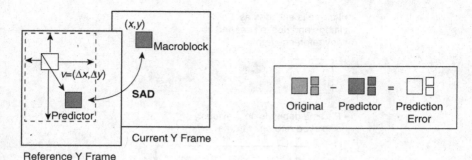

Figure 7.17 Motion estimation process.

described by the macroblock's MV, which is a vector that points from the pixel location of the macroblock in the current frame to the pixel location of its predictor. Video coding standards do not dictate how the MV and prediction error are obtained.

Figure 7.17 illustrates the process of motion estimation. Typically, the motion estimator examines only the luminance portion of the frame, so each macroblock corresponds to 16×16 luminance pixels. The current frame is subdivided into nonoverlapping macroblocks. To each macroblock, the motion estimator assigns a predictor, which must necessarily also be a square region of the size of 16×16 luminance pixels. The predictor can also be considered a macroblock. It is chosen based on the "similarity" between it and the macroblock in the current frame.

The similarity metric for the macroblocks is not specified by video coding standards such as H.264; a commonly used one is the SAD (sum of the absolute difference) metric, which computes the SAD between the values of corresponding luminance pixels in two macroblocks.

All macroblocks in a search region of the reference frame are evaluated against the current macroblock using the SAD metric. A larger SAD value indicates a greater difference between two macroblocks. The predictor macroblock is chosen to be the one which has the lowest SAD.

Many video compression standards require the search region to be rectangular and located about the coordinates of the original macroblock. The dimensions of the rectangle are adjustable but may not exceed a standard-specified maximum value.

The search strategy used to find the best-matching predictor macroblock, called the motion search, is usually not specified by the standard. Many motion search algorithms have been proposed. One possible motion search is an exhaustive (or full) search over all possible macroblocks in the search region; this strategy guarantees a global SAD minimum within the search region. However, exhaustive search is computationally expensive and is therefore primarily adopted by hardware designers, due to its regularity.

Figure 7.18 summarizes bandwidth and storage requirements of different compression methods for 90 minutes of DVD-quality video.

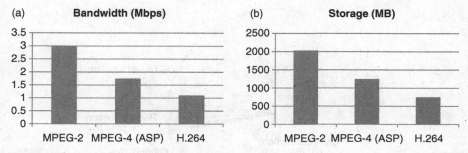

Figure 7.18 Bandwidth (a) and storage (b) of different video compression methods. ASP stands for Active Simple Profile, a version of MPEG-4.

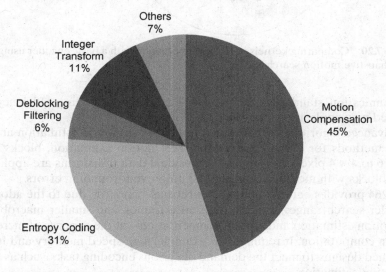

Figure 7.19 Comparing kernels in H.264/AVC decompression.

If we look at the percentage execution time of the operations in a compression or a decompression algorithm, it can be seen that motion compensation and motion estimation usually take the lion's share. For instance, H.264/AVC (Advanced Video Coding) decompression contains four major kernels: motion compensation, integer transform, entropy coding, and deblocking filtering. Motion compensation is the most time-consuming module; see Figure 7.19.

Similar results have been reported for compression as well. For instance, Figure 7.20 shows that motion estimation can take over 95% of execution time in a software H.263 encoder [270].

7.6.2 H.264 Acceleration: Designs

One of the most common digital video formats is H.264. It is an international standard that has been adopted by many broadcasting and mobile

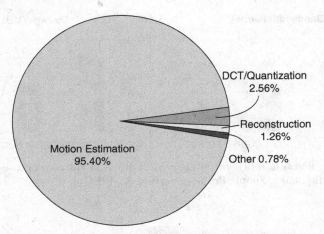

Figure 7.20 Comparing kernels in H.263 compression with a basic encoder using half-pel exhaustive motion search [270].

communication standards, such as DVB and 3G. Its coding efficiency has enabled new applications for streaming video.

Advanced algorithms are included in H.264 for motion estimation and for other methods for video compression. For motion estimation, blocks from 16 × 16 to 4 × 4 pixels are supported. Residual data transforms are applied to 4 × 4 blocks with modified integer DCT to prevent rounding errors.

H.264 provides better results than previous standards, due to the adoption of wider search ranges, multiple reference frames, and smaller macroblocks for motion estimation and motion compensation—at the expense of increased load in computation. It requires, for example, high-speed memory and highly pipelined designs, to meet the demand of various encoding tasks, such as those in motion estimation.

Let us consider two approaches. The first approach is to implement the tasks in programmable or dedicated hardware. For instance, a recent design of a baseline H.264/AVC encoder core [158] has been implemented in various hardware technologies, including:

1. 4CIF (704 × 576) at 30 fps with low-cost FPGAs: Xilinx Spartan-3 and Altera Cyclone-II,
2. 720 pixels (1280 × 720) at 30 fps with high-end FPGAs: Xilinx Virtex-4 and Altera Stratix-II,
3. 1080 pixels (1920 × 1080) at 30 fps with 0.13-μm ASIC.

The features of these implementations are summarized in Table 7.6.

The second approach is to implement the tasks on a software configurable processor introduced in Section 6.5.3, which has an instruction set extension fabric (ISEF) to support demanding operations implemented as custom instructions (also called extension instructions). The one used here is a 300-MHz

TABLE 7.6   FPGA and ASIC Designs for H.264/AVC Encoding [158]

Technology	Approximate Area	Speed (MHz)	Video Throughput
0.13 μm LV 0.9V, 125 C	178K gates + 106 Kbits RAM, optimized for speed	~250	1920 × 1080 (1080p) at 30 fps
0.18 μm slow process	129K gates + 106 Kbits RAM, optimized for area	~50	4 CIF (704 × 576) at 30 fps
StratixllC3	17,511 ALUTs + 5 M512 + 51 M4K + 3 DSPs	~118	1280 × 720 (720p) at 32 fps
CyclonellC6	18,510 M4K + 5 M512 + 51 M4K + 3 DSPs	~65	4 CIF (704 × 576) at 40 fps
Virtex4-12	10,500 slices + 3 multipliers + 33 RAM blocks	~110	1280 × 720 (720p) at 30 fps
Spartan3-4	10,500 slices + 3 multipliers + 33 RAM blocks	~50	4 CIF (704 × 576) at 30 fps

ALUT, Adaptive Lookup Table; M4K, a configurable memory block with a total of 4,608 bits.

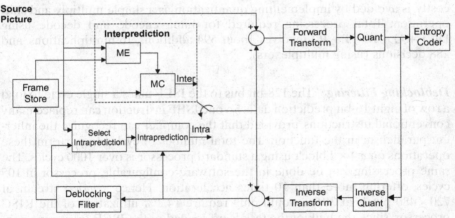

Figure 7.21   H.264 encoder architecture [152]. ME, motion estimation; MC, motion compensation; Quant, quantization.

Stretch S5 processor, which achieves H.264 encoding of Standard Definition (SD) video at 30 fps [152]. We shall look at this approach in more detail below.

Successful real-time video encoding applications have to deliver the best image quality feasible for a particular screen resolution, given real-world operating constraints. For example, an uncompressed video stream has an image size of 720 × 480 pixels and requires 1.5 bytes for color per pixel. Such a stream has 518 KB per frame, and at 30 fps it consumes 15.5 MB per second storage and bandwidth.

Figure 7.21 shows the architecture of an H.264 encoder. The efficiency of the encoder can be found in the implementation of the following functions:

1. forward DCT and IDCT,
2. intraprediction utilizing forward and inverse quantization,
3. deblocking filtering, and
4. motion estimation employing interframe comparisons.

The above are prime candidates for hardware acceleration because of the amount of computation required. Additional acceleration can be achieved by taking advantage of the inherent parallelism in these algorithms.

DCT Consider the processing of 4×4 blocks of luma pixels through a 2-D DCT and quantization step. The computations for the DCT portion of the matrix computation can be reduced to 64 add and subtract operations by taking advantage of symmetry and common subexpressions. All 64 operations can be combined into a single custom instruction for the ISEF.

Quantization (Q) This follows the DCT. The division operation, which is costly, is avoided by implementing quantization as a simple multiply and shift operation. Total processing required for luma encode and decode using DCT + Q + IDCT + IQ involves about 594 additions, 16 multiplications, and 288 decisions (using multiplexers).

Deblocking Filtering The 128-bit bus to the ISEF takes a single cycle to load a row of eight 16-bit prediction data. So one ISEF instruction can replace many conventional instructions, provided that the compiler can recognize the inherent parallelism in the function. The total number of cycles to perform these operations on a 4×4 block using a standard processor is over 1000 cycles. The same processing can be done in the software configurable processor in 105 cycles, offering more than 10 times acceleration. Hence a video stream of 720×480 pixels at 30 fps would only require 14.2% utilization of the RISC processor, since the bulk of the task is off-loaded to the ISEF. Increasing sub-block sizes enhances parallelism: for example, operating on two 4×4 blocks in parallel reduces execution time in half, dropping the utilization of the RISC processor to 7.1% as the ISEF takes on a heavier load.

Accelerating deblocking requires developers to minimize conditional code. Instead of determining which values to calculate, it is often more efficient to create a single custom instruction that calculates all the results in hardware and then select the appropriate result.

Reordering the 128-bit result from the IDCT stage simplifies packing of 16 8-bit edge data pixels into a single 128-bit wide datum to feed the deblocking custom instruction. Precalculating macroblock parameters is another optimization option supported by the state registers inside the ISEF and the instruction.

The filter's inner loop loads the 128-bit register and executes the deblock-Filter() custom instruction, computing two edges per instruction. Because the same custom instruction can be used for both horizontal and vertical filtering, there is zero overhead.

This inner loop takes three cycles and is executed twice (horizontal and vertical), with about 20 cycles for loop overhead. With 64 edges in each MB of data, there are approximately 416 ($64/4 \times 26$) cycles required per MB. For a video stream of resolution 720×480 pixels at 30 fps, this results in 16.8 Mcycles/s, or approximately 5.2% processor utilization.

Motion Estimation   This is known to consume much of the processor budget (50–60%). The key computation requirements are the repeated SAD calculations used in determining the best MV match.

The data calculations and comparisons are repetitive, with many of the intermediate results needing to be reused. These large data sets do not fit well within the limited register space of the traditional processor and digital signal processor (DSP) architectures. Also, these processors and DSP implementations struggle to feed the fixed arithmetic and multiplier units from the data cache.

With the Stretch S5 Software Configurable Processor, the ISEF custom processing unit is capable of performing computations in parallel and holding the intermediate results in the state registers while executing fully pipelined SAD instructions.

Motion estimation consists of potentially 41 SAD and 41 MVs calculations per macroblock. A full motion search on a single macroblock requires 262K operations for a video stream at 30 fps, for a total of 10.6 giga operations per second (GOPS).

By using heuristic algorithms for many implementations, the application developer can minimize the computations to meet target image quality and/or bitrate requirements.

Custom algorithms optimized to perform estimates across different search areas, numbers of frames, or the number of MVs needing to be calculated can easily be converted to ISEF instructions. A single custom instruction can replace multiple computations, as well as pipeline many of the computations using intermediate results.

For example, a single custom instruction can perform 64 SAD calculations. The ISEF maintains the 64 partial sums to reduce the number of data transfers and to reuse the results in the next instruction. The ISEF instructions can be pipelined to improve compute capacity.

Motion estimation also involves various pixel predictions that require nine SADs computed in nine directions around the pixel. By using custom instructions, a 16×16 SAD calculation with quarter pixel precision takes 133 cycles, and a 4×4 SAD calculation with quarter pixel precision takes 50 cycles.

The above discussion covers the Stretch S5 processor. The Stretch S6 processor comes with a programmable accelerator that supports a dedicated hardware block for motion estimation, so there is no need to implement this operation in the ISEF for the S6 processor.

7.7   FURTHER APPLICATION STUDIES

This section covers a number of applications to illustrate the variety of requirements and SOC solutions.

7.7.1   MP3 Audio Decoding

MP3, short for MPEC-1/2 Audio layer-3, is probably the most popular format for high-quality compressed audio. In this section we outline the basic algorithm [42] and describe two implementations: one in ASIC, the other in an FPGA [117].

Requirements   The MPEG-1 standard involves compressing digital video and audio at a combined bitrate of 1.5 Mbps. The standard is divided into a few parts, with Part 3 dealing with audio compression. The audio compression standard contains three layers according to different levels of complexity and performance; the Layer 3 standard—commonly referred to as MP3—performs best but is also the most complex.

The MP3 audio algorithm involves perceptual encoding; a block diagram is shown in Figure 7.22. The algorithm is based on associating a psychoacoustic model to a hybrid sub-band/transform coding scheme. The audio signal is divided into 32 sub-band signals, and a modified discrete cosine transform (MDCT) is applied to each sub-band signal. The transform coefficients are encoded according to a psychoacoustically motivated perceptual error measure, using scalar quantization and variable-length Huffman coding.

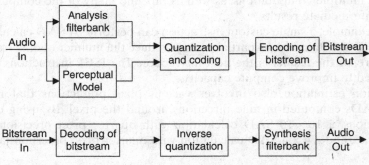

Figure 7.22   Block diagram for perceptual encoding and decoding [42].

The MP3 bitstream is a concatenation of sequence of data "frames," where each frame corresponds to two "granules" of audio such that each granule is defined as precisely 576 consecutive audio samples. A granule may sometimes be divided into three shorter ones of 192 samples each.

There are three main steps involved in decoding an MP3 frame. First, synchronize to the start of the frame and decode header information. Second, decode the side information including scale factor selection information, block splitting information, and table selection information. Third, decode the main data for both granules, including the Huffman bits for the transform coefficients, and scale factors. The main data may overflow into adjoining frames, so multiple frames of data may need to be buffered.

After the frame bits have been parsed, the next stage is to reconstruct the audio for each granule from the decoded bits; the following steps are involved:

1. Dequantizing the transform coefficients from the main and side information. A nonlinear transformation is applied to the decoded coefficients.
2. In the case of short blocks, the dequantized coefficients may be reordered and divided into three sets of coefficients, one per block.
3. In the case of certain stereo signals where the right (R) and left (L) channels may be jointly encoded, the transform coefficients are recast into L and R channel coefficients via a channel transformation.
4. An "alias reduction" step is applied for long blocks.
5. The inverse MDCT (IMDCT) module is applied for coefficients corresponding to each of the 32 sub-bands in each channel.
6. An overlap-add mechanism is used on the IMDCT outputs generated in consecutive frames. Specifically, the first half of the IMDCT outputs arc overlapped and added with the second half of the IMDCT outputs generated in the corresponding sub-band in the previous granule.
7. The final step is performed by an inverse polyphase filterbank for combining the 32 sub-band signals back into a full-bandwidth, time-domain signal.

Design Function-level profiling for an ARM processor and a DSP processor reveals that the synthesis filter bank is the most time-consuming task (Table 7.7).

An ASIC prototype has been fabricated in a five metal layer 350 nm CMOS process from AMI Semiconductor [117]. The chip contains five RAMs including the main memory, and a ROM for the Huffman tables (Table 7.8). The core size is approximately $13\,mm^2$. The power consumption is $40\,mW$ at $2\,V$ and $12\,MHz$. It is possible to lower the clock frequency to 4–$6\,MHz$ while still complying with the real-time constraints.

The real-time requirement for the decoding process is determined by the audio information in an MP3 frame. Table 7.9 presents the computation time for the different sub-blocks for a $24\,MHz$ system clock [117]. The total time

TABLE 7.7   MP3 Profiling Results for ARM and DSP Processors

Module	Percentage Time on ARM	Percentage Time on DSP
Header, side intonnation, decoding scale factors	7	13
Huffman decode, stereo processing	10	30
Alias reduction, IMDCT	18	15
Synthesis filter bank	65	42

TABLE 7.8   MP3 Decoding Blocks in 350-nm ASIC Technology [117]

Decoder blocks	Memory (bits)	ROM Tables (bits)	Equivalent Gate Count
Synchronizer	8192	0	3689
Shared main memory	24,064	0	1028
Huffman	0	45,056	10,992
Requantizer	0	0	21,583
Reorder	0	0	3653
AntiAlias	0	0	13,882
IMDCT	24,064	0	61,931
Filterbank	26,112	0	31,700
I^2S	9216	0	949
Total	91,648	45,056	149,407

TABLE 7.9   Resource Utilization and Computation Time for MP3 Decoding Blocks in Xilinx Virtex-II 1000 FPGA Technology [117]

Decoder blocks	Slices (%)	Block RAM (%)	Computation time (μs)
Synchronizer	15	10	140
Huffman	11	7	120
Requantizer	12	5	140
Reorder	1	12	10
AntiAlias	3	0	83
IMDCT	8	13	678
Filterbank	6	10	1160
Total	56	51	2300

for the decoding process is 2.3 ms, which results in a slack of 24.7 ms. This shows that the clock speed for the decoder can be reduced, and that resources can be shared to lower costs.

The resource utilization on a Virtex-II 1000 FPGA is also reported in Table 7.9. This design takes up 56% of the FPGA slices, 15% of the flip-flops, 45% of the four-input lookup tables, and 57% of the block RAMs. Moreover, a 32×32 bit multiplier, which is shared among the sub-blocks, is made from four of the available 18×18 bit multipliers.

As indicated above, there is scope for reducing the area and power consumption of this design by resource sharing among sub-blocks. However, such resource sharing may complicate control and implementation, for instance by introducing routing bottlenecks; hence, its pros and cons must be evaluated before adoption.

7.7.2 Software-Defined Radio with 802.16

The WiMAX or IEEE 802.16 wireless communications standard, along with a variety of other wireless communication standards, attempts to increase the data transfer rates to meet the demands for end applications and to reduce deployment costs. The techniques used to identify the digital data in the presence of large amounts of noise stress the computational capabilities of most processors. With the standards still evolving and the requirements changing, a programmable solution is particularly attractive.

Requirements   The basic transmitter block diagram for an 802.16 implementation is shown in Figure 7.23 [169]. At the high level, the physical layer (PHY) on the transmitter is responsible for converting the raw digital data stream to a complex data stream ready for upconverting to an analog radio signal. The PHY on the receiver is responsible for extracting the complex data stream and decoding the data back to the original form.

The blocks in PHY that are computationally demanding include fast Fourier transforms (FFT) and its inverse, forward error correction (FEC) including block coding such as Reed–Solomon codec and bit-level coding such as convolution encoding and Viterbi decoding, quadrature amplitude modulation (QAM), interleaving, and scrambling. The media access control (MAC) layer provides the interface between the PHY and the network layer. The MAC processing is much more control oriented as it takes packets from the network layer and schedules the data to be sent according to the quality of service (QoS) requirements; while at the receiver end, the MAC reassembles the data

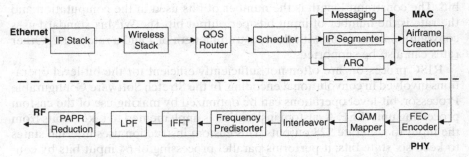

Figure 7.23   802.16 transmitter block diagram [169] IP stack, internet protocol stack; ARQ, automatic repeat reQuest; IFFT, inverse FFT; LPF, low-pass filter; PAPR, peak to average power ratio; RF, radio frequency.

for handing back to the network layer. The MAC layer also includes the necessary messaging to maintain communications between the base and the subscriber stations as well as automatically requesting the retransmission of any bad packets. The network layer is the interface to the application. A TCP/IP network stack is the most common networking stack in use today. For a complete wireless solution, all layers must be connected.

Design   The physical layer PHY in the 802.16 WiMAX standard performs 256-point FFT and orthogonal frequency-division multiplexing (OFDM). On a Stretch S5 Software Configurable Processor (Section 6.5.3), the OFDM can be configured to operate in channel widths of 3.5, 7, and 10 MHz [169]. Modulation support includes BPSK (Binary Phase Shift Keying), QPSK (Quadrature Phase Shift Keying), 16 QAM or 64 QAM. For noisy environments, the FEC is a requirement, with the standard allowing a variety of choices. Note that a conventional RISC or DSP processor does not have enough power to support the high demand of WiMAX baseband processing and the control tasks at the same time. A single software configurable processor meets the demand of all the heavy-duty WiMax signal processing and control tasks such as a base MAC layer and full TCP/IP stack to achieve full bitrate for all three channel widths on a single chip.

The Stretch Software Configurable Processor adopts a Radix-2 FFT design through defining a custom instruction as an extension instruction, which supports sixteen 16×16 multiplies, eight 32-bit adds, and sixteen 16-bit adds with rounding and rescaling operation. This custom instruction makes use of the 128-bit wide registers to pass three sets of four complex values to the ISEF for parallel operations. This results in performing 256-point FFT in $4 \mu s$. Implementing a Radix-4 FFT provides an additional 28% performance improvement.

The FEC block is another one that benefits from flexibility and performance. Forward error correction increases data throughput in the presence of channel noise by introducing data redundancy on the transmitter side, and errors are corrected on the receiver side. In convolutional coding, every encoded bit is generated by convolving the input bit with the previous input bits. The constraint length is the number of bits used in the computation and the rate is the number of input bits per output bit. The WiMax standard uses convolutional encoding with the constraint length of 7 and a rate of 1/2. Other rates can also be supported.

RISC processors are often not sufficiently efficient for the bit-level operations involved in convolutional encoding. In the Stretch Software Configurable Processor, bit-level operations can be optimized by making use of the custom processing unit ISEF. A custom instruction is implemented to take 64 bits from the input to generate 128 outputs. This custom instruction uses internal states to keep six state bits; it performs parallel processing of 64 input bits by convolving the input bits with the state bits to produce 128 outputs.

The bitstreams generated by convolutional encoding can be decoded by using a trellis diagram to find the most likely sequence of codes. A Viterbi decoder is an efficient way to decode the bitstream by limiting the number of sequences needed to be examined. It keeps a record of the most likely path for each state at each trellis stage. Viterbi decoding is computationally demanding; it requires add–compare–selection (ACS) for each state at each stage, as well as keeping the history of the selected path. It involves three main steps: (1) branch metric computation, (2) ACS for each state at each stage, and (3) traceback.

In the trellis diagram, there is a metric associated with each branch, called branch metric, which measures the distance between a received signal and the output branch labels. Branch metric is computed as the Euclidean distance between the received sample and branch label.

One custom instruction, EI_ACS64, is created to perform the branch metric computation, addition of the branch metric with the path metric at the previous stage, comparing the path metrics of the two incoming paths, and updating the path metric with the maximum and then selecting the path. This EI_ACS64 instruction does this ACS operation for all the states at one trellis stage in parallel. In other words, this custom instruction performs 32 butterfly operations in parallel. The 64 path metrics are stored as internal states in ISEF. As we move from one stage to the next stage, EI_ACS64 also updates output wide registers with 1 bit for each state, which indicates the selected path. As we traverse four trellis stages, it will accumulate 4 bits for each state. In total, it accumulates $4 \times 64 = 256$ bits for all the states. Two store instructions (WRAS128IU) can then be used to move these bits to memory.

The actual decoding of symbols back to the original data is accomplished by tracing backwards through the trellis along the maximum likelihood path. The length of the traceback is commonly four to five times the constraint length of the convolutional encoder. In some cases, the entire frame of data is received before beginning traceback. We traverse the trellis in reverse direction to decode the input bitstream. Assume the state reached at the last trellis stage is in a known state, typically state 0. This can be achieved by sending additional $K - 1$ bits of 0 to bring all the states to 0. The bit stored for each state tells which branch to traverse as we traverse from stage j to $j - 1$. Another custom instruction is created, VITERBI_TB, which does traceback for four trellis stages, uses an internal state to keep the previous state for the next round of traceback, and outputs 4 bits for the decoded bitstream. The VITERBI_TB instruction is called twice before the 8-bit decoded bitstream is stored back to memory.

7.8 CONCLUSIONS

We hope that the material in this chapter has illustrated the variety of SOC applications and the range of design techniques and SOC architectures—ranging from embedded ARM processors to reconfigurable devices from Xilinx and Stretch—many of which have been introduced in the preceding chapters. Interestingly, the rapid increase in performance requirements in multimedia, cryptography, communications, and other key applications has led to a wave of start-ups, such as Achronix, Element CXI, Silicon Hive, Stretch, and Tabula; time will tell which are the winners.

We have not, however, attempted to provide a detailed and complete account of design development for a specific application or design style using the latest tools. Such accounts are already available: for instance, Fisher et al [93] and Rowen and Leibson [207] have dedicated their treatment, respectively, to VLIW architectures and to configurable processors. SOC design examples [164] and methodologies [32] from an industrial perspective are also available. Those interested in detailed examples involving application of analytical techniques to processor design are referred to the textbooks by Flynn [96] and by Hennessy and Patterson [118].

7.9 PROBLEM SET

1. How fast would a 32-bit processor with the ARM7 instruction set need to run to be able to support AES for Wi-Fi 802.11b? How about a 64-bit processor?

2. Estimate the number of operations per second involved in computing the DCT for high-resolution images of 1920×1080 pixels at 30 fps.

3. Explain how the JPEG system for the camera in Figure 7.14 can be revised to support 10 megapixel images.

4. Estimate the size in number of rbes of the FPGA and ASIC designs in Table 7.6, assuming that the FPGAs are produced in a 90 nm process.

5. Compare the pros and cons of the FPGA and ASIC designs in Table 7.6, assuming that the FPGAs are produced in a 90 nm process. How would your answer change when both the FPGAs and the ASIC are produced in a 45 nm process?

6. Consider a 3-D graphics application designed to deal with k nonclipped triangles, each covering an average of p pixels and a fraction α of which being obscured by other triangles. Ambient and diffuse illumination models and Gouraud shading are used. The display has a resolution of $m \times n$ pixels, updated at f fps. Estimate:
   (a) the number of floating-point operations for geometry operations,
   (b) the number of integer operations for computing pixel values, and
   (c) the number of memory access for rasterization.

7. Table 7.10 shows data for the ARM1136J-S PXP system. The datapath runs at a maximum of 350 MHz for the 16K instruction cache plus 16K data

TABLE 7.10 MPEG4 Decode Performance on ARM1136J-S PXP System

L1 cache size	16K + 16K	32K + 32K	64K + 64K	16K + 16K	16K + 16K	16K + 16K	32K + 32K	32K + 32K
L2 cache size	—	—	—	128K	256K	512K	256K	512K
Speed (MHz)	350	324	277	350	350	324	324	324
Area (mm²)	2.3	3.3	6	8.3	12.3	21	13.3	22
Run time (ms)	122.6	96.7	93.8	70.6	60.7	60.0	63.6	63.2

Area values include that of L2 where appropriate.

$$\textbf{for } y = 0 \textbf{ to } H_2 - H_1 \textbf{ do}$$
$$\quad \textbf{for } x = 0 \textbf{ to } W_2 - W_1 \textbf{ do}$$
$$\quad Ic_{x,y} = f_3\big($$
$$\qquad \sum_{i=0}^{H_1-1} \sum_{j=0}^{W_1-1} f_{12}(M1_{i,j}, I1_{i,j}, M2_{y+i,x+j}, I2_{y+i,x+j}),$$
$$\qquad \sum_{i=0}^{H_1-1} \sum_{j=0}^{W_1-1} f_{11}(M1_{i,j}, I1_{i,j}),$$
$$\qquad \sum_{i=0}^{H_1-1} \sum_{j=0}^{W_1-1} f_{22}(M1_{y+i,x+j}, I2_{y+i,x+j}))$$
$$\textbf{end for}$$
$$\textbf{end for}$$

Figure 7.24   Convolution algorithm with resulting image I_c.

cache; the 32K + 32K and 64K + 64K implementations are limited in speed by their cache implementations.

(a) Comment on the effect of increasing the size of L1 on performance.

(b) Suggest reasons to explain why the design with the largest cache area is not the fastest.

(c) Compare the fastest design and the one just behind that one. Which one is more cost effective and why?

8. Figure 7.24 shows a convolution algorithm between an $H_1 \times W_1$ image (I_1) and an $H_2 \times W_2$ image (I_2), which have optional masks M_1 and M_2, respectively, of the same width and height. Given that $H_2 > H_1$ and $W_2 > W_1$, and f_3, f_{12}, f_{11}, and f_{22} are pure functions—that is, they have no internal state and their results depend only on their parameters:

(a) What are the values of M_1, M_2 and f_3, f_{12}, f_{11}, and f_{22} for (1) SAD correlation, (2) normalized correlation, and (3) Gaussian blur?

(b) What is the resolution of the result image I_c?

(c) How many cycles are needed to produce the resulting image I_c?

8 What's Next: Challenges Ahead

8.1 INTRODUCTION

With rapid advances in transistor density, it is time to look ahead to the future. One extreme is the completely autonomous system-on-chip (ASOC): a convergence of RFID (radio-frequency identification) technology with SOC technology coupled with transducers, sensor controllers, and battery, all on the same die. The major architectural implication is design for extremely low power (down to $1\,\mu W$ or less) and a strict energy budget. This requires rethinking of clocking, memory organization, and processor organization. The use of deposited thin film batteries, extremely efficient radio frequency (RF) communications, digital sensors, and microelectromechanical systems (MEMS) completes the ASOC plan. Short of this extreme, there are many system configurations providing various trade-offs across power, RF, and speed budgets.

Throughout this text, it is clear that design time and cost are the major SOC limitations now and even more so in the future. One way to address these limitations is to develop a design process in which components can optimize and verify themselves to improve efficiency, reuse, and correctness, the three design challenges identified by the International Technology Roadmap for Semiconductors. Self-optimization and self-verification before and after design deployment are key to future SOC design.

This chapter has two parts. Part I covers the future system: ASOC. Part II covers the future design process: self-optimization and self-verification. There are various challenges which, if met, would enable the opportunities outlined in this chapter. We highlight some of these challenges in the text.

Computer System Design: System-on-Chip, First Edition. Michael J. Flynn and Wayne Luk.

I. THE FUTURE SYSTEM: AUTONOMOUS SYSTEM-ON-CHIP

8.2 OVERVIEW

SOC technology represents an expanding part of the microprocessor marketplace; growing at 20% per annum rate, there's much more to come [134].

The typical SOC consists of multiple heterogeneous processors and controllers, and several types of memory (read-only memory [ROM], cache, and embedded dynamic random access memory [eDRAM]. The various processors are oriented toward one or more types of media processing. Typical applications include cell phones, digital cameras, MP3 players, and various gaming devices.

Another fast-growing chip marketplace is autonomous chips (ACs). These have little processing power or memory, but have RF communications and some type of self-contained power source or power management. The more elaborate ACs also contain or are coupled with some types of sensors. The simple versions include RFID chips [205], smart cards, and chip-implanted credit cards.

The simplest AC is the passively powered RFID. The chip simply reflects the source RF carrier and modulates it (using carrier power) to indicate its ID. More complex examples include the patient monitoring alarm [31] and the Smart Dust research program [63, 181] of the 1990s. Both of these used battery-powered RF to broadcast an ID on a detected sensor input.

The various Smart Cards and Money Cards include VISA cards and Hong Kong's Octopus Card. All (except those that require contact) use a form of RFID. The simplest cards are passive without on-card writeable memory. Records are updated centrally. Implementation is frequently based on Java Card [234]. Based on the extraordinary interest, there are a series of contactless identification cards (RFID) standards:

- ISO 10536 close coupling cards (0–1 cm),
- ISO 14443 proximity coupling cards (0–10 cm),
- ISO 15693 vicinity coupling (0–1 m).

The future autonomous SOC or ASOC is the combination of the SOC with the AC technology (Table 8.1). While conceptually simple, the engineering details are formidable as it involves rethinking the whole of processor architecture and implementation to optimize designs for very low power operation—in the submicrowatt region.

The motivation for ASOC follows the Smart Dust project [63], which started in the early 1990s and pioneered significant work in the sensor and RF areas. That project targeted sensor plus RF integrated into a form factor of the order of 1 mm^3 called motes. As a power source it relied on AA type batteries. That project was targeted at sensing an "event," such as a moving object or a thermal signal.

TABLE 8.1 Some ASOC Examples

System	Passive ID	Active ID	RF Sensor	ASOC
Example	RFID, Smart card (simple)	Smart card, active RFID	Smart Dust; RFID + sensor	
Power source	None	Short-term battery	Battery	Integrated Battery
Maximum memory	ROM ID (1KB)	R/W ID + parameters (2KB)		R/W extensive (100MB)
RF range (meters)	Passive; order of centimeter	Active 1–10	10–20	10+
Compute	None	FSM	FSM	1 or more CPU

FSM represents a simple finite state machine or microcontroller; R/W: Read/Write memory.

ASOC is an updated extension of that work that places more emphasis on computational ability and memory capacity; as well as fully integrating a power source on die.

A simplified classification of ACs, by their level of sophistication, is:

1. Simple identification of the die itself (as in RFID) with RF response.
2. Identification of a sensor-detected "event" with RF response (as in Smart Dust and many Smart Cards).
3. Detection of an "event" and processing (classification, recognition, analyzing) the event (ASOC) with RF response of the result.

The ability of the ASOC to process data is clearly valuable in reducing the amount of sensor data required to be transmitted. It enables applications (such as supporting planetary exploration) where interactive computational support is impossible; so too with the recognition of a rare bird or other species in remote areas; or swallowing an ASOC "pill" for diagnosis of the gastrointestinal tract. Not all dimensions of ASOC are equally important in all applications. A rare species "listening" post may require little size concern and may have ample battery support. We look at ASOC as a toolkit for the new systems designer, offering the ability to configure systems to respond to an almost endless set of environmental and computational requirements.

In the next few sections we consider the evolution of silicon technology, limits on batteries and energy, architecture implications, communications, sensors, and applications.

8.3 TECHNOLOGY

As we saw in the earlier chapters over the next few years transistor and memory density is expected to increase 10-fold [134] to several billion transistors/cm^2. Since a reasonable powerful processor can be realized with a few 100,000 transistors, there are a lot of possibilities for ASOC applications.

This density, however, has a price. Very small devices pose significant performance problems in traditional workstation implementations. Simply the dopant variability (number of dopant atoms needed to create a device) causes variability in delay from device to device. Small structures involve large electric fields causing reliability problems: electromigration in conductors and diaelectric fatigue. These are not significant problems for ASOC at the very low projected power and speed employed.

The main problem for useful ASOC is battery power or stored energy. In dealing with this issue recall two general relationships discussed in Chapter 2, relating silicon area A, algorithmic execution time T, and power consumption P (in these expressions k is a constant):

$$AT^2 = k. \tag{8.1}$$

This result [247] simply related area (the number of transistors) to the execution time required to complete an operation. The more area (transistors) used, the faster (smaller) the execution time. Recall from chapter 2 the relationship between execution time and power [99].

$$T^3 P = k. \tag{8.2}$$

It is easy to see that as voltage is decreased power is reduced by the square but speed is reduced linearly. But in transistors the charging current (representing delay) and voltage have a nonlinear relationship. As we saw in Chapter 2, this gives the cubic result:

$$P_2 / P_1 = (F_2 / F_1)^3. \tag{8.3}$$

So if we want to double the frequency we should expect the design to use eight times more power. While the range of applicability of expression 8.2 is not precise, suppose we use it to project the frequency of a processor design that operates at a microwatt. The best power–performance design of today might consume 1 W and achieve 1 GHz (corresponding perhaps to 1000 million instructions per second [MIPS]); this may be optimistic. Reducing the power by a factor of 10^6 should reduce frequency by a factor of 100 or 10 MHz. Within the past 2 years a sensor processor has been built that achieves almost 0.5 MIPS/μW [271]. While this is an order of magnitude away from our target of 10 MHz/μW, silicon scaling projections may compensate for the difference.

CHALLENGE

Is the $T^3 P = k$ rule robust down to microwatts?

We know that this rule seems valid at the usual operating conditions, but how can we scale it to microwatts? What circuits and devices are required?

8.4 POWERING THE ASOC

The key problems in forming robust ASOC are energy and lifetime. Both relate to the power source, that is, the battery. Batteries can be charged once or are rechargeable (with varying recharge cycles). For ASOC purposes, rechargeable batteries use scavenged energy from the environment. The capacity of the battery is usually measured in milliamp-hours; which we convert

TABLE 8.2   Batteries of ASOC

Type	Energy (J)	Recharge Y/N	Thickness (μm)
Printed	2/cm^2	N	20
Thin film	10/cm^2	Y	100
Button	200	Y	500 stand alone

TABLE 8.3   Some Energy-Scavenging Sources [173, 195, 206]

Source	Charge rate	Comment
Solar	65 (milliwatts per square centimeter)	
Ambient light	2 (milliwatts per square centimeter)	
Strain and acoustic	A force (sound) changes alignment of crystal structure, creating voltage	Piezoelectric effect
RF	An electric field of 10 V/m yields 16 μW/cm^2 of antenna	See Yeatman [266]
Temperature difference (Peltier effect)	40 (microwatts per 5°C difference)	Needs temperature differential

to joules (watt-seconds) at about 1.5 V. Both capacity and rechargeability depend on size, which we assume is generally consistent with the size and weight of the ASOC die (about 1 cm^2 surface area).

In Table 8.2 we list three common battery types: the printed [47, 203] and thin film batteries [67] can be directly integrated into the ASOC die (usually the reverse side); button batteries are external and are less than 1 cm in diameter.

Printed batteries are formed by printing with special inks in a flat surface; thin film batteries are deposited on silicon much as the system die itself.

CHALLENGE

Battery technology that can provide over 100 J in form factor of 1 cm$^2 \times$ 100 μm that can be deposited on a silicon substrate.

Microbattery technology is emerging as a critical new need for many applications.

Energy may be scavenged from many sources (some are illustrated in Table 8.3); usually the larger the battery format, the more the charge. Much depends on the system environment as to which, if any, scavenging is suitable.

Assuming ASOC consumption of 1 μW (when active), the operational lifetime between charges is plotted in Figure 8.1. Duty cycle can play an important

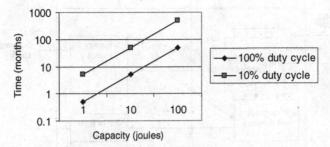

Figure 8.1 Maximum time between recharge for $1\,\mu W$ of continuous power consumption.

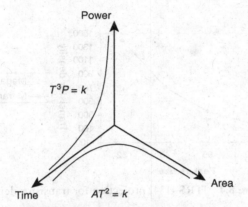

Figure 8.2 The area–time–power trade-off.

role in expending the ASOC serviceability. The assumption is that a passive sensor can detect an event and power up the system for analysis.

Comparing Figures 8.1 and 8.2, if we can configure the ASOC to use of the order of $1\,\mu W$ we should be able to incorporate a suitable battery technology especially if we have the ability to scavenge some addition energy.

CHALLENGE

Scavenge energy from many more sources with ready implementation technologies.

To date, most attention on energy scavenging has been restricted to light and possibly RF (as in RFID). We need an integrated study of alternatives, especially when the amount scavenged is in microwatts. In the past, such low power recovery was considered useless; with ASOC it becomes useful.

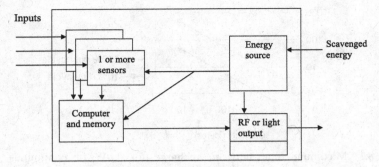

Figure 8.3   An ASOC die.

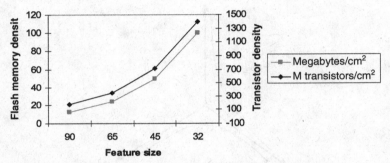

Figure 8.4   ITRS [134] projection for transistor density.

8.5   THE SHAPE OF THE ASOC

The logical pieces of the ASOC die are shown in Figure 8.3. It consists of the power source, sensors(s), main computer and memory, and the communications module. What distinguishes the ASOC from the earlier RFID plus sensor technology is the compute power and memory. It is this facility that enables the system to analyze and distinguish patterns, to synthesize responses before communicating with the external environment.

Physically the ASOC is just a silicon die, probably $1\,cm^2$ in surface area. Surface size is dictated by cost, which is determined by defect density. Current technology gives excellent yields for $1\,cm^2$ and smaller die sizes. Much below $1\,cm^2$ costs are limited by testing and handling so this represents the preferred size for most applications. Die thickness is limited by wafer fabrication considerations and is about $600\,\mu m$. A thin film battery deposited in the reverse side might add another $50\,\mu m$. The resultant ASOC would be $65\,mm^3$ and weigh about $0.2\,g$. From Figure 8.4 it could have of the order of 1 billion transistors. These transistors would realize the sensors, computer, memory, and RF; the battery is on the reverse side.

8.6   COMPUTER MODULE AND MEMORY

With a power budget of only $1\,\mu W$ the microarchitecture of the computer is considerably different from the conventional processor:

1. Asynchronous clocking: Data state transitions must be minimized to reduce dynamic power. There may be only one-tenth asynchronous transitions required compared to a clocked system.
2. Use of VLIW: Transistors are plentiful but power is scarce, so the effort is to use any available parallelism to recover performance.
3. Beckett and Goldstein [39] have shown that by careful device design (lowering drive current and managing leakage), it is possible to arrange for overall die power to be a reducing function of die area. This sacrifices maximum operating frequency but the additional area can more than compensate by parallelizing aspects of the architecture.
4. Minimum and simple cache system: The memory and processor are in relatively closer time proximity if the processor is performing an action once every $0.1\,\mu s$ and the flash memory has access time between 1 and $10\,\mu s$. A small instruction cache and explicitly managed data buffers seem most suitable in the context of specified applications.

The flash memory is another essential piece of the system as it has a persistent data image even without power. Current densities (NAND-based flash) give excellent access times, $10\,\mu s$, and ASOC capacity of perhaps 16–64 MB.

As the technology is currently configured, Flash is largely incompatible with integrated CMOS technology and seems restricted to off-die implementations. However, there are a number of Flash variants that are specifically designed to be compatible with ordinary SOC technology. SONOS [233] is a nonvolatile example and Z-RAM [91] is a DRAM replacement example. Neither seems to suffer from the conventional Flash rewrite cycle limitations (the order of 100,000 writes).

Even though the Flash memory consumes no power when it is not being used, when it is accessed the power consumption is proportional to the active memory array size; that is, the number of memory cells connected to each bit and word-line (assuming 2-D square structure). In the context of ASOC this implies a memory partitioned into smaller units, which may be most effective from both a power and access time basis.

8.7   RF OR LIGHT COMMUNICATIONS

One of the great challenges of ASOC is communications. There are two obvious approaches: laser and RF communications.

CHALLENGE

Extremely low power processors that achieve perhaps 1/100 of the performance of a conventional processor with microwatt power.

This requires a rethinking of processor design issues from the device level (absolutely minimum static power) to new circuit technology (sub-threshold or adiabatic circuits); new clocking; and finally, a completely new look at architectures.

8.7.1 Lasers

Integrating laser with silicon is an emerging technology. A recent development [85] uses an Indium Phosphide laser with silicon waveguide bonded directly to a silicon chip. Using lasers for optical free-space communications has possibilities and difficulties.

Optical sensors are quite responsive [136]; reception of $1\,\mu W$ supports about 100 MHz data rates (Figure 8.5). The difficulty is that reception is subject to ambient light (noise). In general the signal must be 10 times greater than the noise. The other difficulty is beam divergence (especially in laser diodes). This requires optics to collimate the beam for low divergence [192].

The beam should not be too narrow (focused) as communications with the receiver must be spatially and temporally synchronized. With a coherent narrow beam, light must be diffused to allow for movement between source and receiver. A slight movement (vibration) can cause an angular displacement of α either vertically or horizontally over distance d. This results in an uncertainty of δ at the receiver. So the receiver must accommodate signals across a box of area $R \times R$; see Figure 8.6.

Since $R > \delta = \alpha d$ in both x- and y-axes, signal is lost at a rate of $k(1/d^2)$.

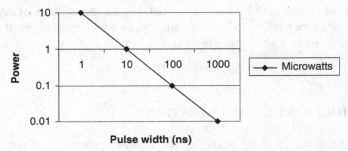

Figure 8.5 Photo detector sensitivity is a function of pulse width.

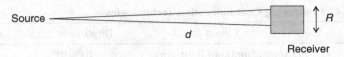

Figure 8.6   Free space light communications.

Given the limitations, the use of laser free space (as distinct from fiber optics) for communication is probably a secondary prospect for ASOC.

8.7.2   RF

The work of the Smart Dust program seems to the most relevant and useful here [63, 181]. That program demonstrated the integration of low-power RF into an SOC chip. To summarize some of their many findings:

1. A feasibility study realized a transceiver achieving 100 Kbps over a 20-m distance with an energy budget of 25 nJ/bit. This corresponds to about 10^{11} bits/J/m. One joule of battery energy allows 100 Gbits to be transferred across 1 m [181].
2. Expressing data volume on a per-meter basis (as above) might imply a linear relation between signal loss and distance. This is incorrect. As with light, RF signal strength is a function of at least distance, d, squared; but it is also a function of frequency, f. At best the RF signal is proportional to $k(1/fd^2)$. In many situations the signal may be reflected and arrives at the receiver in multiple uncoordinated modes. This multipath signal represents additional signal loss. It is usually expressed as $k(1/fd^2)$ $(d_0/d)^n$, where d_0 is a standard distance (usually 1 m) and typically n is 3 or 4.
3. Communications with less than 1 mW was not only feasible but likely to be commercialized. With typical duty cycle of less than 1% the average power consumption was between 1 and 10 μW.
4. There is a large data packet overhead (including start-up and synchronization, start symbol, address, packet length, encryption, and error correction). Short messages can have as little as 3% payload packet efficiency. It is better to create fewer longer messages.
5. As a result of (2) and (3), the system designer will want to minimize the number of transmissions and maximize the data packet payload.

8.7.3   Potential for Laser/RF Communications

Table 8.4 summarizes and compares the communications (data volume or total number of bits) potential per joule of energy. While laser light seems to offer more bits per joule, its limitations restrict its use.

TABLE 8.4 Comparing Communication Technologies

Sources	Losses	Bits/J/m at 10 m	Comment
Laser	Distance; ambient light noise	10^{10}–10^{12}	
RF at 1 GHz	Distance; multipath, frequency	10^8–10^{11}	[63, 181]

CHALLENGE

Adaptive and optimized communications including hyperdirectional antennae for RF and adaptive special synchronization for light and transmission.

Protocols are needed to support short broadly directional initial transmission, which enables sender and receiver to align for optimum path transmission.

8.7.4 Networked ASOC

In many situations multiple ASOCs form a network connecting an ultimate sender and receiver across several intermediate nodes. For such a system to be viable and connected, the ASOC placement must be constrained to a maximum average distance between nodes. This maximum distance depends on path loss characteristics. In RF, the Smart Dust experiment showed that this distance could vary from 1 km to 10 m as n varies from 2 to 4. It is important to remember that the message bits passed across the network comes with a (sometimes large) overhead due to synchronization. Spatial and temporal synchronization requires adaptation and signaling overhead. This can be of the order of 100 bits/message for time synchronization alone. Ideally, the system would have infrequent but long messages so as to minimize this overhead.

CHALLENGE

Communications technology that minimizes synchronization (both special and temporal) overhead.

In order to enable efficient short message communications, it is essential to reduce overhead to the order of 10s of bits rather than much more.

8.8 SENSING

8.8.1 Visual

Vision and motion sensors are usually configured as an array of photodiodes, with array sizes varying from 64×64 to 4000×4000 or more [144]. Each photodiode represents a pixel in the image (for grayscale digital images). Three or more diodes are needed for colored and multiple spectrum images. To conserve power and reduce state transitions an ASOC would probably implement the vision processor as an array with a single element per pixel.

In either image recognition or motion detection and recognition, it is necessary to find either the correspondence with a reference image or the direction in which a block in one image shifts with respect to a previous image [65]. Determining the match between two images or successive frames of the same scene requires that the image be partitioned into blocks. The blocks of one image are compared to the reference or previous image block by block in a spiral pattern. Each comparison involves computing the SAD (sum of absolute difference) index. When the image configuration with the minimum SAD index is found, the recognition or motion flow is resolved. While image recognition should be possible in milliseconds, the challenge for vision sensors is to meet the computational requirements of relatively fast-moving objects (Figure 8.7).

While it is clear that the image sensors can be integrated in the ASOC, optics for focusing distant object in varying amounts of light can improve performance.

8.8.2 Audio

As mentioned above the piezoelectric effect applied to silicon crystal can be used to record sounds and is the basis for many simple sound detection and microphone systems. Alternatively, in specialized applications such as hearing aids, it is sometimes important to mimic the action of the ear. Various cochlear chips have been realized using a sequence of low-pass filters to emulate the operation of the cochlea. In one silicon implementation [251], 360 cells each containing dual low-pass filters are arranged as a linear array. Cochlea-type implementations are usually preferred when speech recognition is required:

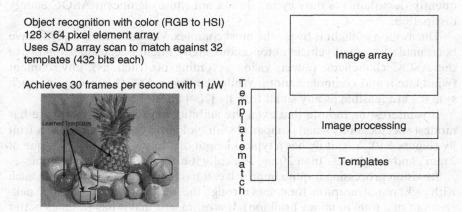

Object recognition with color (RGB to HSI)
128 × 64 pixel element array
Uses SAD array scan to match against 32
templates (432 bits each)

Achieves 30 frames per second with 1 μW

Learned Templates

T e m p l a t e m a t c h

Image array

Image processing

Templates

Figure 8.7   Visual processing.

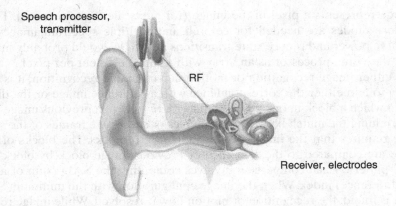

Speech processor, transmitter

RF

Receiver, electrodes

Figure 8.8 Audio processing (Cochlear implant from Wikipedia).

they form the frontend signal processing of the auditory system, separating sound waves and mapping them into the frequency domain (Figure 8.8).

Since audible sound frequencies are relatively low there are few real-time constraints for an ASOC.

8.9 MOTION, FLIGHT, AND THE FRUIT FLY

Of course, the ultimate ASOC can both move and fly. Given a weight of only 0.2 g motion per se is not a problem when the ASOC has associated MEMS. MEMS and nanomotors are used to anchor and move the ASOC across a surface. The energy required to move on a surface is simply the force to start (accelerate) and then to overcome friction. One joule of energy translates into 10^7 ergs. An erg is the energy required to move a gram for 1 cm with the force of a dyne. So slow motion (order of 1–2 cm/s) that occurs relatively infrequently (less than 1% duty cycle) should not cause significant ASOC energy dissipation.

The motion of flight is by far the most complex. Various attempts [273] have been made for small vehicle autonomous flight. Flight encapsulates many of the ASOC challenges: power, vision (avoiding obstructions), environment (wind, etc.), and communications. While the flying ASOC is a way off, such systems are feasible as any small fruit fly [209] knows!

It is interesting to note that even the ambitious ASOC described here has modest specifications when compared with biological creatures such as a fruit fly (Figure 8.9). A fruit fly has a typical length of 2.5 mm, occupies a volume of 2 mm³, and weighs less than 20 mg. Typically it has only a 1-month lifetime.

Its vision processing is quite impressive. It has 800 vision receptor units, each with eight photoreceptors for colors through the ultraviolet (using 200,000 neurons out of a total of about 1 million). It is estimated that it has 10 times better

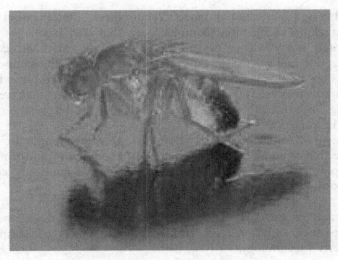

Figure 8.9   The fruit fly (from Wikipedia).

temporal vision than the human vision system. When coupled with processing for olfaction, audition, learning/memory, and communications with other nodes (flies), it represents an elegant ASOC. Its ability in flight just further impresses: its wings beat 220 times per second and can move at 10 cm/s and rotate 90 degrees in 50 ms. Its energy source is scavenged rotting fruit.

There have been recent proposals about the development of robotic flies with control systems inspired by the real ones [255]. Clearly the designer of silicon-based ASOC described here has much to learn from the fruit fly.

CHALLENGE

Sensor miniaturization and integration of transducers for measurement of temperature and strain, and movement and pressure.

At present, there is an assumption that these units will be off die and hence large. At issue is how to miniaturize and integrate these into an ASOC.

II.   THE FUTURE DESIGN PROCESS: SELF-OPTIMIZATION AND SELF-VERIFICATION

8.10   MOTIVATION

The remaining sections of this chapter cover an approach that can be used to develop advanced SOC including the ASOC described earlier.

A good design is efficient and meets requirements. Optimization enhances efficiency, while verification demonstrates that requirements are met. Unfortunately, many existing designs are either inefficient, incorrect, or both.

Optimization and verification are recognized to be of major importance at all levels of abstraction in design. A recent International Technology Roadmap for Semiconductors listed "cost-driven design optimization" and "verification and testing" as two of the three overall challenges in design; the remaining challenge is "reuse."

What would a future be like in which these three challenges are met? Let us imagine that building blocks for use in design are endowed with the capability of optimizing and verifying themselves. A new design can be completed in the following ways:

1. Characterize the desired attributes of the design that define the requirements, such as its function, accuracy, timing, power consumption, and preferred technology.
2. Develop or select an architecture that is likely to meet the requirements and explore appropriate instantiations of its building blocks.
3. Decide whether existing building blocks meet requirements; if not, either start a new search, or develop new optimizable and verifiable building blocks, or adapt requirements to what can be realized.
4. After confirming that the optimized and verified design meets the requirements, organize the optimization and verification steps to enable the design to become self-optimizing and self-verifying.
5. Generalize the design and the corresponding self-optimization and self-verification capabilities to enhance its applicability and reusability.

A key consideration is to be able to preserve self-optimization and self-verification in the design process: starting from components with such properties, the composite design is also self-optimizing and self-verifying. In the next few sections, we include more information about this approach.

8.11   OVERVIEW

Optimization can be used to transform an obvious but inefficient design into one that is efficient but no longer obvious. Verification can then show, for instance, that the optimization preserves functional behavior subject to certain preconditions. A common error in design is to apply optimizations disregarding such preconditions. Verification can also be used to check whether a design possesses desirable properties, such as safety and security, to a particular standard.

Optimization and verification, when combined with a generic design style, supports reuse in three main ways. First, an optimized generic design provides abstraction from details, enabling designers to focus on the available optimization options and their effects. Second, a generic design offers choices at multiple levels of abstraction, from algorithms and architectures to technology-specific elements. Third, a verified optimization process improves confidence in the correctness of its optimized designs. Correctness must be established before a design can be reused. In the event of errors, one can check whether the verification is incorrect or whether the design is applied in a context outside the scope of the verification.

We take a broad view of self-optimization and self-verification. One way is to think of a design—which can include both hardware and software—and its characterization about the key properties that an implementation should possess. Such properties include functional correctness, type compatibility, absence of arithmetic underflow or overflow, and so on. The characterization can include prescriptions about how the design can be optimized or verified by specific tools locally or remotely. Various mechanisms, from script-driven facilities to machine learning procedures, can be used in the self-optimization and self-verification processes, making use of context information where available. Designers can focus on optimizing and verifying particular aspects; for instance, one may wish to obtain the smallest design for computing Advanced Encryption Standard (AES) encryption on 128-bit data streams with a 512-bit key at 500 MHz.

The proposed design flow involves self-optimization and self-verification before and after deployment (Table 8.5). Before deployment, compilation produces an initial implementation and its characterization. The characterization contains information about how the design has been optimized and verified, and also about opportunities for further optimization and verification; such opportunities can then be explored after deployment at run time for a particular context to improve efficiency and confidence of correctness.

The self-optimization of a design depends on context. Before deployment, the context is the design tool environment; the context can be acquired by identifying parameters that affect design tool performance. While automated facilities, possibly self-improving, attempt to figure out what combinations of

TABLE 8.5 Context for Predeployment and Postdeployment

	Predeployment	Postdeployment
Focus context	Designer productivity design tool environment, often static	Design efficiency operation environment, often dynamic
Acquire context	From parameters affecting tool performance	From data input, for example, sensors
Optimize/verify	Optimize/verify initial postdeployment design	Optimize according to situation
Planning	Plan postdeployment optimize/ verify	Plan to meet postdeployment goals
External control	Frequent	Infrequent

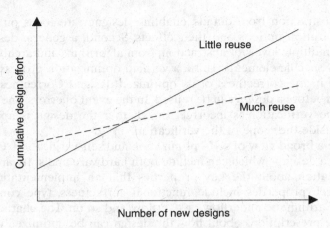

Figure 8.10   Design effort: The impact of reuse.

libraries and tools would produce a design that best meets the requirements, designers can optionally control the tools to ensure such self-optimization and self-verification proceed in the right direction. In contrast, after deployment such external control is usually less frequent, for instance if the design is part of a spacecraft. To summarize, predeployment tasks are mainly strategic and try to proactively determine possible courses of action that might take place at run time; postdeployment tasks are mainly tactical and must choose between the set of possible actions to react to the changing run-time context.

Our approach has three main benefits. First, it enhances confidence in design correctness and reliability by automating the verification process. Second, it improves design efficiency by automating the optimization process and exploiting run-time adaptivity. Third, it raises productivity by enabling reuse of designs and their optimization and verification.

However, adopting systematic design reuse—especially when self-optimization and self-verification are involved—can require more initial effort than doing a one-off design. The designer needs to organize, generalize, and document the designs appropriately. Only after some time, design reuse would become worthwhile (Figure 8.10). Moreover, there can be large overheads involved in supporting optimization and verification after deployment. In the long term, however, those who invest in capabilities for design reuse and design adaptability are likely to achieve substantial improvement in design efficiency and productivity.

8.12   PRE-DEPLOYMENT

Before deployment, a designer has the characterization of a desired design and has access to building blocks and their characterization. The task is to develop an architecture that defines how selected building blocks are instanti-

CHALLENGE

Capture composable generic descriptions of design and context, together with their optimization and verification characterization, at various levels of abstraction.

Composition is a convenient way of reuse, but it may not be straight-forward, other than for those that adopt simple communication regimes such as streaming. In particular, before composing heterogeneous components, they may need to be transformed to support a common communication and synchronization infrastructure. System-level design composition is challenging, since not only the designs themselves are composed, but also their corresponding optimization and verification procedures.

ated and composed to produce an initial design that either meets the requirements, or can be further optimized to do so, after deployment at run time. Postdeployment optimization and verification have to be planned carefully to avoid becoming an unaffordable overhead.

We assume that, at compile time before deployment,

1. the available computing resources are adequate to support the design and the tools, but
2. there is a limit on how much optimization and verification can take place since, for instance, some data values useful for optimization are only known at run time, and it is impractical to compute all possibilities for such values.

As a simple example, given that one of the two operands of an n-bit adder is a constant whose value is only known after deployment at run time, we wish to optimize the adder by constant propagation. It is, however, impractical to precompute the configuration of all 2^n possibilities, unless n is a small number. Fortunately, if we target a bit-slice architecture, then it may suffice to precompute only two configurations for each of the n bits so that, at run time when the value is known, the appropriate configuration can be placed at the right location at the right time [216].

Designers may have to prioritize or to change their requirements until a feasible implementation is found. For instance, one may want the most power-efficient design that meets a particular timing constraint or the smallest design that satisfies a given numerical accuracy. Other factors, such as safety or security issues, may also need to be taken into account.

Given that predeployment optimization is to produce an optimized design that would, where appropriate, be further optimized after deployment, the

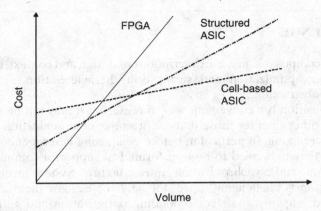

Figure 8.11 Comparing cost and volume for FPGA and ASIC technologies.

following are some examples of optimizations that can take place before deployment:

1. Choose a circuit technology in which the design would be implemented. The two common technologies are application-specific integrated circuit (ASIC) and field-programmable gate array (FPGA); the choice of technology depends on volume and flexibility (Figure 8.11). For instance, cell-based ASIC tends to be cheaper at large volume since they have large nonrecurring engineering cost, while FPGA is the other way around with structured ASIC somewhere in between. While ASIC technology can be used to implement adaptive instruction processors with, for instance, custom instruction extensions [29] or a reconfigurable cache [76], all the options for reconfiguration have to be known before fabrication. Adaptive instruction processors can also be implemented in FPGA technology [77, 269], which allows them much more flexibility at the expense of speed and area overheads in supporting reconfigurability.

2. Choose the granularity and synchronization regime for the configurable units. Current commercial FPGAs are mainly fine-grained devices with one or more global clocks, but other architectures are emerging: there are coarse-grained devices containing an array of multi-bit ALUs (arithmetic logic units) executing in parallel [25, 80], as well as architectures based on self-synchronizing technology to enhance scalability [52]. Generally, fine-grained devices have a better chance to be tailored to match closely with what is required. For instance, if a 9-bit ALU is needed, nine bit-level cells in an FPGA would be configured to form that 9-bit ALU. For a coarse-grained device containing cells with 8-bit ALUs, two such cells would be needed. However, fine-grained devices tend to have a large overhead in speed, area, power consumption, and so on,

since there are more resources that can be configured. Coarse-grained devices, in contrast, have lower overheads at the expense of flexibility.

3. For instruction processors with support for custom instructions [29, 77], choose the granularity of custom instructions to achieve the right balance between speed and area. Coarse-grained custom instructions are usually faster but require more area than fine-grained ones. For instance, if the same result can be achieved using: (a) one coarse-grained custom instruction, or (b) 50 fine-grained custom instructions, then (a) is likely to be more efficient since there are fewer instruction fetch/decode, and there are more opportunities to customize the instruction to do exactly what is needed. However, since the more coarse-grained an instruction, the more specific it can become, there would be fewer ways for reusing a coarse-grained custom instruction than a fine-grained one.

4. Choose the amount of parallelism and hardware/software partitioning to match performance or size constraints by determining, for instance, the number of processing elements, the level of pipelining, or the extent of task sharing for each processing element. Various factors, such as the speed and size of control logic and on-chip memory, and interfaces to other elements such as memory or sensors, would also need to be taken into account. As an example, Figure 8.12 shows how speedup varies with the number of processors targeting an FPGA for a multiprocessor architecture specialized for accelerating inductive logic programming applications [89]. Since the amount of FPGA on-chip memory is fixed, increasing the number of processors reduces the amount of cache memory for each processor; hence, the linear speedup until there are 16 processors. After

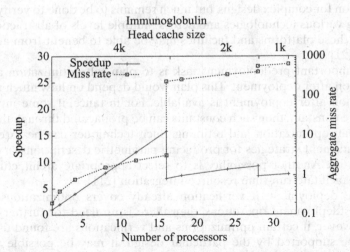

Figure 8.12 Variation of speedup and aggregate miss rate against the number of processors for the Arvand multiprocessor system targeting the XC2V6000 FPGA.

this optimal point, adding more processors reduces the speedup since the cache for each processor becomes too small.

5. Choose data representations and the corresponding operations. Trade-offs in adopting different kinds of arithmetic representations are well known: for instance, redundant arithmetic tends to produce faster designs, since no carry chain is required at the expense of size. Since fine-grained FPGAs support designs with any word length, various static and dynamic word-length optimization algorithms can be used for providing designs with the best trade-off between performance, size, power consumption, and accuracy in terms of, for instance, signal-to-noise ratio [62]. Models and facilities to support exceptions, such as arithmetic overflow and underflow, should also be considered [153].

6. Choose placement strategies for processing and memory elements on the physical device, such as those interacting frequently are placed close to one another to improve performance, area, and power consumption. It may be possible to automate the optimization of placement by a combination of heuristics and search-based autotuners [27] that generate and evaluate various implementation options; such methods would need to take into account various architectural constraints, such as the presence of embedded computational or memory elements [36].

Each example above has aspects that would benefit from verification, from high-level compilation [43] to flattening procedures [168] and placement strategies [196]. There are verification platforms [236] enabling consistent application of verification facilities such as symbolic simulators, model checkers, and theorem provers. Such platforms show promise in supporting self-verification for complex designs, but much remains to be done to verify designs involving various technologies and across multiple levels of abstraction. Also, many of these platforms and facilities may be able to benefit from automatic tuning [121].

One important predeployment task is to plan self-optimization and self-verification after deployment. This plan would depend on how much run-time information after deployment is available. For instance, if some inputs to a design are constant, then such constants can be propagated through the design by boolean optimization and retiming. Such techniques can be extended to cover placement strategies for producing parametric descriptions of compact layout [168]. Another possibility is to select appropriate architectural templates to facilitate run-time resource integration [211].

Before deployment, if verification already covers optimizations and all other postdeployment operations, then there is no need for further verification. However, if certain optimizations and verifications are found useful but cannot be supported by the particular design, it may be possible for such optimizations and verifications to take place remotely, so that the optimized and verified design would be downloaded securely into the running system at an appropriate time, minimizing interruption of service.

> **CHALLENGE**
>
> Develop techniques and tools for specifying and analyzing require-
> ments of self-optimizing and self-verifying systems, and methods for
> automating optimization and verification of operations and data
> representations.
>
> Relevant optimization techniques include scheduling, retiming, and
> word-length optimization, while relevant verification techniques include
> program analysis, model checking, and theorem proving. Their effective
> tuning and combination, together with new methods that explore, for
> instance, appropriate arithmetic schemes and their impact, would enable
> efficient designs to be produced with reduced effort.

8.13 POST-DEPLOYMENT

The purpose of optimization is to tailor a design to best meet its requirements.
Increasingly, however, such requirements no longer stay the same after the
design is commissioned; for instance, new standards may need to be met, or
errors may need to be fixed. Hence there is a growing need for upgradable
designs that support postdeployment optimization. Besides upgradability,
postdeployment optimization also enables resource sharing, error removal,
and adaptation to run-time conditions—for instance, selecting appropriate
error-correcting codes depending on the noise variation.

Clearly any programmable device would be capable of postdeployment
optimization. As we described earlier, fine-grained devices have greater opportunities of adapting themselves than coarse-grained devices, at the expense of
larger overheads.

In the following we focus on two themes in postdeployment optimization:
situation-specific optimization and autonomous optimization control. In both
cases, any untrusted postdeployment optimizations should be verified by light-
weight verifiers; possible techniques include proof-carrying code checkers
[252]. Such checkers support parameters that capture the safety conditions for
particular operations. A set of proof rules are used to establish acceptable ways
of constructing the proofs for the safety conditions.

As mentioned in the preceding section, should heavy-duty optimizations
and verifications become desirable, it may be possible for such tasks to be
carried out by separate trusted agents remotely and downloaded into the
operational device in a secure way, possibly based on digital signatures that
can verify senders' identity. Otherwise it would be prudent to include a time-
out facility to prevent nontermination of self-optimization and self-verification
routines that do not produce results before completion.

Besides having a time-out facility, postdeployment verification should be capable of dealing with other forms of exceptions, such as verification failure or occurrence of arithmetic errors. There should be error recovery procedures, together with techniques that decide whether to avoid or to correct similar errors in the future. For some applications, on-chip debug facilities [120] would be useful; such facilities can themselves be adapted to match the operational and buffering requirements of different applications.

8.13.1 Situation-Specific Optimization

One way to take advantage of postdeployment optimization in a changing operational environment is to continuously adapt to the changing situation, such as temperature, noise, process variation, and so on. For instance, it has been shown [241] that dynamic reconfiguration of a Viterbi decoder to adapt the error-correcting convolutional codes to the variation of communication channel noise conditions can result in almost 70% reduction in decoder power consumption, with no loss of decode accuracy.

Figure 8.13 shows a reconfiguration schedule that optimally adapts to the program phase behavior of the SPECviewperf benchmark 9 [232]. A program phase is an interval over which the working set of the program remains largely constant; our purpose is to support a dynamic optimization regime that makes use of program phase information to optimize designs at run time. The regime consists of a hardware compilation scheme for generating configurations that exploit program branch probability [231] and other opportunities to optimize for different phases of execution, and a run-time system that manages interchange of configurations to maintain optimization between phase transitions. The idea is to accelerate the hardware for branches that occur frequently in a particular program phase; when the beginning of the next program phase is detected, the hardware would be reconfigured to optimize the new program phase.

In addition to improving performance by exploiting, for instance, program phase behavior, postdeployment optimization also has the potential to improve

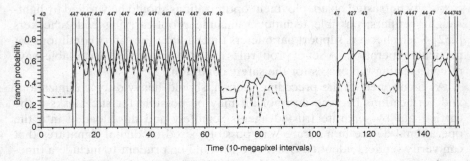

Figure 8.13 Optimal reconfiguration schedule for upper bound performance measure, SPECviewperf benchmark 9. The dotted and solid lines show, respectively, the branch probabilities of the inner and outer loop over time.

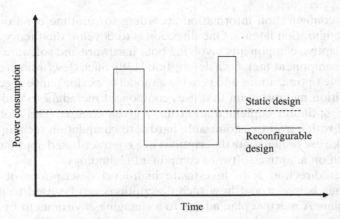

Figure 8.14 Possible variation of instantaneous power consumption over time. The two narrow spikes indicate power consumption during two reconfigurations for run-time optimization.

power consumption. Figure 8.14 shows a possible variation of power consumption over time. Comparing to a static design, a postdeployment optimizable design can be configured to a situation-specific design with the lowest possible power consumption for that situation, although there could be power surges when the device is being reconfigured. Techniques have been proposed for FPGAs that would automatically adjust their run-time clock speed [49] or exploit dynamic voltage scaling [57]; related methods have been reported for microprocessors [73]. Such techniques would be able to take advantage of run-time conditions after deployment, as well as adapting to effects of process variation in deep submicron technology.

A useful method for supporting situation-specific optimization is to integrate domain-specific customizations into a high-performance virtual machine, to which both static and dynamic information from postdeployment instrumentation is made available. Such information can be used in various situations for self-optimization and self-verification, such as optimizing the way hardware or software libraries are used based on special properties of the library code and context from postdeployment operation.

8.13.2 Autonomous Optimization Control

"Autonomic computing" [139] has been proposed for systems that support self-management, self-optimization, and even self-healing and self-protection. It is motivated by the increasing complexity of computer systems that require significant efforts to install, configure, tune, and maintain. In contrast, we focus on the design process that can support and benefit from self-optimizing and self-verifying components.

An evolving control strategy for self-optimization can be based on event-driven, just-in-time reconfiguration methods for producing software code and hardware configuration information according to run-time conditions, while hiding configuration latency. One direction is to develop the theory and practice for adaptive components involving both hardware and software elements, based on component metadata description [138]. Such descriptions characterize available optimizations and provide a model of performance together with a composition metaprogram that uses component metadata to find and configure the optimum implementation for a given context. This work can be combined with current customizable hardware compilation techniques [245], which make use of metadata descriptions in a contract-based approach, as well as research on adaptive software component technology.

Another direction is to investigate high-level descriptions of desirable autonomous behavior and how such descriptions can be used to produce a reactive plan. A reactive plan adapts to a changing environment by assigning an action toward a goal for every state from which the goal can be reached [238]. Dynamic reconfiguration can be driven by a plan specifying the properties a configuration should support.

Other promising directions for autonomous optimization control include those based on machine learning [6], inductive logic programming [89], and self-organizing feature maps [200]. Examples of practical self-adaptive systems, such as those targeting space missions [140], should also be studied to explore their potential for widening applicability and for inspiring theoretical development. It would be interesting to find an appropriate notion of verifiability for these optimization methods.

CHALLENGE

Find strategies that provide the best partitioning between co-optimization and coverification before and after deployment.

The more work is done before deployment, the more efficient the postdeployment design for a given application tends to become, but at the expense of flexibility. Strategies for getting the right balance between predeployment and postdeployment optimization and verification will be useful.

8.14 ROADMAP AND CHALLENGES

In the short term, we need to understand how to compose self-optimizing and self-verifying components, such that the resulting composite design is still self-optimizing and self-verifying. A key step is to provide both theoretical and practical connections between relevant design models and representations, as well as their corresponding optimization and verification procedures, to ensure consistency between semantic models and compatibility between interfaces of different tools.

It seems a good idea to begin by studying self-optimizing and self-verifying design in specific application domains. Experience gained from such studies would enable the discovery of fundamental principles and theories concerning the scope and capability of self-optimizing and self-verifying design that transcend the particularities of individual applications.

Another direction is to explore a platform-based approach for developing self-optimizing and self-verifying systems. Promising work [236] has been reported in combining various tools for verifying complex designs; such work provides a basis on which further research on self-optimization and self-verification can be built. Open-access repositories that enable shared designs and tools would be useful; in particular, the proposed approach would benefit from, and also contribute to, the verified software repository [43], currently being developed as part of the UK Grand Challenge project in dependable systems evolution.

Clearly, much research remains to be done to explore the potential for self-optimizing and self-verifying design. Progress in various areas is required to enhance self-optimization and self-verification for future development.

Challenge. So far, we focus on designing a single element that may operate autonomously. The criteria for optimality and correctness become more complex for a network of autonomous elements, especially if the control is also distributed. We need to develop theoretical and practical connections between the optimality and correctness of the individual elements, and the optimality and correctness of the network as a whole.

Challenge. Design reuse would only become widespread if there are open standards about the quality of the re-usable components as well as the associated optimization and verification processes. Such standards cover a collection of methods for verifying functional and performance requirements, including simulation, hardware emulation, and formal verification, at different levels of abstraction.

Challenge. There is a clear need for a sound foundation to serve as the basis for engineering effective self-optimization and self-verification methodologies that closely integrate with design exploration, prototyping, and testing. The challenge is that adaptability, while improving flexibility, tends to complicate optimization and verification.

8.15 SUMMARY

There is a whole new field to be explored based on the next generation of SOC and ASOC. As we have seen, transistor density improvements will enable a billion transistors per square centimeter. This enormous computational potential has a major limitation: limited electrical energy. There is a new direction opening in computer architecture, *nanocomputing*, to contrast with historical efforts in supercomputing. The target of this field is to produce the algorithms and architectural approaches for high performance at less than 1 millionth of the current levels of power dissipation, freeing the chip from external power coupling.

For untethered operation, a form of wireless communication is required. This is another significant challenge, especially with a power budget also in the order of microwatts. While RF is the conventional approach, some form of light or infrared may offer an alternative.

In addition, digitizing the sensors and even the transducers offers a final challenge where multiple sensors are integrated into a seamless SOC.

The chapter also projects a vision of design with self-optimizing and self-verifying components, to address the design challenges identified by the International Technology Roadmap for Semiconductors. Tasks for self-optimization and self-verification before and after deployment are described, together with a discussion of possible benefits and challenges. Making progress in theory and practice for self-optimization and self-verification would contribute to our goal: enabling designers to produce better designs more rapidly.

The best designs anticipate system complexity and deal effectively with the unanticipated. System complexity includes many issues overlooked in this chapter: component design and suppliers, design tools, validation and testing, security, and so on. Successful trade-offs across a myriad of issues define effective design.

While there is little expectation that all of the ASOC components discussed here will actually be integrated into a single die, there are many different possible combinations. Each combination with its own system requirements must be optimized across all of the constituent components. Designers, with the help of a self-optimizing and self-verifying development approach, are now no longer concerned about a component but only about the final system; they become the ultimate *systems engineers*.

APPENDIX
Tools for Processor Evaluation

Given the complexity of many processor configurations, it is not always possible to predict performance or the area required for many designs without the help of simulation or prediction tools. In this text, we provide simple tools that can give reasonable estimates of many design parameters.

The SimpleScalar tool set is used for exploring the design space for instruction processors. Its backend has been precompiled to support four architectures: Alpha, ARM, PISA (a variant of MIPS), and x86.

Figure A.1 shows the setting for the SimpleScalar web interface. Figures A.2 and A.3 present two simulated results using different L1 cache configurations and different translation lookaside buffer (TLB) configurations.

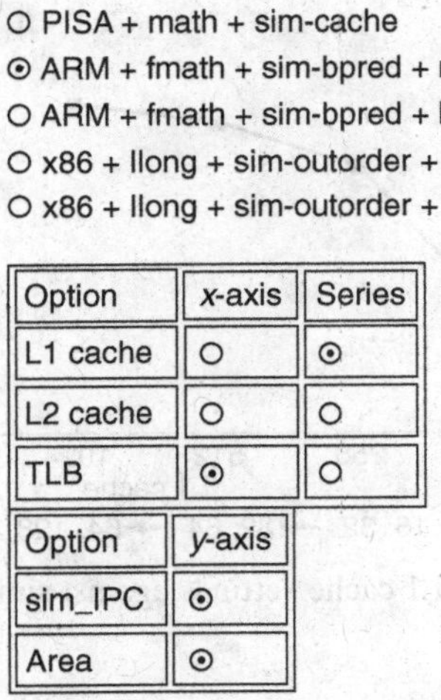

○ PISA + math + sim-cache

⊙ ARM + fmath + sim-bpred + not-taken

○ ARM + fmath + sim-bpred + bimod with large table size

○ x86 + llong + sim-outorder + 2 i-ALU + 2 f-ALU

○ x86 + llong + sim-outorder + 6 i-ALU + 6 f-ALU

Option	x-axis	Series
L1 cache	○	⊙
L2 cache	○	○
TLB	⊙	○

Option	y-axis
sim_IPC	⊙
Area	⊙

Figure A.1 Web interface for selecting different user options.

Computer System Design: System-on-Chip, First Edition. Michael J. Flynn and Wayne Luk.
© 2011 John Wiley & Sons, Inc. Published 2011 by John Wiley & Sons, Inc.

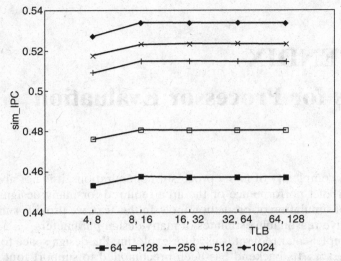

Figure A.2 Variations of different TLB settings against simulated IPC.

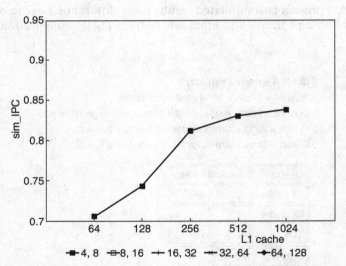

Figure A.3 Variations of different L1 cache settings against simulated IPC.

This web interface provides the following key features to users:

- enabling different instruction set architectures (ISAs) such as PISA, ARM, and x86;
- enabling different benchmark programs such as math.c, fmath.c, and llong.c;

- enabling different SimpleScalar simulators for various processor information; and
- providing a dynamic and real-time update to the generated figure from the web user browser.

If we want to produce a figure from the SimpleScalar web interface, we need to first select the architecture, then select the option according to the type of simulation that we want, such as getting the L1 cache or the TLB information. Finally, we can choose the simulated instructions per cycle (IPC) value or area information.

As shown in Figure A.2, the x-axis shows different TLB values and the y-axis shows different simulated IPC values. Each line in the plot refers to a single configuration of the L1 cache value.

REFERENCES

[1] S. Abraham and K. Padmanabhan, "Performance of direct binary n-cube networks for multiprocessors," *IEEE Transactions on Computers*, 38(7):1000–1111, 1989.

[2] Actel, Axcelerator Family FPGAs, v2.8, 2009.

[3] Actel, IGLOO Handbook, v1.2, 2009.

[4] Actel, ProASIC Plus Family Flash FPGAs, v3.5, 2004.

[5] Actel, ProASIC3 Handbook, v1.4, 2009.

[6] F. Agakov et al., "Using machine learning to focus iterative optimization," *Proceedings of the International Symposium on Code Generation and Optimization*, IEEE, 2006, pp. 295–305.

[7] A. Agarwal, Analysis of Cache Performance of Operating Systems and Multiprogramming, PhD thesis, Computer Systems Laboratory, Stanford University, published as CSL-TR-87-332, 1987.

[8] A. Agarwal, "Limits on interconnection network performance," *IEEE Transactions on Parallel and Distributed Systems*, 2(4):398–412, 1991.

[9] K. Ajo, A. Okamura and M. Motomura, "Wrapper-based bus implementation techniques for performance improvement and cost reduction," *IEEE Journal of Solid-State Circuits*, 39(5):804–817, 2004.

[10] Altera, Avalon Interface Specifications, Version 1.2, 2009.

[11] Altera, Nios embedded processor, http://www.altera.com/products/ip/processors/nios/nio-index.html, 2010.

[12] Altera, Nios II Processor Reference Handbook Ver. 9.1, 2009.

[13] Altera, Nios II Performance Benchmarks, 2010.

[14] Altera, Stratix II Device Handbook, SII5V1-4.4, 2009.

[15] Altera, Stratix III Device Handbook, Version 2.0, 2010.

[16] Altera, Stratix IV Device Handbook, Version 4.2, 2010.

[17] H. Amano, "Japanese dynamically reconfigurable processors," *Proceedings of ERSA*, 2009, pp. 19–28.

[18] AMD, AMD Geode Brochure, 2005.

[19] ARC, ARC 600, Configurable 32-bit CPU core Description, 2005.

[20] ARM, ARM 1020E, Technical Reference Manual, rev. r1p7, 2003.

[21] ARM, AMBA Bus Standard Specifications, 2010.

Computer System Design: System-on-Chip, First Edition. Michael J. Flynn and Wayne Luk.
© 2011 John Wiley & Sons, Inc. Published 2011 by John Wiley & Sons, Inc.

[22] ARM, AMBA Specification, Rev 2.0, ARM-IHI-0011A.

[23] ARM, ARM VFP11, Vector Floating-Point Coprocessor for ARM1136JF-S Processor r1p5, Technical Reference Manual, 2007.

[24] ARM, ARM1136J(F)-S Processor Specifications, 2010.

[25] J.M. Arnold, "The architecture and development flow of the S5 software configurable processor," *Journal of VLSI Signal Processing*, 47(1):3–14, 2007.

[26] Arteris, "A comparison of network-on-chip and busses," White Paper, 2005.

[27] K. Asanovic et al., The landscape of parallel computing research: A view from Berkeley, Technical Report No. UCB/EECS-2006-183, 2006.

[28] K. Atasu et al., "CHIPS: Custom hardware instruction processor synthesis," *IEEE Transactions on Computer-Aided Design*, 27(3):528–541, 2008.

[29] K. Atasu et al., "Optimizing instruction-set extensible processors under data bandwidth constraints," *Proceedings of Design, Automation and Test in Europe Conference*, IEEE, 2007, pp. 1–6.

[30] T. Austin, E. Larson and D. Ernst, "SimpleScalar: An infrastructure for computer system modeling," *IEEE Computer*, 35(2):59–67, 2002.

[31] B. Bacheldor, "Belgium hospital combines RFID, sensors to monitor heart patients," *RFID Journal*, March 6, 2007.

[32] B. Bailey, G. Martin and A. Piziali, *ESL Design and Verification: A Prescription for Electronic System-Level Methodology*, Morgan Kaufmann, 2007.

[33] J.E. Barth et al., "Embedded DRAM design and architecture for the IBM 0.11-μm ASIC offering," *IBM Journal of Research and Developmental*, 46(6):675–689, 2002.

[34] S. Baskiyar and N. Meghanathan, "A survey of contemporary real-time operating systems," *Informatica*, 29:233–240, 2005.

[35] J. Becker, M. Hubner, G. Hettich, R. Constapel, J. Eisenmann and J. Luka, "Dynamic and partial FPGA exploitation," *Proceedings of the IEEE*, 95(2):438–452, 2007.

[36] T. Becker, W. Luk and P.Y.K. Cheung, "Enhancing relocatability of partial bitstreams for run-time reconfiguration," *Proceedings of the IEEE International Symposium on Field-Programmable Custom Computing Machines*, 2007, pp. 35–44.

[37] T. Becker, W. Luk and P.Y.K. Cheung, "Parametric design for reconfigurable software-defined radio," *Reconfigurable Computing: Architectures, Tools and Applications*, LNCS 5453, J. Becker et al. (eds.), Springer, 2009.

[38] T. Becker, W. Luk and P.Y.K. Cheung, "Energy-aware optimisation for run-time reconfiguration," *Proceedings of the IEEE Symposium on Field-Programmable Custom Computing Machines*, 2010, pp. 55–62.

[39] P. Beckett and S. Goldstein, "Why area might reduce power in nanoscale CMOS," *IEEE International Symposium on Circuits and Systems*, 3:2329–2332, 2005.

[40] L. Benini and G. De Micheli, "Networks on chips: A new SOC paradigm," *IEEE Computer*, 35(1):70–78, 2002.

[41] D.P. Bhandarkar, "Analysis of memory interference in multiprocessors," *IEEE Transactions on Computers*, C-24(9):897–908, 1975.

[42] V. Bhaskaran and K. Konstantinides, *Image and Video Compression Standards: Algorithms and Architectures*, (2nd ed.), Kluwer, 1997.

[43] J. Bicarregui, C.A.R. Hoare and J.C.P. Woodcock, "The verified software repository: A step towards the verifying compiler," *Formal Aspects of Computing*, 18(2):143–151, 2006.

[44] M. Birnbaum and H. Sachs, "How VSIA answers the SOC dilemma," *IEEE Computer*, 32(6):42–50, 1999.

[45] P. Biswas et al., "ISEGEN: Generation of high-quality instruction set extensions by iterative improvement," *Proceedings of DATE*, 2005, pp. 1246–1251.

[46] P. Boehm and T. Melham, Design and verification of on-chip communication protocols, Oxford University Computing Laboratory Research Report, RR-08-05, 2008.

[47] K. Bonsor, "How power paper will work," *How Stuff Works*, 12 January 2001.

[48] M. Borgatti et al., "A reconfigurable system featuring dynamically extensible embedded microprocessor, FPGA, and customizable I/O," *IEEE Journal of Solid-State Circuits*, 38(3):521–529, 2003.

[49] J.A. Bower et al., "Dynamic clock-frequencies for FPGAs," *Microprocessors and Microsystems*, 30(6):388–397, 2006.

[50] P. Brisk, A. Kaplan and M. Sarrafzadeh, "Area-efficient instruction set synthesis for reconfigurable system-on-chip designs," *Proceedings of DAC*, 2004, pp. 395–400.

[51] D.C. Burger and T.M. Austin, "The SimpleScalar Tool Set, Version 2.0," *Computer Architecture News*, 25(3):13–25, 1997.

[52] M. Butts, A.M. Jones and P. Wasson, "A structural object programming model, architecture, chip and tools for reconfigurable computing," *Proceedings of the IEEE International Symposium on Field-Programmable Custom Computing Machines*, IEEE, 2007, pp. 55–64.

[53] Cadence Design Systems Inc, Palladium Datasheet, 2004.

[54] CEVA, Ceva X-1620 Product Note, 2005.

[55] K. Chen et al., "Predicting CMOS speed with gate oxide and voltage scaling and interconnect loading effects," *IEEE Transactions of the Electron Devices*, 44(11):1951–1957, 1997.

[56] D. Chen, J. Cong and P. Pan, "FPGA design automation: A survey," *Foundations and Trends in in Electronic Design Automation*, 1(3):139–169, 2006.

[57] C.T. Chow, L.S.M. Tsui, P.H.W. Leong, W. Luk and S. Wilton, "Dynamic voltage scaling for commercial FPGA," *Proceedings of the IEEE International Conference on Field-Programmable Technology*, National University of Singapore, 2005, pp. 173–180.

[58] S. Ciricescu et al., "The reconfigurable streaming vector processor (RSVP)," *IEEE/ACM International Symposium on Microarchitecture MICRO-36*, pp. 141–150, 2003.

[59] ClearSpeed, ClearSpeed CSX600 Datasheet, 2006.

[60] K. Compton and S. Hauck, "Totem: Custom reconfigurable array generation," *Proceedings of the Symposium on Field-Programmable Custom Computing Machines*, IEEE Computer Society Press, 2001, pp. 111–119.

[61] K. Compton and S. Hauck, "Reconfigurable computing: A survey of systems and software," *ACM Computing Surveys*, 34(2):171–210, 2002.

[62] G.A. Constantinides, "Word-length optimization for differentiable nonlinear systems," *ACM Transactions on Design Automation of Electronic Systems*, 11(1): 26–43, 2006.

[63] B.W. Cook, S. Lanzisera and K.S.J. Pister, "SoC issues for RF Smart Dust," *Proceedings of the IEEE*, 94(6):1177–1196, 2006.

[64] CrossBow Technologies, Xfabric Core Connectivity Junction, Preliminary Product Specification, 2004.

[65] R. Etienne-Cummings, P. Pouliquen and M.A. Lewis, "A vision chip for color segmentation and pattern matching," *EURASIP Journal on Applied Signal Processing*, 2003(7):703–712, 2003.

[66] U. Cummings, "PivotPoint: Clockless crossbar switch for high-performance embedded systems," *IEEE Micro*, 24(2):48–59, 2004.

[67] Cymbet, The POWER FAB (Thin Film Lithium Ion Cell) Battery System, 2007.

[68] Cypress semiconductor, CY8C41123 and CY8C41223 Linear Power PSoC Devices, 2005.

[69] J. Daemen and V. Rijmen, *The Design of Rijndael: AES—The Advanced Encryption Standard*, Springer-Verlag, 2002.

[70] W.J. Dally, "Performance analysis of *k*-ary *n*-cube interconnection networks," *IEEE Transactions on Computers*, 39(6):775–785, 1990.

[71] W.J. Dally and B. Towles, "Route packets, not wires: On-chip interconnection networks," *Proceedings of the Design Automation Conference*, 2001.

[72] W.J. Dally and B. Towles, *Principles and Practices of Interconnection Networks*, Morgan Kaufmann, 2004.

[73] S. Das et al., "A self-tuning DVS processor using delay-error detection and correction," *IEEE Journal of Solid-State Circuits*, 41(4):792–804, 2006.

[74] K. DeHaven, "Extensible processing platform ideal solution for a wide range of embedded systems," Xilinx White Paper WP369 (v1.0), 2010.

[75] J.A. DeRosa and H.M. Levy, "An evaluation of branch architectures," *Proceedings of the 14th Annual Symposium on Computer Architecture*, ACM, 10–16, 1987.

[76] A.S. Dhodapkarm and J.E. Smith, "Tuning adaptive microarchitectures," *International Journal of Embedded Systems*, 2(1/2):39–50, 2006.

[77] R. Dimond, O. Mencer and W. Luk, "Application-specific customisation of multi-threaded soft processors," *IEE Proceedings—Computers and Digital Techniques*, 153(3):173–180, 2006.

[78] J. Duato, S. Yalamanchili and L. Ni, *Interconnection Networks*, Morgan Kaufmann, 2003.

[79] S. Dutta, "Architecture and implementation of multiprocessor SOCs for advanced set-top boxes and digital TV systems," *Proceedings of the 16th Symposium on Integrated Circuits and System Design*, 2003, pp. 145–146.

[80] C. Ebeling et al., "Implementing an OFDM receiver on the RaPiD reconfigurable architecture," *IEEE Transactions on Computers*, 53(11):1436–1448, 2004.

[81] E. El-Araby, I. Gonzalez and T. El-Ghazawi, "Exploiting partial runtime reconfiguration for high-performance reconfigurable computing," *ACM Transactions on Reconfigurable Technology and Systems*, 1(4):21, 2009.

[82] Elixent Corporation, DFA 1000 Accelerator Datasheet, 2003.

[83] Embedded Access, MQX RTOS Product Description, 2010.

[84] Fairchild Semiconductor, Two Input NAND Gate Layout, 1966.

[85] A. Fang et al., "Integrated hybrid silicon evanescent racetrack laser and photodetector," *12th OptoElectronics and Communications Conference*, 2007.

[86] A. Fauth, M. Freericks and A. Knoll, "Generation of hardware machine models from instruction set descriptions," *Proceedings of the IEEE Workshop VLSI Signal Processing*, IEEE, 242–250, 1993.

[87] A. Fauth, J. Van Praet and M. Freericks, "Describing instruction set processors using nML," *Proceedings of DATE*, IEEE, 503–507, March 1995.

[88] Federal Information Processing Standards publication 180-2, *Secure Hash Standard*, August 2002.

[89] A.K. Fidjeland and W. Luk, "Customising application-specific multiprocessor systems: A case study," *Proceedings of the IEEE International Conference on Application-Specific Systems, Architectures and Processors*, IEEE, 239–244, 2005.

[90] A. Fidjeland, W. Luk and S. Muggleton, "A customisable multiprocessor for application-optimised inductive logic programming," *Proceedings of the Visions of Computer Science—BCS International Academic Conference*, September 2008, pp. 319–330.

[91] D. Fisch, A. Singh and G. Popov, "Z-RAM ultra-dense memory for 90nm and below," Hot Chips 18, August 2006.

[92] J.A. Fisher, "Very long instruction word architectures and the ELI-512," *Proceedings of the 10th Symposium on Computer Architecture*, ACM, 140–150, 1983.

[93] J.A. Fisher, P. Faraboschi and C. Young, *Embedded Computing*, Elsevier, 2005.

[94] J.A. Fisher, P. Faraboschi and C. Young, "Customizing processors: Lofty ambitions, stark realities," *Customizable Embedded Processors*, P. Ienne and R. Leupers (eds.), pp. 39–55, Morgan Kaufmann, 2007.

[95] D. Flynn, "AMBA: Enabling reusable on-chip designs," *IEEE Micro*, 17(4):20–27, 1997.

[96] M.J. Flynn, *Computer Architecture*, Jones and Bartlett, 1995.

[97] M.J. Flynn, "Some computer organizations and their effectiveness," *IEEE Transactions on Computing*, 21(9):948–960, 1972.

[98] M.J. Flynn and P. Hung, "Microprocessor design issues: Thoughts on the road ahead," *IEEE Micro*, 25(3):16–31, 2005.

[99] M.J. Flynn, P. Hung and K.W. Rudd, "Deep-submicron microprocessor design issues," *IEEE Micro*, 19(4):11–22, 1999.

[100] C.W. Fraser, D.R. Hanson and T.A. Proebsting, "Engineering a simple, efficient code-generator generator," *ACM Letters on Programming Languages and Systems*, 1(3):213–226, 1992.

[101] Freescale Semiconductor, Freescale e600 Core Product Brief, Rev.0, 2004.

[102] Freescale Semiconductor, Freescale MPC8544E PowerQUICC III Integrated Processor, Hardware Specifications, Rev.2, 2009.

[103] Fujitsu, MB93555A Product Description, 2010.

[104] H. Fujiwara, *Logic Testing and Design for Testability*, MIT Press, 1985.

[105] S. Furber and J. Bainbridge, "Future trends in SoC interconnect," *Proceedings of the International Symposium on System-on-Chip*, 2005, pp. 183–186.

[106] Gaisler, Leon 4 Product Description, 2010.

[107] K. Gaj and P. Chodowiec, "Fast implementation and fair comparison of the final candidates for advanced encryption standard using field programmable gate arrays," *Proceedings of the RSA Security Conference*, 2001, pp. 84–99.

[108] A. Gerstlauer et al., "Electronic system-level synthesis methodologies," *IEEE Transactions on Computer-Aided Design*, 28(10):1517–1530, 2009.

[109] S.K. Ghandi, *VLSI Fabrication Principles*, (2nd ed.), Morgan Kaufmann Publishers, 1994.

[110] D. Goodwin and D. Petkow, "Automatic generation of application specific processors," *Proceedings of the International Conference on Compilers, Architecture and Synthesis for Embedded Systems*, 2003, pp. 137–147.

[111] H.H. Goode and R.E. Machol, *System Engineering—An Introduction to the Design of Large-Scale Systems*, McGraw-Hill, 1957.

[112] P. Guerrier and A. Grenier, "A generic architecture for on-chip packet-switched interconnections," *Proceedings of the IEEE Design Automation and Test in Europe*, IEEE, 250–256, 2000.

[113] I.J. Haikala, Program behavior in memory hierarchies, PhD thesis (Technical Report A-1986-2), University of Helsinki, 1986.

[114] A. Halambi and P. Grun, "Expression: A language for architecture exploration through compiler/simulator retargetability," *Proceedings of DATE*, March 1999, pp. 485–490.

[115] J. Hayter, *Probability and Statistics for Engineers and Scientists*, Duxbury Press, 2006.

[116] J. Heape and N. Stollon, "Embedded logic analyzer speeds SoPC design," *Chip Design Magazine*, August/September 2004.

[117] H. Hedberg, T. Lenart and H. Svensson, "A complete MP3 decoder on a chip," *Proceedings of the IEEE International Conference on Microelectronic Systems Education*, 2005, pp. 103–104.

[118] J.L. Hennessy and D.A. Patterson, *Computer Architecture: A Quantitative Approach*, (4th ed.), Morgan Kaufmann, 2006.

[119] M. Hohenauer and R. Leupers, *C Compilers for Asips: Automatic Compiler Generation with LISA*, Springer, 2009.

[120] A.B.T. Hopkins and K.D. McDonald-Maier, "A generic on-chip debugger for wireless sensor networks," *Proceedings of the 1st NASA/ESA Conference on Adaptive Hardware and Systems*, IEEE, 338–342, 2006.

[121] F. Hutter et al., "Boosting verification by automatic tuning of decision procedures," *Proceedings of the International Conference on Formal Methods in Computer-Aided Design*, IEEE, 27–34, 2007.

[122] K. Hwang and F.A. Briggs, *Computer Architecture and Parallel Processing*, McGraw-Hill, 1984.

[123] IBM, 128-Bit Processor Logic Bus—Architecture Specification, Version 4.4, SA-14-2538-02, 2001.

[124] IBM, CoreConnect Bus Architecture, https://www-01.ibm.com/chips/techlib/techlib.nsf/productfamilies/CoreConnect_Bus_Architecture, 2010.

[125] IBM, Embedded DRAM Comparison Charts, IBM Microelectronics Presentation, December 2003.

[126] IBM, On-chip Peripheral Bus—Architecture Specification, Version 2.1, SA-14-2528-02, 2001.

[127] P. Ienne and R. Leupers (eds.), *Customizable Embedded Processors*, Morgan Kaufmann, 2007.

[128] K. Illgner et al., "Programmable DSP platform for digital still cameras,' *Proceedings of the International Conference on Acoustics, Speech, and Signal Processing*, 4:2235–2238, 1999.

[129] Infineon, TriCore2, Synthesizable Processor Core, 2010.

[130] InSpeed, InSpeed SOC320, Emulex Overview, 2010.

[131] Intel, Intel IOP333 I/O Processor Datasheet, July 2005.

[132] Intel, Intel PXA27x Overview, 2010.

[133] ITRS, International Technology Roadmap for Semiconductors, 2009.

[134] ITRS, ITRS Roadmap Summary, 2006.

[135] M. Johnson, *Superscalar Microprocessor Design*, Prentice-Hall, 1991.

[136] D. Johnson, Handbook of Optical through the Air Communications, Imagineering E-Zine, 2008.

[137] J.R. Jump and S. Lakshmanamurthy, "NETSIM: A general-purpose interconnection network simulator," *International Workshop on Modeling, Analysis and Simulation of Computer and Telecommunication Systems*, H.D. Schwetman et al. (eds.), pp. 121–125, Society for Computer Simulation International, 1993.

[138] P.H.J. Kelly et al., "THEMIS: Component dependence metadata in adaptive parallel applications," *Parallel Processing Letters*, 11(4):455–470, 2001.

[139] J.O. Kephart and D.M. Chess, "The vision of autonomic computing," *IEEE Computer*, 36(1):41–50, 2003.

[140] D. Keymeulen et al., "Self-adaptive system based on field programmable gate array for extreme temperature electronics," *Proceedings of the 1st NASA/ESA Conference on Adaptive Hardware and Systems*, IEEE, 296–300, 2006.

[141] M. Kistler, M. Perrone and F. Petrini, "Cell multiprocessor communication network: Built for speed,' *IEEE Micro*, 26(3):10–23, 2006.

[142] L. Kleinrock, *Queueing Systems: Theory, Vol. 1, Theory*, John Wiley and Sons, 1975.

[143] F. Kobayashi et al., "Hardware technology for Hitachi M-880 processor group," *Proceedings of the Electronic Components and Technologies Conference*, 693–703, 1991.

[144] T. Komuro, S. Kagami and M. Ishikawa, "A dynamically reconfigurable simd processor for a vision chip," *IEEE Journal of Solid-State Circuits*, 39(1):265–268, 2004.

[145] C. Kruskal and M. Snir, "The performance of multistage interconnection networks for multiprocessors," *IEEE Transactions on Computers*, C-32(12):1091–1098, 1983.

[146] I. Kuon and J. Rose, "Measuring the gap between FPGAs and ASICs," *IEEE Transactions on Computer-Aided Design of Integrated Circuits and Systems*, 26(2):203–215, 2007.

[147] K. Kutaragi et al., "A microprocessor with a 128 bit CPU, 10 floating-point MACs, 4 floating-point dividers, and an MPEG2 decoder," *IEEE International Solid-State Circuits Conference*, IEEE, 256–257, 1999.

[148] S.K. Lam and T. Srikanthan, "Rapid design of area-efficient custom instructions for reconfigurable embedded processing," *Journal of Systems Architecture*, 55(1):1–14, 2009.

[149] Lattice Semiconductor, *Lattice XP2 Family Handbook*, HB1004 Version 02.5, 2010.

[150] D. Lawrie, "Access and alignment of data in an array processor," *IEEE Transactions on Computers*, 24(12):1145–1154, 1975.

[151] E.A. Lee, "Embedded software," *Advances in Computers*, 56:56–97, 2002.

[152] F. Lee and A. Dolgoeorodov, "Implementation of H.264 encoding algorithms on a software-configurable processor," *Proc. GSPx*, 2005.

[153] D. Lee et al., "Accuracy-guaranteed bit-width optimization," *IEEE Transactions on Computer-Aided Design*, 25(10):1990–2000, 2006.

[154] J.K.F. Lee and A.J. Smith, "Analysis of branch prediction strategies and branch target buffer design," *IEEE Computer*, 17(1):6–22, 1984.

[155] O. Lehtoranta et al., "A parallel MPEG-4 encoder for FPGA based multiprocessor SOC," *Proceedings of the IEEE ISCAS*, 2005.

[156] S. Leibson, "NOC, NOC, NOCing on heaven's door: Beyond MPSOCs," *Electronics Design, Strategy, News*, 8 December 2005.

[157] G. Lemieux and D. Lewis, *Design of Interconnect Networks for Programmable Logic*, Kluwer, 2004.

[158] V. Liguori and K. Wong, "Designing a real-time *HDTV* 1080p baseline H.264/ AVC encoder core," *Proceedings of DesignCon*, 2006.

[159] W. Luk et al., "A high-level compilation toolchain for heterogeneous systems," *Proceedings of the IEEE International SOC Conference*, 2009, pp. 9–18.

[160] D. Lyonnard, S. Yoo, A. Baghdadi and A.A. Jerraya, "Automatic generation of application-specific architectures for heterogeneous multiprocessor system-on-chip," *Proc. Design Automation Conference*, 518–523, IEEE, May 2001.

[161] P. Lysaght and D. Levi, "Of gates and wires," *International Parallel and Distributed Processing Symposium*, 2004.

[162] P. Machanick, "SMP-SOC is the answer you get if you ask the right questions," *Proceedings of SAICSIT*, SAICSIT, 12–21, 2006.

[163] T. Makimoto, "The hot decade of field programmable technologies," *Proceedings of the IEEE International Conference on Field-Programmable Technology*, IEEE, 3–6, 2002.

[164] G. Martin and H. Chang (eds.), *Winning the SoC Revolution*, Kluwer, 2003.

[165] M.M. Mbaye, N. Blanger, Y. Savaria and S. Pierre, "A novel application-specific instruction-set processor design approach for video processing acceleration," *Journal of VLSI Signal Processing Systems*, 47(3):297–315, 2007.

[166] G. McFarland, CMOS Technology Scaling and its Impact on Cache Delay, PhD thesis, Stanford University, 1997.

[167] J. McGregor, Interconnects target SoC design, Microprocessor Report, 2004.

[168] S. McKeever and W. Luk, "Provably-correct hardware compilation tools based on pass separation techniques," *Formal Aspects of Computing*, 18(2):120–142, 2006.

[169] B. McNamara, M. Ji and M. Leabman, "Implementing 802.16 SDR using a software-configurable processor," *Proceedings of GSPx*, 2005.

[170] C.A. Mead and L.A. Conway, *Introduction to VLSI Systems*, Addison-Wesley, 1980.

[171] B. Mei et al., "ADRES: An architecture with tightly coupled VLIW processor and coarse-grained reconfigurable matrix," *Field-Programmable Logic and Applications*, LNCS 2778, P.Y.K. Cheung, G.A. Constantinides and J.T. de Sousa (eds.), Springer, 2003.

[172] A. Mello, L. Moller, N. Calazans and F. Moraes, "MultiNoC: A multiprocessing system enabled by a network on chip," *Proceedings of Design, Automation and Test in Europe*, IEEE, 234–239, 2005.

[173] S. Meninger et al., "Vibration-to-electric energy conversion," *IEEE Transactions of the VLSI Systems*, 9(1):64–76, 2001.

[174] Mentor Graphics, Atsana Semiconductor J2211 Product Description, 2010.

[175] Mentor Graphics, Nucleus Operating System, 2010.

[176] Microprocessor Report, Matsushita Integrated Platform, 2005.

[177] Microprocessor Report, MicroBlaze Can Float, 5/17/05-02, 2005.

[178] Microprocessor Report, XAP3 Takes the Stage, 6/13/05-01, 2005.

[179] P. Mishra and N. Dutt (eds.), *Processor Description Languages, Applications and Methodologies*, Morgan Kaufmann, 2008.

[180] S. Mirzaei, A. Hosangadi and R. Kastner, "FPGA implementation of high speed FIR filters using add and shift method," *Proceedings of ICCD*, 2006, pp. 308–313.

[181] A. Molnar et al., "An ultra low power 900 MHz RF transceiver for wireless sensor output," *Proceedings of the Custom Integrated Circuits Conference*, IEEE, 2004, pp. 401–404.

[182] A.C. Murray, R.V. Bennett, B. Franke and N. Topham, "Code transformation and instruction set extension," *ACM Transactions on Embedded Computing*, 8(4), Article 26, 2009.

[183] MIPS, MIPS 74K Core Product Description, 2010.

[184] NetSilicon, NET+Works for NET+ARM, Hardware Reference Guide, 2000.

[185] NetSilicon, NetSilicon NS9775 Datasheet, Rev. C, January 2005.

[186] NXP, LH7A404, 32-Bit System-on-Chip, Preliminary data sheet, July 2007.

[187] M. Oka and M. Suzuoki, "Designing and programming the Emotion Engine," *IEEE Micro*, 19(6):20–28, 1999.

[188] Open Core Protocol International Partners, Open Core Protocol Specification 1.0, OCP-IP Association, Document Version 002, 2001.

[189] OpenCores, Wishbone B4, 2010.

[190] OpenCores, OpenRISC, 2010.

[191] I. Page and W. Luk, "Compiling occam into FPGAs," *FPGAs*, W. Moore and W. Luk (eds.), pp. 271–283, Abingdon EE&CS books, 1991.

[192] R. Paschotta, Encyclopedia of Laser Physics and Technology, RP Photonics, 2010.

[193] S. Pasricha and N. Dutt, *On-Chip Communication Architectures*, Morgan Kaufmann, 2008.

[194] J.H. Patel, "Performance of processor–memory interconnections for multiprocessors," *IEEE Transactions on Computers*, 30(10):771–780, 1981.

[195] L.D. Partain, *Solar Cells and Their Applications*, Wiley, 2004.

[196] O. Pell, "Verification *of FPGA* layout generators in higher order logic," *Journal of Automated Reasoning*, 37(1–2):117–152, 2006.

[197] O. Pell and W. Luk, "Instance-specific design," *Reconfigurable Compuing*, S. Hauck and A. DeHon (eds.), pp. 455–474, Morgan Kaufmann, 2008.

[198] P. Pelgrims, T. Tierens and D. Driessens, Evaluation Report OCIDEC-Case, De Nayer Instituut., 2003.

[199] Philips, Nexperia PNX1700 Connected Media Processor, 2007.

[200] M. Porrmann, U. Witkowski and U. Rueckert, "Implementation of self-organizing feature maps in reconfigurable hardware," *FPGA Implementations of Neural Networks*, A.R. Omondi and J.C. Rajapakse (eds.), 247–269, Springer, 2006.

[201] E.J. Prinz et al., "Sonos: An embedded 90 nm SONOS flash EEPROM utilizing hot electron injection programming and 2-sided hot hole injection erase," *IEDM Conference Record*, 2002.

[202] S. Przybylski, M. Horowitz and J. Hennessy, "Characteristics of performance optimal multi-level cache hierarchies," *Proceedings of the 16th Symposium on Computer Architecture*, ACM, 114–121, June 1989.

[203] V.L. Pushparaj et al., "Flexible energy storage devices based on nanocomposite paper," *Proceedings of the National Academy of the USA*, 104(34):13574–13577, 2007.

[204] C.V. Ravi, "On the bandwidth and interference in interleaved memory systems," *IEEE Transactions on Computers*, 21(8):899–901, 1972.

[205] RFID Journal, http://www.rfidjournal.com.

[206] S. Roundy et al., "Power sources for wireless sensor networks," *Proceedings of the 1st European Workshop on Wireless Sensor Networks*, 2004, pp. 1–17.

[207] C. Rowen and S. Leibson, *Engineering the Complex SoC*, Prentice Hall, 2004.

[208] R.M. Russell, "The CRAY-1 computer system," *Communications of the ACM*, 21(1):63–72, 1978.

[209] S. Sane, "The aerodynamics of insect flight," *The Journal of Experimental Biology*, 206:4191–4208, 2003.

[210] J. Schmaltz and D. Borrione, "A generic network on chip model," *Theorem Proving in Higher Order Logics*, LNCS 3603, J. Hurd and T. Melham (eds.), pp. 310–325, Springer, 2005.

[211] P. Sedcole et al., "Run-time integration of reconfigurable video processing systems," *IEEE Transactions on VLSI Systems*, 15(9):1003–1016, 2007.

[212] P. Sedcole and P.Y.K. Cheung, "Parametric yield modelling and simulations of FPGA circuits considering within-die delay variations," *ACM Transactions on Reconfigurable Technology and Systems*, 1(2), Article 10, 2008.

[213] S. Seng, W. Luk and P.Y.K. Cheung, "Run-time adaptable flexible instruction processors," *Field Programmable Logic and Applications*, LNCS 2438, M. Glesner, P. Zipf and M. Renovell (eds.), pp. 545–555, 2002.

[214] R.A. Shafik, B.H. Al-Hashimi and K. Chakrabarty, "Soft error-aware design optimization of low power and time-constrained embedded systems," *Proceedings of DATE*, IEEE, 1462–1467, 2010.

[215] L. Shannon and P. Chow, "SIMPPL: An adaptable SoC framework using a programmable controller IP interface to facilitate design reuse," *IEEE Transactions on VLSI Systems*, 15(4):377–390, 2007.

[216] N. Shirazi, W. Luk and P.Y.K. Cheung, "Run-time management of dynamically reconfigurable designs," *Field-Programmable Logic and Applications*, LNCS 1482, R.W. Hartenstein and A. Keevallik (eds.), pp. 59–68, Springer, 1998.

[217] M. Shirvaikar and L. Estevez, "Digital camera design with JPEG, MPEG4, MP3 and 802.11 features," *Embedded Systems Conference*, 2006.

[218] M.L. Shooman, *Reliability of Computer Systems and Networks: Fault Tolerance, Analysis, and Design*, Wiley, 2001.

[219] SiliconBlue, iCE65 Ultra Low-Power Mobile FPFA Family, 2.1.1, 2010.

[220] Silicon Hive, Avispa block accelerator, Product Brief, 2003.

[221] A.J. Smith, "Cache evaluation and the impact of workload choice," *Proceedings of the 12th International Symposium on Computer Architecture*, pp. 64–73, ACM, 1985.

[222] J.E. Smith, "A study of branch prediction strategies," *Proceedings of the Symposium on Computer Architecture*, pp. 135–148, ACM, 1981.

[223] A.J. Smith, "Cache memories," *ACM Computing Surveys*, 14(3):473–530, 1982.

[224] A.J. Smith, "Cache evaluation and the impact of workload choice," *Proceedings of the International Symposium on Computer Architecture*, pp. 64–73, ACM, 1985.

[225] Sonics Inc, Sonics μNetwork Technical Overview, Document Revision 1, 2002.

[226] B. Stackhouse el al. "A 65 nm 2-billion-transistor quad-core Itanium processor," *IEEE Journal of Solid-State Circuits*, 44(1):18–31, 2009.

[227] T. Starnes, Programmable Microcomponent Forecast through 2006, Gartner Market Statistics, 2003.

[228] H.S. Stone, *High-Performance Computer Architecture*, (2nd ed.), AddisonWesley, 1990.

[229] W.D. Strecker, Analysis of the Instruction Execution Rate in Certain Computer Systems, PhD thesis, Carnegie-Mellon University, 1970.

[230] Stretch, "The S6000 family of processors," Architecture White Paper, 2009.

[231] H.E. Styles and W. Luk, "Exploiting program branch probabilities in hardware compilation," *IEEE Transactions on Computers*, 53(1):1408–1419, 2004.

[232] H.E. Styles and W. Luk, "Compilation and management of phase-optimized reconfigurable systems," *Proceedings of the International Conference on Field-Programmable Logic and Applications*, IEEE, 311–316, 2005.

[233] T. Sugizaki et al., "Novel multi-bit sonos type flash memory using a high-k charge trapping layer," *IEEE Symposium on VLSI Technology, Digest of Technical Papers*, IEEE, 27–28, June 2003.

[234] Sun, "Java Card 3 Platform," White Paper, 2008.

[235] Sun, OpenSPARC T1 FPGA Implementation, Release 1.6 Update, 2008.

[236] K.W. Susanto, "An integrated formal approach for system on chip," *Proceedings of the International Workshop in IP Based Design*, 119–123, October 2002.

[237] M. Suzuoki et al., "A microprocessor with a 128-bit CPU, ten floating-point MAC's, four floating-point dividers, and an MPEG-2 decoder," *IEEE Journal of Solid-State Circuits*, 34(11):1608–1618, 1999.

[238] D. Sykes et al., "Plan-directed architectural change for autonomous systems," *Proceedings of the International Workshop on Specification and Verification of Component-Based Systems*, 2007, pp. 15–21.

[239] Target Compiler Technologies, The nML Processor Description Language, 2002.

[240] Tensilica, Tensilica Instruction Extension (TIE) Language Reference Manual, 2006.

[241] R. Tessier et al., "A reconfigurable, power-efficient adaptive Viterbi decoder," *IEEE Transactions on VLSI Systems*, 13(4):484–488, 2005.

[242] J.E. Thornton, *Design of a Computer: The Control Data 6600*, Scott, Foresman and Co., 1970.

[243] Texas Instruments, TMS320C6713B, Floating point digital signal processor Datasheet, Rev. B, 2006.

[244] T.J. Todman et al., "Reconfigurable computing: Architectures and design methods," *IEE Proceedings—Computers and Digital Techniques*, 152(2):193–207, 2005.

[245] T. Todman, J.G. de, F. Coutinho and W. Luk, "Customisable hardware compilation," *The Journal of Supercomputing*, 32(2):119–137, 2005.

[246] R.M. Tomasulo, "An efficient algorithm for exploiting multiple arithmetic units," *IBM Journal of Research and Development*, 11(1):25–33, 1967.

[247] J.D. Ullman, *Computational Aspects of VLSI*, Computer Science Press, 1984.

[248] J. Villarreal, A. Park, W. Najjar and R. Halstead, "Designing modular hardware accelerators in C with ROCCC 2.0," *Proceedings of the IEEE Symposium on Field-Programmable Custom Computing Machines*, 2010.

[249] Virtual Socket Interface Alliance, On-Chip Bus DWG, Virtual Component Interface (VCI) Specification Version 2, OCB 2 2.0, 2001.

[250] W.J. Watson, "The TI ASC: A highly modular and flexible super computer architecture," *Proceedings of the AFIPS*, 41(1):221–228, 1972.

[251] B. Wen and K. Boahen, "Active bidirectional coupling in a cochlear chip," *Advances in Neural Information Processing Systems 17*, B. Sholkopf and Y. Weiss (eds.), MIT Press, 2006.

[252] N. Whitehead, M. Abadim and G. Necula, "By reason and authority: A system for authorization of proof-carrying code," *Proceedings of the IEEE Computer Security Foundations Workshop*, IEEE, 236–250, 2004.

[253] S.J.E. Wilton et al., "A synthesizable datapath-oriented embedded FPGA fabric for silicon debug applications," *ACM Transactions on Reconfigurable Technology and Systems*, 1(1), Article 7, 2008.

[254] Wind River, Wind River VxWorks, http://www.windriver.com/products/vxworks, 2010.

[255] R. Wood, "Fly, robot fly," *IEEE Spectrum*, 45(3):21–25, 2008.

[256] C.-L. Wu and T.-Y. Feng, "On a class of multistage interconnection networks," *IEEE Transactions on Computers*, 29(8):694–702, 1980.

[257] Xelerated, Xelerator X10q Network Processors, Product Brief, 2004.

[258] Xilinx, MicroBlaze Processor Reference Guide, EDK 11.4, 2009.

[259] Xilinx, Microblaze Processor Reference Guide, 2004.

[260] Xilinx, MicroBlaze Soft Processor Core, http://www.xilinx.com/tools/microblaze.htm, 2010.

[261] Xilinx, PowerPC 405 Processor Block Reference Guide, 2003.

[262] Xilinx, Virtex II Datasheet, 2004.

[263] Xilinx, Virtex 4 FPGA User Guide, v2.6, 2008.

[264] Xilinx, Virtex 5 FPGA User Guide, v5.3, 2010.

[265] Xilinx, Virtex-6 Family Overview, v2.2, 2010.

[266] E.M. Yeatman, "Advances in power sources for wireless sensor nodes," *Proceedings of the 1st International Workshop on Body Sensor Networks*, 2004.

[267] T.-Y. Yeh and Y.N. Patt, "Alternative implementations of two-level adaptive branch prediction," *Proceedings of the International Symposium on Computer Architecture*, ACM, 124–134, May 1992.

[268] T.-Y. Yeh and Y.N. Patt, "Two-level adaptive training branch prediction," *Proceedings of the International Symposium on Microarchitecture*, IEEE, 51–61, November 1991.

[269] P. Yianancouras, J.G. Steffan and J. Rose, "Exploration and customization of FPGA-based soft processors," *IEEE Transactions on Computer-Aided Design*, 26(2):266–277, 2007.

[270] A.C. Yu, Improvement of Video Coding Efficiency for Multimedia Processing, PhD thesis, Stanford University, 2002.

[271] B. Zhai et al., "A 2.60pJ/inst subthreshold sensor processor for optimal energy efficiency," *IEEE Symposium on VLSI Circuits, Digest of Technical Papers*, IEEE, 2006, pp. 154–155.

[272] Z. Zhang et al., "AutoPilot: A platform-based ESL synthesis system," *HighLevel Synthesis: From Algorithm to Digital Circuit*, P. Coussy and A. Morawiec (eds.), Springer Publishers, 2008.

[273] J. Zufferey and D. Floreano, "Toward 30-gram autonomous indoor aircraft: Vision-based obstacle avoidance and altitude control," *Proceedings of the IEEE International Conference on Robotics and Automation*, 2005, pp. 2594–2599.

INDEX

Computer System Design: System-on-Chip, First Edition. Michael J. Flynn and Wayne Luk.
© 2011 John Wiley & Sons, Inc. Published 2011 by John Wiley & Sons, Inc.